Economic Growth & Fiscal Planning

Economic Growth & Fiscal Planning

NEW YORK IN THE 1990s

Roy Bahl and
William Duncombe

CENTER
FOR URBAN
POLICY RESEARCH

WIDENER UNIVERSITY
WOLFGRAM
LIBRARY
CHESTER, PA.

DISCARDED
WIDENER UNIVERSITY

Copyright ©1991 by Rutgers, the State University of New Jersey
All rights reserved

Published by the Center for Urban Policy Research
New Brunswick, New Jersey 08903

Printed in the United States of America

Library of Congress Cataloging-in-Publication Data

Bahl, Roy W.
 Economic growth and fiscal planning: New York in the 1990s /
Roy Bahl and William Duncombe.
  p. cm.
 Includes bibliographical references and index.
 ISBN 0-88285-134-9

 1. New York (State)—Economic conditions. 2. Economic forecasting—
New York (State). 3. Fiscal policy—New York (State). I. Duncombe, William.
II. Title.
HC107.N7B34 1991
330.9747′001′12—dc20

91-7516
CIP

To Esther

On behalf of all her students

Contents

Tables

Chapter 3. Personal Income

Part II. New York's Fiscal Performance and Health

Chapter 4. The Public Sector in New York in the 1980s

Chapter 5. Explaining Government Growth in New York

Chapter 6.   Fiscal Health and Responsiveness

Appendix A.   Geographic Definitions

Appendix B. Population Data

Appendix C. Employment Data

Appendix D. Personal Income Data

Appendix E.   Fiscal Data

Figures

Part II.   New York's Fiscal Performance and Health

Chapter 4.   The Public Sector in New York in the 1980s

Appendix A.   Geographic Definitions

Preface

This book is the result of many years of studying the relationships among the national economy, the New York economy, and the finances of New York state and local governments. Our research is drawn to a close here with a pulling together of the hard evidence and analytic work about those relationships. The end of the story we tell is that the mistakes and successes of the past can teach us some important policy lessons for the future. If there is a single message here, it is that New York must begin a process of long-term fiscal planning—one based more on hard data and a realistic view of the future.

We learned much, from many people, in the course of doing this research, and we can not begin to mention them all. We received significant support for this work from the Metropolitan Studies Program of The Maxwell School of Citizenship and Public Affairs at Syracuse University and the Policy Research Program of the College of Business Administration at Georgia State University. The staff assistance we received at Georgia State University and at Syracuse University was excellent and improved the manuscript considerably. This was in no small part due to the efforts of Esther Gray, Vanessa Jamison, and Sharon Weaver. Despite all this good help and advice, some errors, misstatements, and controversial conclusions doubtless remain, and we accept responsibility for these.

Introduction

The total 1986 income in New York was $362.7 billion, about the same as in Canada. Based on its per capita income, New York State would rank as the richest nation in the world.[1] The state is home to some of the largest corporations and leading universities; it is blessed with good seaports and has developed a strong transportation infrastructure; its politicians are and always have been national leaders; and New York's rich melting pot history has made the economy a center of economic development energy. Metropolitan New York City is one of the world's largest urban agglomerations and, as the leading financial center, is one of the most important.

Despite these advantages and despite its great economic and political power, New York cannot balance its budget. New York City went broke in 1975 and its finances were monitored by a state-appointed control board. Several other New York cities, most notably Yonkers and Buffalo, were on the edge. Now the state government finds itself in a fiscal deficit position and must rely on short-term borrowing to fill its revenue shortfall. All of this seems a mystery to the outsider. Particularly with the very strong growth in the state's income in the 1980s, one would have expected the issue to be how to dispose of the fiscal surplus. Instead, the public debate has been about deficit reduction.

What keeps New York in fiscal trouble? Are things likely to get better or worse in the 1990s, and, either way, what kinds of discretionary government policies should be followed? Can New York learn something from its fiscal problems and performance in the 1970s and 1980s that will help in the 1990s? These are the policy questions addressed in this book.

We begin with the premise that one cannot separate an evaluation of fiscal performance from an evaluation of economic performance. Accordingly, the three chapters in Part I describe and analyze the patterns of population, employment, and personal income growth. Part II of this book is a telling of the story of state and local government finances in New York since 1970 and a recounting of the fiscal adjustments that were taken in the face of slower (in the 1970s) and then faster (in the 1980s) growth in the economy. The lessons from the 1980s and prospects for the 1990s are the subject of Part III.

The conclusions of this work are not upbeat—the state and its local governments are in for the fiscal belt-tightening that was postponed over the last several years. This will be an especially difficult proposition if the economy turns down and/or federal assistance to New York is cut dramatically. The advice we offer is that the state take a longer run and more comprehensive view in planning the development, and probably the retrenchment, of its government sector.

Note

1. These income comparisons are based on gross state product (GSP) estimates for New York and gross national product (GNP) estimates for countries. This comparison slightly understates the relative size of the New York economy because total GSP is lower than GNP in the United States. See Vernon Renshaw, Edward Trott, Jr., and Howard Freidenberg, "Gross State Product by Industry, 1963–86," *Survey of Current Business* 68 (May 1988): 30–46; and the World Bank, *World Development Report 1988* (New York: Oxford University Press, 1988), pp. 222–223.

PART I

New York's Economy in the 1980s

1

Population

Population trends are one of the most publicized (and probably least understood) indicators of state economic health. The rapid population declines of the 1970s in New York State brought out-migration to the forefront of the economic policy agenda. During the 1970s, the state lost nearly 700,000 people (almost 4 percent of the 1970 population), with most of this loss occurring in New York City. There has been a pronounced reversal of this population decline, with the state gaining almost 400,000 people since 1980. Most of this growth has occurred in New York City.

These aggregate statistics tell only part of the story. There have been important changes in the demographic and migration patterns that underlie these trends that have significant implications for New York public policy. This review attempts a look beneath the general trends.[1]

General Trends

There is no question that the population declines of the 1970s were reversed in the 1980s. Total state population grew by 2.2 percent from 1980 to 1989 (0.2 percent per year). This compares to a decline of 3.7 percent during the 1970s (Figure 1; Table 1). However, this recovery must be kept in perspective. Population growth was still well below that in other northeastern states or in the nation as a whole. If New York State had grown at the national rate, it would have added close to 1.3 million more people since 1980. This below-average

FIGURE 1

Population Trends (1970–1989)
New York, Other Northeast Region, and Total United States

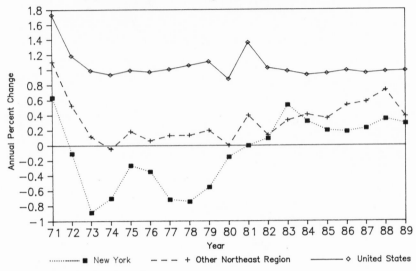

Source: U.S. Bureau of the Census

growth is forecast to continue through this century, although the gap is expected to narrow.

Even within the Northeast region, population growth in New York State has continued to lag behind (Table 2). Only Pennsylvania and Massachusetts have experienced similar slow growth rates. If New York State had grown at the average rate for other Northeast states, it would have added 300,000 residents since 1980. The relatively slow population growth in New York and the other northeastern states implies that they have declined as a share of the total U.S. population. New York's share has fallen from 9.0 percent in 1970 to 7.2 percent in 1989. By the end of the century, New York is projected to account for less than 7 percent of the U.S. population and will be surpassed by Texas as the second largest state. The effect of New York's declining share of population on its economy and finances is unclear; however, one certain result is the declining political representation in the U.S. Congress of New York and most northeastern states in the 1990s. As will be discussed more fully in chapter 6, this may have a significant influence on the distribution of federal aid and contracts.

TABLE 1

Population Trends and Projections: Resident Population for New York,
The Northeast Region, and the United States
(In Thousands)

Year	New York State			Other Northeast States[a]			Total United States	
	Population	Annual Percent Change	Share of United States (Percent)	Population	Annual Percent Change	Share of United States (Percent)	Population	Annual Percent Change
1960	16,782		9.4	27,896		15.6	179,323	
1970	18,241	0.8	9.0	30,820	1.0	15.2	203,302	1.3
1975	18,003	−0.3	8.4	31,408	0.4	14.6	215,465	1.2
1980	17,558	−0.5	7.8	31,577	0.1	13.9	226,546	1.0
1983	17,670	0.2	7.5	31,854	0.3	13.6	234,284	1.1
1988	17,909	0.3	7.3	32,697	0.5	13.3	245,807	1.0
1989	17,950	0.2	7.2	32,822	0.4	13.2	248,239	1.0
Projections:								
1990[b]	18,023	0.3	7.2	32,982	0.4	13.2	249,891	1.0
2000	18,548	0.3	6.9	34,453	0.4	12.9	267,748	0.7
Long-term Trends:								
1970–80		−0.4			0.2			1.1
1980–89		0.2			0.4			1.0

[a]Includes the Mideast and New England regions as defined by the Bureau of the Census except for New York.
[b]Percent change from 1980 to 1990.

Source: U.S. Department of Commerce, Bureau of the Census, *Current Population Reports*, Nos. 1044 and 1053; *U.S. Census of Population: 1960, 1970, and 1980,* and press release, December 29, 1989 (with 1989 population estimates); and New York State Data Center, *Official Population Projections for New York State Counties: 1980–2010,* April 1985.

TABLE 2

Population Trends
New York Compared to Other Northeast States

	Annual Percent Change		Percent of United States		
	1970–80	1980–89	1970	1980	1989
New York	–0.4	0.2	9.0	7.8	7.2
Connecticut	0.2	0.5	1.5	1.4	1.3
Maine	1.2	0.9	0.5	0.5	0.5
Massachusetts	0.1	0.3	2.8	2.5	2.4
New Hampshire	2.2	2.1	0.4	0.4	0.4
New Jersey	0.3	0.5	3.5	3.3	3.1
Pennsylvania	0.1	0.2	5.8	5.2	4.9
Rhode Island	0.0	0.6	0.5	0.4	0.4
Vermont	1.4	1.2	0.2	0.2	0.2
Other Northeast	0.2	0.4	15.2	13.9	13.2
Total United States	1.1	1.0	100.0	100.0	100.0

Source: U.S. Department of Commerce, Bureau of the Census, *Current Population Reports*, No. 998, and press release, December 29, 1989 (with 1989 population estimates).

There has been a major shift in the geographic pattern of population growth rates within the state, as described in Table 3 and Figure 2. The decline in the 1970s was due primarily to a major population loss in New York City—800,000 people in total or an annual rate of 1.1 percent for the decade. This was accompanied by a deconcentration in the New York City area as population grew rapidly in the distant suburbs of Putnam, Rockland, and Suffolk counties and in the mid-Hudson region of Dutchess, Orange, and Ulster counties.[2] There were also population declines in many of the central city counties in upstate New York, with populations in Erie, Chemung, and Broome counties all declining by at least 0.4 percent per year.

These patterns changed in the 1980s. New York City had been one of the fastest growing areas of the state (0.5 percent per year).[3] Population increased by more than 280,000 in New York City between 1980 and 1988—80 percent of the state population growth during this period. Growth has actually been slower in the New York

TABLE 3
Population Trends and Projections: Resident Population
In New York City, New York City Suburbs, and the Rest of the State
(In Thousands)

Year	New York City			New York City Suburbs[a]			Rest of New York State		
	Population	Annual Percent Change	Share of New York State (Percent)	Population	Annual Percent Change	Share of New York State (Percent)	Population	Annual Percent Change	Share of New York State (Percent)
1960	7,782		46.4	2,944		17.5	6,056		36.1
1970	7,896	0.1	43.3	3,737	2.4	20.5	6,609	0.9	36.2
1975	7,480	-1.1	41.5	3,781	0.2	21.0	6,742	0.4	37.4
1980	7,072	-1.1	40.3	3,809	0.1	21.7	6,677	-0.2	38.0
1983	7,177	0.5	40.6	3,835	0.2	21.7	6,658	-0.1	37.7
1988	7,353	0.5	41.1	3,853	0.1	21.5	6,703	0.1	37.4
Projections:									
1985	7,191	0.0	40.5	3,873	0.5	21.8	6,711	0.5	37.8
1990	7,180	0.0	39.8	3,978	0.5	22.1	6,865	0.5	38.1
2000	7,261	0.1	39.1	4,144	0.4	22.3	7,144	0.4	38.5
Long-term Trends:									
1970–80		-1.1			0.2			0.1	
1980–88		0.5			0.1			0.0	

[a]Includes Nassau, Putnam, Rockland, Suffolk, and Westchester counties.

Source: U.S. Department of Commerce, Bureau of the Census, and New York State Data Center, unpublished population estimates for New York, and *Official Population Projections for New York State Counties, 1980–2000,* April 1985.

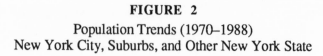

FIGURE 2

Population Trends (1970–1988)
New York City, Suburbs, and Other New York State

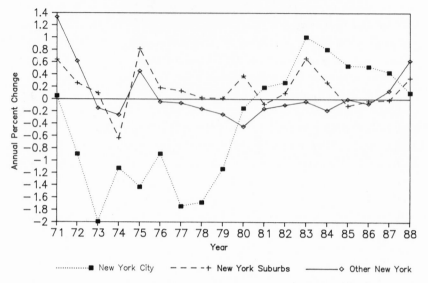

Sources: New York State Data Center; U.S. Bureau of the Census

City suburban counties than in the city. This pattern was clearly not anticipated even by the demographers in the New York State Data Center. New York City has surpassed the level of population projected for the year 2000 in the recent state forecasts.[4]

There has been slight population growth in the rest of the state. The western and central regions of the state generally fared the worst in the 1980s and in some cases grew even less than in the 1970s.[5] Particularly hard hit were the traditional manufacturing centers of Buffalo, Elmira, Utica, and Binghamton. The State Data Center has forecast slow growth in these areas in the 1990s.

The most rapid growth occurred in the mid-Hudson region of Dutchess, Orange, and Ulster counties, where population grew at the national rate. This appears to be driven by rapid in-migration from within the state and has been accompanied by rapid employment growth (close to 3 percent per year). This is consistent with the continued deconcentration of population and economic activity in the New York City metropolitan area.

Population growth in urban and rural areas appeared to have returned to their historic patterns in the 1980s. In the 1970s, population declined sharply in central cities (1.1 percent per year) while non-metropolitan areas and suburban counties experienced population growth (0.7 percent per year). New York State fit the general national patterns of nonmetropolitan area growth and deconcentration within urban areas.[6] This was a reversal of the long-term trend for population growth in urban areas to exceed that of rural areas.

The relative decline of metropolitan areas in New York appears to have ended in the 1980s.[7] This is consistent with national trends and with growth patterns in New Jersey and Pennsylvania. However, several of the New England states, particularly Connecticut and Massachusetts, continue to experience more rapid growth in nonmetropolitan areas.[8] It should be pointed out that the population of New York metropolitan areas without New York City has grown less than 0.1 percent per year since 1980, well below the growth rate for nonmetropolitan areas. The New York State Data Center has projected that the patterns of the 1970s will continue until the end of the century; that is, nonmetropolitan and suburban counties will be the main source of growth in the 1990s.

Changes in Population Composition

The last several decades have also been a time of significant changes in the composition of the New York State population. In the 1970s, the population in the state grew older, more racially diverse, and was increasingly apt to be in "nontraditional" households.[9] These trends appear to have continued in the 1980s and may have significant repercussions on the tax base and the demand for government services.

The changing demographic patterns between 1970 and 1980 have been well documented in other sources.[10] Unfortunately, there is limited availability of demographic information in noncensus years, but this section will attempt to present some evidence on patterns in the 1980s. Specifically, we examine changes in the age structure and racial composition of New York during the 1980s using several recent census publications.[11] Combined with information on national trends in household composition and poverty, it is possible to draw inferences about the changing status of families and children during the 1980s.

Age Structure

The well-documented aging of the American population has occurred in New York State as well. The median age of the population increased from 30.3 years in 1970 to 31.8 in 1980 and 34.0 in 1989.[12] This parallels national trends, although New York State has long had an older population. There has been a sharp decline in the percent of the population below twenty-five years of age (Table 4). The percentage of total population in New York below twenty-five years of age fell from 43 percent in 1970 to 35 percent in 1989. The decline in the relative share of children has not been as sharp in New York as it has been in other northeastern states or for the nation as a whole. This appears to be due to less of a decline in New York City, which may be partially explained by the sizable foreign immigration of families in their childbearing years into the city. These trends are expected to continue through the remainder of the century in New York State and in the nation.

Most of the population growth has occurred in the early middle-age years as the baby boom generation has passed from the young adult years, which experienced rapid growth in the 1970s.[13] The percentage of New York State population between thirty-five and fifty-four years old increased from 22.5 percent in 1980 to 25.5 percent in 1989. By the turn of the century, this category is expected to account for more than 30 percent of the total population.

There has been strong growth in the number of the elderly in New York State in the 1980s, with most growth occurring in the age bracket of more than seventy-five years. Growth is expected to continue in the 1990s; the percent of population sixty-five years or older is forecast to grow from 12.3 percent in 1980 to 13.7 percent in 2000. However, most of this growth will be in the sixty-five to seventy-four age group—the "young old." This group is less dependent on outside assistance and more apt to migrate out of state. New York State has consistently had one of the highest out-migration rates for the elderly in the country.[14]

These trends in the age distribution of the population appear to be statewide.[15] Growth in the relative importance of the elderly is expected to be particularly significant in western and central New York, less because of growth in the numbers of the elderly than because of the continued high out-migration of young adults (twenty to thirty-four) from these regions. The decline in the young population has been quite sharp in upstate New York. The population below twenty years of age is expected to fall from approximately 38 percent of total population in 1970 to 25 percent by the turn of the century in many upstate areas.

Households, Race, and Poverty

New York is one of the most racially and ethnically diverse states in the nation. The percentage of the population that is nonwhite increased from 13.2 percent in 1970 to 18.3 percent in 1985 (see Table 4). This compares respectively to 7.6 and 9.8 percent for other northeastern states and 12.5 and 15.2 percent for the United States as a whole (Box 1).

The arithmetic of this change is that the white population in New York decreased in absolute numbers in both the 1970s and 1980s (0.8 and 0.2 percent per year, respectively) while there has been moderate growth in the nation (0.8 percent per year) and slight growth in other northeastern states (0.1 percent per year). In contrast, there was strong population growth in black and other racial groups in both New York State and the country (approximately 2 percent per year). In addition, the Hispanic population grew by 2.6 percent per year in New York State and 4.2 percent nationally from 1980 to 1985.

The nonwhite population is heavily concentrated in the nation's and New York's metropolitan areas. In the mid 1980s, more than 90 percent of the nonwhite population was in metropolitan areas in New York (75 percent nationally), 83 percent was in central city counties, and 74 percent was in New York City. Twenty-seven percent of the population in central counties is nonwhite (32 percent in New York City) compared to 3 percent in nonmetropolitan areas and 9 percent in suburban counties.

Although most growth in the nonwhite population has also been in the primary working age years (twenty to sixty-four), the decline in the young age groups has been much less than that for whites. Accordingly, minorities account for an increasing portion of the nation's and New York's children. Minorities are expected to account for 40 percent of New York's children in 1990 and 46 percent by the end of the century. This compares to 31 and 34 percent, respectively, for the nation as a whole.[16]

An increasing portion of these children are in single-parent households headed by women. Although detailed data on households

TABLE 4

Changes in the Demographic Composition of the Population
For New York City, State, Northeast Region, and the United States
(Percent of Total Population)[a]

	New York City[b]						New York State					
	1970	1980	1985	2000	1970	1980	1985	1989	2000
Age Distribution:									
Under 25	31.3	28.1	26.8	25.3	42.9	39.0	36.6	34.8	32.1
25–34	22.2	25.6	27.3	20.9	12.4	15.8	16.5	16.9	14.4
35–54	23.2	22.4	23.0	29.2	23.8	22.5	23.8	25.5	30.1
55–64	11.3	10.4	10.1	10.0	10.1	10.4	10.4	9.8	9.6
Over 65	12.0	13.5	12.8	14.6	10.7	12.3	12.7	13.0	13.7
Racial Composition:									
White	76.6	72.2	69.2	NA	86.8	83.5	81.7	NA	78.2
Black	21.1	24.3	26.1	NA	11.9	14.3	15.4	NA	17.6
Other Races	2.3	3.5	4.7	NA	1.3	2.2	2.9	NA	4.2
Hispanic[c]	NA	17.7	19.8	NA	NA	9.4	10.6	NA	NA

	Other Northeast Region					Total United States				
	1970	*1980*	*1985*	*1989*	*2000*	*1970*	*1980*	*1985*	*1989*	*2000*
Age Distribution:										
Under 25	44.0	39.3	36.0	34.0	31.5	46.0	41.4	38.3	36.4	33.9
25–34	11.6	15.6	16.7	17.1	13.6	12.3	16.4	17.6	17.7	13.8
35–54	24.1	21.9	23.2	25.1	31.2	22.8	21.4	22.8	24.7	30.3
55–64	9.9	10.8	10.6	9.7	9.4	9.2	9.6	9.4	8.7	9.0
Over 65	10.5	12.4	13.5	14.0	14.4	9.8	11.3	12.0	12.5	13.0
Racial Composition:										
White	92.4	91.1	90.2	NA	88.2	87.5	85.8	84.8	NA	82.6
Black	7.1	7.9	8.3	NA	9.3	11.1	11.8	12.1	NA	13.1
Other Races	0.5	1.0	1.5	NA	2.5	1.4	2.4	3.1	NA	4.3
Hispanic[c]	NA	2.8	3.3	NA	NA	NA	6.3	7.3	NA	NA

[a] Percentages may not add to total due to rounding.

[b] Age distribution based on population below twenty and twenty to thirty-four, and calculated for 1984 instead of 1985.

[c] Hispanic category includes persons categorized in the white, black, and other categories.

Source: U.S. Department of Commerce, Bureau of the Census, *Current Population Reports*, Nos. 998, 1017, 1040–RD-1, 1044, 1053, and 1058; *U.S. Census of Population, 1970*, and unpublished data from the "Experimental County Estimates by Age, Sex, Race and Year", and New York State Data Center, *Official Population Projections for New York State Counties: 1980–2010*, April 1985.

Box 1. Data on Racial Composition
The definition of nonwhite population used in this paper includes all residents not counted as white by the U.S. Bureau of the Census. Unfortunately, the data on racial composition in the 1980 census are not comparable, without modification, with previous censuses and interim estimates. Comparisons of nonwhite population between the 1980 and previous censuses, such as those made in the *1986-87 New York State Statistical Yearbook* (Table A-10), would appear to be incorrect.

Comparability problems are due primarily to differences in the classification of the Hispanic population. In the past, Hispanics were classified according to the racial category to which they belonged, either white or black. In the 1980 census, most Hispanics were placed in a residual category ("Other, not specified"), which could not be separated by racial category. Since many would have been classified as white under previous censuses, the estimate of the white population is undercounted in 1980.

This problem appears to have been corrected in several recent census estimates used for this paper. These estimates attempt to classify Hispanics according to their racial category to be consistent with previous censuses. Estimates for 1980 and 1984 for New York State are from the U.S. Bureau of the Census, "Experimental County Estimates by Age, Sex, Race and Year," prepared for the National Cancer Institute. Estimates for states are from "Population Estimates by Race and Hispanic Origin for States, Metropolitan Areas, and Selected Counties: 1980 to 1985," *Current Population Reports*, Series P-25, No. 1040-RD-1 (Washington, D.C.: U.S. Government Printing Office, May 1989). Based on telephone discussions and correspondence with census officials, we judged these estimates to be definitionally comparable.[a]

---

[a] For a good review of this issue, see Jeffrey S. Passel and David L. Word, "Problems in Analyzing Race and Hispanic Origin Data for the 1980 Census: Solutions Based on Constructing Consistent Populations from Micro-Level Data." Paper presented at the 1987 Annual Meeting of the Population Association of America, Chicago, April-May 1987.

are not readily available, there are several recent estimates for New York State. The number of households has continued growing much faster (0.9 percent per year from 1980 to 1989) than total population.[17] In 1980, more than 50 percent of black and 40 percent of Hispanic family households were headed by a single parent, compared to 15 percent for white families in New York. Nationally, there appears to have been continued relative growth of such households in the 1980s. Single-parent family households grew from 44 percent in 1980 to 50 percent of black households in 1988 and from 25 to 30 percent for Hispanics. Within the New York City metropolitan area, single-parent households rose from 50 to 55 percent of black households and 41 to 52 percent of Hispanic households.[18] Recent projections indicate that there will be a continued rapid growth of single-parent households (particularly female-headed) in New York through the rest of the century.[19]

Recent research suggests that the growth in black families headed by women has been driven not by divorce but by an increase in the number of never-married mothers.[20] Since such families are at an economic disadvantage, it is not surprising that an increasing number of minority children are growing up in poverty.[21] For the nation as a whole in 1988, more than 50 percent of black and Hispanic families and close to 30 percent of white single-parent families headed by women were below the poverty line. There has been little improvement in the poverty rate for such families in the last several decades.[22] It has been estimated in New York State in 1984 that 45 percent of black children and 60 percent of Hispanic children grew up in poverty compared to 15 percent for whites.[23] As summarized by Wetzel:

> The poverty gap between children and adults has increased significantly since the early 1970s, a trend that is inexorably linked to out-of-wedlock childbearing and to divorce. Social science research has repeatedly shown that ... children raised in poverty are at higher risk of low educational attainment, more frequent involvement with the criminal justice system and out-of-wedlock childbearing themselves.[24]

The racial mix of New York's population suggests a much higher incidence of poverty than in the rest of the country. Using longitudinal data from the panel study of income dynamics,[25] Adams, Duncan, and Rodgers estimate that blacks constitute 21 percent of the national population but 51 percent of the poor and 66 percent of the persistently poor.[26]

About 20 percent of New York City's population had an income below the poverty line in 1980 and 10 percent are persistently poor.[27] These are approximately median levels by comparison with the nineteen largest U.S. cities, but the absolute numbers—2 million poor people in New York City in 1980—are the highest in the nation.[28] Ehrenhalt has updated these statistics using census data. He estimates that 24 percent of the city's population lived in poverty in the mid-

1980s, up from 15 percent in 1976, and argues that this is sharply above the national average of 15 percent.[29]

Migration and Natural Increase

To understand why the sharp declines in population in the 1970s were reversed in the 1980s, and what this implies for state policy, requires a deeper look at the components of population change. In particular, it is necessary to have an understanding of the pattern of natural increase, migration by origin and destination, and characteristics of migrants. Unfortunately, no single source can provide this information. Using several different sources of data on natural increase and migration, we attempt to piece together a story about how New York's population grew in the 1980s. Although there are still some major gaps, especially in the migration data, it is possible to sketch out an overall picture of population change in New York State.

Natural Increase

The Bureau of the Census, as part of its annual population estimates, calculates components of population change. These trends for 1980 to 1988 are presented in Table 5. It is clear that the population increases in the 1980s were due primarily to the natural increase of the resident population. However, the rate of natural increase in New York (4 percent of the 1980 population) has lagged behind growth in the total United States (6 percent) because of the lower birthrates in New York.

New York has consistently had lower fertility rates than most of the country, for example, 1.65 for New York compared to 1.83 for the nation in 1980.[30] Although it is not possible to calculate fertility rates from these census estimates, it is possible to compare average annual births from 1980 to 1988 to the 1980 population. Rates for New York (1.5 percent) are lower than those for the nation (1.7 percent).

The most recent population forecasts by the State Data Center (1985) assume that the fertility rates for the state will slowly increase until the end of the century. Alba and Trent estimate that if these rates remained at their 1980 levels, then, ceteris paribus, total population in the year 2000 would be 300,000 less than presently forecast.[31] This shows the substantial sensitivity of these forecasts to changes in fertility assumptions.

With regard to the other component of the natural increase estimates—mortality—New York State tends to more closely follow national trends. From 1980 to 1988, deaths averaged 1.0 percent of the 1980 population for New York State compared to 0.9 percent for the total United States. Although mortality rates will obviously vary with age distribution, based on past trends, New York State should follow national rates.

Recent census estimates permit examination of the racial composition of the natural increase from 1980 to 1985.[32] The fastest natural increase in the population has occurred in black and Hispanic families. The average annual growth rates for births, deaths, and natural increase among white families has been 1.3, 1.0, and 0.3 percent, respectively, in New York and 1.6, 1.0, and 0.6 percent, respectively, nationally. This compares to rates of 2.2, 0.8, and 1.4 percent, respectively, for blacks and 2.3, 0.5, and 1.7 percent, respectively, for Hispanics both nationally and in New York. The higher birthrates among these groups are driven in part by the higher percent of young adults but also by higher fertility rates.[33]

Migration

The major cause of population decline in New York State over the last several decades has been migration to other states. Understanding the magnitude, composition, and causes of this migration is important for thoroughly evaluating future population prospects in the state. It is beyond the scope of this study to examine, in depth, the complex causes in intrastate and interstate migration. Instead, in this section, we hope to shed some light on recent migration trends using several different sources of migration data (Box 2).

The 1970s were a time of volatile migration trends. During this decade, the well-publicized migration from the northeastern and Great Lakes states to the Sunbelt took place. New York was one of the major contributors to this population shift. Based on census estimates of net migration, it appears that the state lost, on average, 140,000 people per year. Most of this out-migration took place between 1973 to 1979, with annual flows exceeding 200,000 in several years.[34]

Net out-migration decreased during the 1980s, but it still averaged more than forty thousand persons per year. New York's net out-migration rate (2 percent of 1980 population) has exceeded that in all northeastern states but is lower than that in several states in the

Box 2. Sources of Migration Data

Ideally, migration data would provide information on the origin and destination of migrants by substate area, as well as the socioeconomic characteristics of migrants. Unfortunately, no one source provides information on all these aspects. The U.S. Bureau of the Census estimates net migration for substate areas on an annual basis (Table 5). However, these estimates do not indicate the origin or destination of migrants or their characteristics.

The most commonly used source of detailed migration data has been the decennial census. As part of the census, people are asked where they lived five years before compared to their present residence. Combined with the extensive demographic data collected as part of the census, this is by far the most detailed information on migration available.

Since the last data collected were for migration from 1975 to 1980, this does not help us analyze changes in migration trends in the 1980s. Moreover, because these data measure migration over a five-year period, they miss much of the return migration. There is growing evidence that this return migration is important and that those returning are different from those moving on (for example, they tend to be less educated and skilled).[a] The census also carries out an annual population survey that does include migration questions.[b] Unfortunately, the small sample size does not permit estimation of migration trends at the state level with a high degree of confidence.

The other primary source of migration data is based on IRS income tax records. The Census Bureau, in arrangement with the IRS, counts annual migrants based on changes in address on the tax forms. Using information on the tax forms, they are able to estimate in- and out-migration by origin and destination (down to the county level). However, these data do not include characteristics of migrants and capture only those migrants filing federal income tax returns. Data on characteristics of nonfilers are not readily available; still, one would expect that they would tend to have lower incomes. Although an imperfect estimate of total migration, these data probably are a good indicator of annual migration trends and are used here to examine both interstate and intrastate migration trends for New York State. The results are presented in Table 6.

---

[a] See Julie DaVanzo, "Repeat Migration in the United States: Who Moves Back and Who Moves On?" *Review of Economics and Statistics* 65 (November 1983): 552–559; and Peter A. Morrison and Julie DaVanzo, "The Prism of Migration: Dissimilarities Between Return and Onward Movers," *Social Science Quarterly* 67 (September 1986): 504–516.

[b] The U.S. Bureau of the Census uses the *Current Population Survey* to make estimates of the origin, destination, and characteristics of migrants between regions. For recent estimates, see U.S. Bureau of the Census, "Geographic Mobility: 1987," *Current Population Reports*, Series P-20, No. 430 (Washington, D.C.: U.S. Government Printing Office, April 1989).

Midwest (see Table 5). The big gainers from migration continue to be southern and western states, particularly Florida, California, and Arizona.

Within New York State, the major losers were in western and central New York, with net out-migration from 1980 to 1988 exceeding 3 percent of the 1980 population.[35] Especially hard hit were Buffalo and Elmira, which lost 8.0 and 9.3 percent, respectively, of their 1980 population. In contrast, most of the eastern and downstate areas experienced lower migration rates. The net out-migration from New York City, which had averaged more than 110,000 residents per year in the 1970s, was quite low (4,250 per year) during the 1980s. The only area to experience net in-migration was the mid-Hudson region due to a large inflow from other areas of the state. Unfortunately, these census estimates are only for net migration and do not provide any information on migrant origin or destination.

Migration data from the Internal Revenue Service (IRS) provide more detailed information. Net migration levels and trends using the IRS data correspond fairly closely with census estimates of net migration. According to this source, the largest net out-migration occurred in the late 1970s, with annual flows of close to 200,000. This has decreased significantly in the 1980s and now averages 100,000 per year (Table 6).[36] Most of the change between decades occurred in the amount of *gross* out-migration. Out-migration, which approached 400,000 people per year in the late 1970s, had dropped to around 300,000 by the mid-1980s. There were more out-migrants from New York State than from any other state between 1975 and 1980. However, New York's out-migration *rate* (migration as a percent of population) was not among the highest in the country even in the late 1970s.[37]

Not surprisingly, the destination of most New York out-migrants has been the Sunbelt and neighboring northeastern states. The South has consistently received more than 50 percent of New York migrants, with Florida alone receiving more than 20 percent. Northeastern states, such as New Jersey and Connecticut, have attracted 20 to 30 percent of New York out-migrants. There has been some decrease in the relative importance of the South in recent migration, with poor economic conditions in oil states such as Texas the major cause. There was actually a net in-migration, on average, from the Southwest from 1984 to 1988.

TABLE 5

Components of Population Change (1980–1988):
Comparison of New York, Northeast, and Other Regions[a]
(Resident Population, in Thousands)

	Total Population Change (1980–88)	Percent of 1980 Population	Natural Increase (1980–88)	Percent of 1980 Population	Net Migration (1980–88)	Percent of 1980 Population
Other Northeast:	1,106	3.5	1,069	3.4	38	0.1
Connecticut	125	4.0	125	4.0	0	0.0
Maine	80	7.1	48	4.3	32	2.9
Massachusetts	152	2.6	198	3.5	-46	-0.8
New Hampshire	164	17.8	56	6.1	109	11.8
New Jersey	356	4.8	276	3.7	80	1.1
Pennsylvania	137	1.2	309	2.6	-172	-1.4
Rhode Island	46	4.9	29	3.1	17	1.8
Vermont	46	9.0	28	5.5	18	3.5
Midwest:	1,012	1.7	3,172	5.4	-2,159	-3.7
Ohio	57	0.5	523	4.8	-466	-4.3
Michigan	-22	-0.2	502	5.4	-524	-5.7
Iowa	-80	-2.7	124	4.3	-204	-7.0

South:	9,283	12.3	4,771	6.3	4,511	6.0
Florida	2,589	26.6	319	3.3	2,270	23.3
Georgia	879	16.1	391	7.2	488	8.9
Texas	2,612	18.4	1,494	10.5	1,117	7.9
West:	7,507	17.4	3,966	9.2	3,540	8.2
Arizona	771	28.4	270	9.9	501	18.4
California	4,646	19.6	2,130	9.0	2,516	10.6
New York State:	351	2.0	700	4.0	−348	−2.0
New York City	281	4.0	315	4.5	−34	−0.5
New York Suburbs	44	1.2	126	3.3	−82	−2.2
Rest of State	26	0.4	259	3.9	−232	−3.5

aNet migration by region includes intraregional migration between states within a region. Subcategories may not add to total due to rounding.

Source: U.S. Department of Commerce, Bureau of the Census, and New York State Data Center, unpublished data on components of population change.

TABLE 6

Net In-Migration to New York State[a]: By Region of Origin/Destination[b]
(Average Annual Migration)

Region	1970–73	Percent of Total	1975–79	Percent of Total	1980–84	Percent of Total	1984–88	Percent of Total
New England	-18,658	12.1	-15,978	8.6	-9,313	8.9	-14,363	11.8
Mid-Atlantic	-32,131	20.8	-27,690	14.8	-18,302	17.5	-32,687	26.9
East North Central	-4,279	2.8	-6,787	3.6	2,611	-2.5	-253	0.2
West North Central	-1,964	1.3	-3,148	1.7	252	-0.2	371	-0.3
South Atlantic	-63,146	40.9	-76,288	40.9	-53,003	50.8	-63,660	52.5
East South Central	-2,070	1.3	-4,383	2.3	-1,007	1.0	-1,161	1.0
West South Central	-4,830	3.1	-13,944	7.5	-9,669	9.3	1,708	-1.4
Mountain	-11,191	7.2	-14,483	7.8	-6,274	6.0	-3,143	2.6
Pacific	-16,109	10.4	-23,961	12.8	-9,724	9.3	-8,113	6.7
Total United States	-154,376	100.0	-186,661	100.0	-104,428	100.0	-121,301	100.0
In-migration	138,560		181,683		198,609		191,578	
Out-migration	292,936		368,344		303,037		312,879	

[a]In-migrants minus out-migrants. This is based on individuals claimed as exemptions on federal income tax returns. Residence is assumed to be where tax returns were filed, which may not reflect in all cases the actual address of residence. This does not measure migration of those individuals not filing federal tax returns. Percentages may not add up to 100 due to rounding. Net in-migration by region may not add to United States total due to rounding.

[b]Regions are those defined by the U.S. Bureau of the Census.

Source: U.S. Department of the Treasury, Internal Revenue Service, Statistics of Income Division, Area Migration Flow Data, unpublished data provided by the IRS.

In-migration into New York State has remained fairly stable, ranging between 175,000 and 200,000 since the mid-1970s. New York State, along with the Great Lakes states, has had one of the nation's lowest in-migration rates since the 1960s. As summarized by Long, "the distinctly low rates of migration to 'rustbelt' states developed long before the economic dislocations of the 1970s."[38]

The origin of in-migrants tends to follow closely the destinations of out-migrants. This finding is consistent with hypotheses concerning the importance of return migration. The major source of in-migrants has been other northeastern states (close to 40 percent), particularly New Jersey, Pennsylvania, and Connecticut. The South is also a major source of in-migrants (more than 30 percent), with Florida again the major origin.

The IRS data also make it possible to track migration flows within the state.[39] Generally, the out-of-state migration flows have been a much more important source of migration than within-state migration. The highly publicized city-to-suburb migration would appear to have been a relatively insignificant component of total migration, except for the New York City area.

The rate of net, out-of-state migration has decreased since the late 1970s but is still high in the western and central Metropolitan Statistical Areas (MSAs), especially Buffalo and Elmira. Consistently, the South has been the region receiving most of this net out-migration (often accounting for 50 percent or more). Migration to neighboring states, such as Connecticut and New Jersey, from the New York City area is also quite important.

Ideally, this analysis of migration trends would be accompanied by information about the demographic characteristics of out-migrants and in-migrants. Unfortunately, the IRS migration data do not contain demographic information. The only generally accepted source of such information is the decennial census. Several reviews of these trends for New York State find that New York State out-migrants tend to fit national patterns.[40] Most migrants tend to be young adults (twenty to thirty-four years old) who are more highly educated and affluent than the population as a whole. New York's out-migration rates among this age group have been very similar to the national average. These results imply that New York State has been losing a disproportionate share of its young, educated, and affluent work force. There is a second peak in migration in the sixty-four to seventy age group.

These older migrants are moving for retirement reasons and also tend to be relatively more affluent. New York State out-migration among this age group has been well above the national average.[41] A recent study of New York State migration, using information from the 1985 *Current Population Survey*, confirmed these patterns.[42]

A census report estimated the racial composition of migration from 1980 to 1985.[43] The major source of out-migration for New York State and the other northeastern states has been among white residents. New York has an out-migration rate of more than 2 percent, among the highest in the nation. Most of these white households are relocating in the South and West. In contrast, there has been a strong in-migration among blacks and Hispanics in New York and the Northeast in general.

Ultimately, the issue of most interest to state policymakers is the reason for in-migration and out-migration. There has been extensive research on the determinants of intrastate and interstate migration. Not surprisingly, most studies put employment opportunities at the top of the list of determinants.[44] This has been confirmed by survey research among recent in-migrants and out-migrants from New York State.[45] Of those interviewed, 44 percent of out-migrants and 57 percent of in-migrants cited employment-related factors as the primary reason for migration. Family-related concerns was the primary reason stated by 21 percent of in-migrants and 18 percent of out-migrants. Cost of living (for example, high taxes and the price of housing) was cited as the primary reason for migration among 11 percent of the out-migrants. Also important to out-migrants were quality of life considerations, such as crime and climate.[46]

Foreign Immigration

Foreign immigration has averaged between 80,000 and 100,000 persons per year in New York based on data collected by the Immigration and Naturalization Service.[47] New York State has continued to be the second most important destination for foreign immigrants (after California), with New York City receiving 90 percent of these immigrants. Based on 1980 census data, it would appear that more than 40 percent of those migrating to New York were from abroad.[48] Armstrong estimates that the foreign-born share of New York City's population was about 36 percent in 1987. By the year 2000, she estimates that 56 percent of New Yorkers will have been born outside the U.S. mainland.[49]

Although the determinants of a foreign immigrant's location decision are complex and may vary significantly by nationality, there is strong evidence that the location of family members or individuals from the same country is important.[50] Since New York City has been one of the major destinations of immigrants over the last several decades, this should encourage continued sizable immigration in the near future. One possible constraint on this may be the availability of affordable housing within New York City. As stressed by Alba and Trent,

> We find it difficult to believe that immigration into the city, which is by far the greatest part of immigration into the state, can be sustained at its present levels without some easing of the city's tight housing markets.[51]

Foreign immigration has primarily involved young families who have provided a disproportionate share of the state's children.[52] They generally have been of average educational background and have had above-average labor force participation rates. Most are concentrated in lower paying jobs and accordingly have had below-average family income. However, they are not more likely than the population in general to fall below the poverty line. They represent a significant share of the lower paid service and manufacturing work force in New York City and are probably not unusually high demanders of public assistance services.

Conclusions

Some would like to point to New York population growth in the past decade as a sign that the corner has been turned on the absolute and relative decline of the New York State economy.[53] While it is quite clear that the economy in the 1980s performed better than in the 1970s, policymakers would do well to look beneath the aggregate population statistics and to think through the more specific implications of these demographic changes for public policy.

In fact, New York population did rebound from its sharp declines in the 1970s. Still, the growth during the 1980s was below the national and even the regional rate of increase, and it was due to natural increase and foreign immigration. There continued to be a net out-migration of population, more than forty thousand persons per year, with the primary destinations the Sunbelt and neighboring northeastern states. Low in-migration rates also have continued, with a significant portion of this in-migration coming from foreign countries. The major location of population growth was New York City, which reversed its decline of the 1970s. Most of the rest of the state experienced slow population growth or absolute decline.

There has continued, on average, to be an aging of the population as the baby boom generation hits middle age. In the near future, this will swell population in the prime working years and could lead to generally higher productivity and income growth. Accompanying these trends has been a continuation of the racial diversification within the state and rapid growth of single-parent households. A growing percentage of the state's children live in poverty.

These demographic changes can have significant repercussions on the welfare of the state's population and demand for government services. Blacks and Hispanics have lower educational achievement and are disadvantaged in the job market. They tend to have higher unemployment and lower labor force participation rates. Accordingly, their incomes tend to be significantly lower than the average household, and a much higher percent are below the poverty line.

In summary, New York's population has been increasing but, perhaps as important, the mix of population has been changing dramatically. It is likely that out-migration of more affluent, working age, and better-educated New Yorkers has been more than replaced by immigration of less well-educated, less skilled, and poorer foreign immigrants. This "replacement" effect, coupled with an increasing concentration of the elderly and poorer, nonwhite households with children, suggests that social welfare needs will place an increasing claim on the state's resources. Underlying all of this is the fact that net out-migration from New York to the rest of the country continued in the 1980s and that in-migration from other states to New York has not changed since the 1970s. All of this taken together means that the "new" population growth observed for New York in the 1980s may not indicate a new competitive edge.

Notes

1. For excellent analyses of the changing New York State population, see Richard Alba and Katherine Trent, *The People of New York: Population Dynamics of a Changing State; New York State Project 2000, Report on Population* (Albany: Rockefeller Institute of Government, 1986); and Richard Alba and Michael Batutis, *The Impact of Migration on New York State* (Albany: Business Council of New York State and New York State Job Training Partnership Council, September 1984).

2. See Table B-1 in Appendix B for population trends for substate areas in New York State. See Appendix A for the definitions of substate areas used in this book.

3. Of the 186 cities in the United States with more than 100,000 inhabitants in 1988, population growth (from 1980 to 1988) in New York City (4 percent overall) ranked below the median (104 out of 186). However, of the twenty-three large cities in the Northeast region, New York City experienced the most rapid population growth during the 1980s. Based on information in the U.S. Bureau of the Census, *Statistical Abstract of the United States, 1990* (Washington, D.C.: U.S. Government Printing Office, 1989).

4. The projections were based on detailed demographic information for each county in New York State, adjusted to reflect special circumstances, such as the existence of military facilities and large university or institutional populations. For a detailed review of the projection methodology, see New York State Data Center, *Official Population Projections for New York State Counties: 1980-2010* (Albany: New York State Department of Commerce, 1985).

5. See Table B-1 in Appendix B.

6. See John D. Kasarda, "The Implications of Contemporary Redistribution Trends for National Urban Policy," *Social Science Quarterly* 61 (December 1980): 373–400; and Daniel Lichter and Glenn V. Fuguitt, "The Transition to Nonmetropolitan Population Deconcentration," *Demography* 19 (May 1982): 211–221.

7. See Table B-1 in Appendix B.

8. See U.S. Bureau of the Census, "Patterns of Metropolitan Area and County Population Growth: 1980 to 1987," *Current Population Reports,* Series P-25, No. 1039 (Washington, D.C.: U.S. Government Printing Office, June 1989).

9. These include family households headed by single parents, or nonmarried parents, and nonfamily households.

10. See Alba and Trent, *The People of New York: Population Dynamics of a Changing State; New York State Project 2000, Report on Population*.

11. See, in particular, U.S. Bureau of the Census, "State Population and Household Estimates, with Age, Sex and Components of Change: 1981–88," *Current Population Reports*, Series P-25, No. 1044 (Washington, D.C.: U.S. Government Printing Office, August 1989); "Population Estimates by Race and Hispanic Origin for States, Metropolitan Areas, and Selected Counties: 1980 to 1985," *Current Population Reports*, Series P-25, No. 1040-RD-1 (Washington, D.C.: U.S. Government Printing Office, May 1989); and "Projections of the Population of States, by Age, Sex and Race: 1988 to 2010," *Current Population Reports*, Series P-25, No. 1017 (Washington, D.C.: U.S. Government Printing Office, October 1988). For estimates of age and racial composition for substate areas in New York, the primary source was the "Experimental County Estimates by Age, Sex, Race and Year," which was prepared by the Bureau of the Census for the National Cancer Institute. For a general review of methodology, see U.S. Bureau of the Census, "Methodology for Experimental Estimates of the Population of Counties, by Age and Sex: July 1, 1975," *Special Studies*, Series P-23, No. 103 (Washington, D.C.: U.S. Government Printing Office, May 1980).

12. U.S. Bureau of the Census, "General Population Characteristics: New York," *1970 Census of Population*, Report PC(1)-B34 (Washington, D.C.: U.S. Government Printing Office, 1971); and U.S. Bureau of the Census, "State Population and Household Estimates: July 1, 1989," *Current Population Reports*, Series P-25, No. 1058 (Washington, D.C.: U.S. Government Printing Office, March 1990).

13. The transition would have been even more rapid had out-migration not decreased in the 1980s. This is because out-migration is heaviest among young adults.

14. See Larry Long, *Migration and Residential Mobility in the United States* (New York: Russell Sage Foundation, 1988).

15. Estimates of population composition for substate areas are available from the authors upon request.

16. Minorities are defined as including all races except whites and white Hispanics. See Joe Schwartz and Thomas Exter, "All Our Children," *American Demographics* 11 (May 1989): 34–37.

17. The faster growth of households than population occurred for the nation as well. See U.S. Bureau of the Census, "State Population and Household Estimates: July 1, 1989," Table 11.

18. U.S. Bureau of the Census, "Household and Family Characteristics," *Current Population Reports*, Series P-20, Nos. 366 and 437 (Washington, D.C.: U.S. Government Printing Office, March 1980 and May 1989); and "Households, Families, Marital Status, and Living Arrangements: March 1989 (Advanced Report)," *Current Population Reports*, Series P-20, No. 441 (Washington, D.C.: U.S. Government Printing Office, November 1989).

19.   New York Council on Children and Families, "Household Projections: New York State," unpublished manuscript, 1984.

20.   Roger Wojtkiewicz, Sara McLanahan, and Irwin Garfinkel, "The Growth of Families Headed by Women: 1950–80," *Demography* 27 (February 1990): 19–30; and James Wetzel, "American Families: 75 Years of Change," *Monthly Labor Review* 113 (March 1990): 4–13.

21.   A household includes all persons who occupy a housing unit where occupants share common living and eating facilities. The poverty line was initially defined in 1964 (three times the cost of the least costly of four "nutritionally adequate" food plans designed by the U.S. Department of Agriculture) and has been modified in 1969 and 1984. These levels are updated annually using the Consumer Price Index. However, there is no attempt to account for differences in the cost of living within the United States. The poverty line in 1988 for a family of four was $12,091. See the U.S. Bureau of the Census, "Money Income and Poverty Status in the United States 1988," *Current Population Reports,* Series P-60, No. 166 (Washington, D.C.: U.S. Government Printing Office, October 1989).

22.   Ibid., Table 18.

23.   See Alba and Trent, *The People of New York: Population Dynamics of a Changing State; New York State Project 2000, Report on Population.*

24.   Wetzel, "American Families: 75 Years of Change," p. 11.

25.   Survey Research Center, *User Guide to the Panel Study of Income Dynamics* (Ann Arbor: University of Michigan, 1984).

26.   Terry K. Adams, Gregg J. Duncan, and Willard R. Rodgers, "Persistent Urban Poverty: Prevalence, Correlates and Trends." Paper presented at "The Kerner Report: 20 Years Later," a conference held in Racine, Wisconsin on February 27 to 29, 1988. "Persistent poverty" is defined as a family being below the poverty line at least 80 percent of the time between 1974 and 1983.

27.   Ibid.

28.   Ibid.

29.   Samuel Ehrenhalt, "Looking to the 1990s: Continuity and Change." Paper presented at the 20th Annual Institute of Challenges of the Changing Economy of New York City, sponsored by the New York City Council on Economic Education, July 1987, pp. 12–14.

30.   As summarized by Alba and Trent, this is "... defined as the number of children a woman would be expected to bear in her lifetime if her behavior at each age recapitulated the prevailing fertility rate specific to that age." See Alba and Trent, *The People of New York: Population Dynamics of a Changing State; New York State Project 2000, Report on Population,* p. 11.

31.   Ibid., p. 14.

32.   U.S. Bureau of the Census, "Population Estimates by Race and

Hispanic Origin for States, Metropolitan Areas, and Selected Counties: 1980 to 1985."

33. U.S. Bureau of the Census, "Fertility of American Women: June 1988," *Current Population Reports,* Series P-20, No. 436 (Washington, D.C.: U.S. Government Printing Office, May 1989).

34. Based on census estimates provided by the New York State Data Center.

35. Migration trends for substate areas are available from the authors upon request.

36. The differences between the IRS and census net migration estimates may be due partly to the undercounting of foreign immigration in the IRS data.

37. Generally, the states with the highest out-migration rates were in the West. See Long, *Migration and Residential Mobility in the United States,* Tables 3–1 and C-1.

38. Ibid., chapter 3, p. 17.

39. A summary of migration trends for the major metropolitan areas in New York State is available from the authors upon request.

40. See Alba and Batutis, *The Impact of Migration on New York State;* and Richard Alba and Katherine Trent, "Population Loss and Change in the North: An Examination of New York's Migration to the Sunbelt," *Social Science Quarterly* 67 (December 1986): 690–706.

41. Long, *Migration and Residential Mobility in the United States,* Figure 3–4.

42. Cornell Institute for Social and Economic Research and Public Policy Institute of New York State, *Patterns of Migration in New York State, 1980 to 1985* (Albany: Public Policy Institute, July 1987). See also John D. Kasarda, Michael Irwin, and Holly Hughes, "Demographic and Economic Shifts in the Sunbelt." Paper presented at the Sunbelt Research Conference, Miami, Florida, November 3 to 6, 1985. The *Current Population Survey* is a national sample of approximately 60,000 households carried out by the Bureau of the Census. It is used to develop estimates of a number of demographic and economic variables.

43. U.S. Bureau of the Census, "Population Estimates by Race and Hispanic Origin for States, Metropolitan Areas, and Selected Counties: 1980 to 1985." Results are reported in Table B-2 in Appendix B.

44. See, for example, Michael J. Greenwood, "Human Migration: Theory, Models, and Empirical Studies," *Journal of Regional Science* 25 (November 1985): 521–544; Richard J. Cebula, *The Determinants of Human Migration* (New York: D.C. Health and Co., 1979); and R. Paul Shaw, *Migration Theory and Fact* (Philadelphia: Regional Science Research Institute, 1975).

45.   Cornell Institute for Social and Economic Research and Public Policy Institute of New York State, *Patterns of Migration in New York State, 1980 to 1985.*

46.   A recent empirical analysis that finds a relationship between mild climate and migration is in Joseph Schachter and Paul G. Althaus, "An Equilibrium Model of Gross Migration," *Journal of Regional Science* 29 (May 1989): 143–160.

47.   See Table B-3 in Appendix B. These include only those admitted as lawful permanent residents. Excluded are those with temporary visas or residing in the country illegally. For definitions and immigration statistics, see the U.S. Department of Justice, Immigration, and Naturalization Service, *1988 Statistical Yearbook of the Immigration and Naturalization Service* (Washington, D.C.: U.S. Department of Commerce, August 1989). Foreign in-migration and out-migration were removed from the IRS migration statistics due to the undercounting in this data.

48.   U.S. Bureau of the Census, "Geographic Mobility for States and the Nation," *1980 Census of Population,* Report PC80-2-2A (Washington, D.C.: U.S. Government Printing Office, September 1985), Table 25, p. 168. For an excellent review of immigration to New York, see Alba and Trent, *The People of New York: Population Dynamics of a Changing State; New York State Project 2000, Report on Population,* chapter 3.

49.   Regina Armstrong, "Immigration," *Citizens Budget Commission Quarterly* 9 (Winter 1989): 5.

50.   See Ann P. Bartel, *Location Decisions of the New Immigrants to the United States,* NBER Working Paper No. 2049 (Cambridge: National Bureau of Economic Research, October 1986).

51.   Alba and Trent, *The People of New York: Population Dynamics of a Changing State; New York State Project 2000, Report on Population,* p. 67.

52.   Using census data, it appears that 56 percent of foreign immigrants are between twenty and forty-four years of age. See Alba and Trent, *The People of New York: Population Dynamics of a Changing State; New York State Project 2000, Report on Population,* chapter 3.

53.   A good example is "Population's Rise in the Northeast Reverses a Trend," *New York Times* (April 7, 1985), p. 1.

2

Employment

Above all else, it was the loss of 450,000 jobs in the city and 300,000 manufacturing jobs in the state during the 1970s that prompted concern about the future of the New York economy.[1] The picture has improved dramatically, with employment increasing by more than 1 million since 1980 and with 30 percent of this growth in New York City. Moreover, the unemployment rate for the state remained below the national average during the 1980s.

Despite this better record, there are still many employment problems facing New York State. This chapter describes and interprets employment trends in New York and suggests what they imply for the future of the New York economy. Emphasis is given to examining the detail of the structural changes and to two commonly cited solutions to the loss of manufacturing jobs—the promotion of high-technology and export-oriented industries.

General Trends

Employment in New York rebounded from the stagnant period of the 1970s, growing by an average of 1.5 percent per year since 1980 (Table 7). Growth has been almost as rapid as that in the rest of the Northeast and only slightly below the average for the United States. New York State employment was hurt much less by the 1981–82 recession than were the regional or national economies and much less than it was during the 1973–75 recession.

In the recovery since 1983, employment has grown by more than 2 percent per year. However, this lags behind the regional and national growth rates (Figure 3). Compared to the other northeastern states, employment growth lags behind all but Pennsylvania, especially since 1983 (Table 8). The growth rates in Maine, New Hampshire, New Jersey, and Vermont actually exceeded that for the nation.

If New York State employment had grown at the national rate during this expansion, more than 500,000 *additional* jobs would have been added since 1983. While this is a large number, it is well below the corresponding growth gap of close to 2 million jobs during the 1970s.[2] Employment growth rates were less than half those of the United States as a whole for 1988 and 1989 and are projected to continue lagging behind those of other states in the region and the nation during the 1990s.

The unemployment rate, which was consistently above the national average during the 1970s, has been below the average rate since 1981 (see Figure 3).[3] However, as will be discussed below, not all occupations, demographic groups, and regions of the state have benefited from what appears to be a tighter labor market in New York. One issue is displaced or dislocated workers.[4] The New York State Job Service estimates that the highest incidence of dislocated workers in New York is not in manufacturing but in the service sector and that the incidence is heavily concentrated in New York City.[5]

The total labor force participation rate and that for blacks are both lower in New York than in the rest of the nation. This lower labor force participation rate takes something away from the euphoria about New York's low unemployment rate. Ehrenhalt emphasizes this for New York City: "The proportion of New Yorkers employed holds at about ten percentage points below the nation, a gap that has been developing over the years. It means that it would take something on the order of 450,000 New Yorkers employed to lift the New York City experience up to the nation. This points to a considerable job deficit and a substantial number of New Yorkers outside the mainstream of the economy."[6]

The major reason for the reversal in employment trends during the 1980s has been the rebound of the New York City economy.[7] New York City lost 12 percent of its employment, or close to a half-million jobs, during the 1970s. It was particularly hard hit by the 1973–75 recession, with a decline of more than 7 percent in total jobs. Employment continued to fall during the early years of the

TABLE 7

Employment Trends and Projections: Nonagricultural Employment for New York,
The Northeast Region, and the United States
(In Thousands)

Year	New York State			Other Northeast Region[a]			United States	
	Employment	Annual Percent Change	Share of United States (Percent)	Employment	Annual Percent Change	Share of United States (Percent)	Employment	Annual Percent Change
1960	6,182		11.4	9,427		17.4	54,189	
1970	7,156	1.5	10.1	11,482	2.0	16.2	70,880	2.7
1975	6,830	-0.9	8.9	11,793	0.5	15.3	76,945	1.7
1980	7,207	1.1	8.0	13,295	2.4	14.7	90,406	3.3
1986	7,908	1.6	7.9	14,514	1.5	14.6	99,525	1.6
1987	8,059	1.9	7.9	14,915	2.8	14.6	102,200	2.7
1988	8,186	1.6	7.8	15,274	2.4	14.5	105,584	3.3
1989	8,265	1.0	7.6	15,413	0.9	14.2	108,581	2.8
Projections[b]:								
2000	8,944	0.7		17,122	1.0		123,270	1.2

Business Cycles[c]:			
Expansion 1971–73	0.9	2.9	3.8
Contraction 1973–75	-2.1	-0.9	0.1
Expansion 1975–79	1.3	2.9	3.9
1980–81	1.1	0.4	0.8
Contraction 1981–82	-0.4	-1.6	-1.7
Expansion 1982–89	1.9	2.3	2.8
Long-term Trends:			
1970–80	0.1	1.5	2.5
1980–89	1.5	1.7	2.1

[a]Includes Connecticut, Maine, Massachusetts, New Hampshire, New Jersey, Pennsylvania, Rhode Island, and Vermont.

[b]Based on the projected growth rates for nonfarm employment for 1988 to 2000 by the U.S. Bureau of Economic Analysis.

[c]These are only rough approximations of the business cycles because they are based on annual averages.

Source: U.S. Department of Labor, Bureau of Labor Statistics, *Employment, Hours and Earnings, States and Areas,* and *Employment and Earnings,* March 1990; and U.S. Department of Commerce, Bureau of Economic Analysis, *Survey of Current Business,* May 1990.

FIGURE 3

Employment Trends and Unemployment Rates (1970–1989)

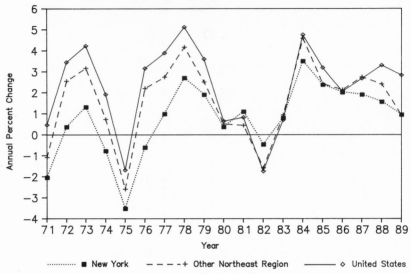

EMPLOYMENT TRENDS (1970–1989)
NEW YORK, OTHER NORTHEAST REGION, AND TOTAL UNITED STATES

.... ■ New York   – – – –+ Other Northeast Region   ———— ◇ United States

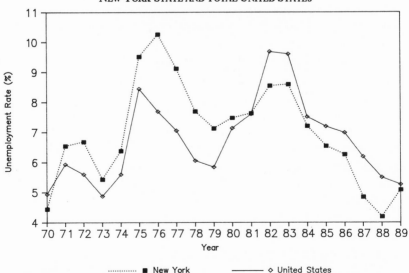

UNEMPLOYMENT RATES (1970–1989)
NEW YORK STATE AND TOTAL UNITED STATES

.... ■ New York   ———— ◇ United States

Sources: New York State Department of Labor; U.S. Bureau of Labor Statistics

TABLE 8
Employment Trends
New York Compared to Other Northeast States

	Annual Percent Change		Percent of United States[a]		
	1970–80	*1980–89*	*1970*	*1980*	*1989*
New York	0.1	1.5	10.1	8.0	7.6
Connecticut	1.8	1.8	1.7	1.6	1.5
Maine	2.3	3.0	0.5	0.5	0.5
Massachusetts	1.7	1.8	3.2	2.9	2.9
New Hampshire	4.1	3.5	0.4	0.4	0.5
New Jersey	1.6	2.2	3.7	3.4	3.4
Pennsylvania	0.9	0.8	6.1	5.3	4.7
Rhode Island	1.5	1.6	0.5	0.4	0.4
Vermont	3.1	3.0	0.2	0.2	0.2
Other Northeast	1.5	1.7	16.2	14.7	14.2
Total United States	2.5	2.1	100.0	100.0	100.0

[a]Percentages for the other Northeast states may not add to total due to rounding.

Source: U.S. Department of Labor, Bureau of Labor Statistics, *Employment, Hours and Earnings, States and Areas*, and *Employment and Earnings*, March 1990.

recovery, when national employment was growing by 4 percent per year (Table 9; Figure 4). Unemployment rates were consistently one to two points above the national average.

Since 1980, New York City has gained back 70 percent of the jobs lost in the 1970s, an increase of more than 300,000. In contrast to the 1973–75 recession, New York City fared much better in the 1981–82 recession than the rest of the nation. Since 1982, though, employment growth has been less than 50 percent of the growth rate for the country and is projected to lag behind state and national growth. Had New York City grown at national rates, it would have added close to 400,000 additional jobs since 1980. There has been "near flat" job growth for the entire region since 1987, suggesting an economic slowdown.[8] Unemployment rates have improved considerably in New York City since the early 1980s due to a sharp drop in the number of unemployed (see Figure 4).[9]

The most rapid employment growth and lowest unemployment rates continue to be enjoyed by the suburbs surrounding New York

TABLE 9

Employment Trends and Projections: Nonagricultural Employment in
New York City, New York City Suburbs, and the Rest of the State
(In Thousands)

Year	New York City			New York City Suburbs[a]			Rest of New York State		
	Employ-ment	Annual Percent Change	Share of New York State (Percent)	Employ-ment	Annual Percent Change	Share of New York State (Percent)	Employ-ment	Annual Percent Change	Share of New York State (Percent)
1960	3,538		57.2	720		11.6	1,923		31.1
1970	3,746	0.6	52.3	1,101	4.3	15.4	2,310	1.9	32.3
1975	3,286	-2.6	48.1	1,179	1.4	17.3	2,365	0.5	34.6
1980	3,302	0.1	45.8	1,362	2.9	18.9	2,544	1.5	35.3
1986	3,541	1.2	44.8	1,616	2.9	20.4	2,752	1.3	34.8
1987	3,591	1.4	44.6	1,648	2.0	20.4	2,820	2.5	35.0
1988	3,605	0.4	44.0	1,666	1.1	20.4	2,915	3.4	35.6
1989	3,609	0.1	43.7	1,675	0.5	20.3	2,981	2.3	36.1
Projections[b]:									
1990	3,699	1.1	43.9	1,773	2.3	21.0	2,961	1.7	35.1
2000	3,927	0.6	42.8	2,008	1.3	21.9	3,244	0.9	35.3

Business Cycles[c]:			
Expansion 1971–73	–1.0	3.7	3.0
Contraction 1973–75	–3.7	–0.4	–1.0
Expansion 1975–79	–0.1	3.2	1.6
1980–81	1.7	1.5	–1.6
Contraction 1981–82	–0.4	1.5	0.3
Expansion 1982–89	1.1	2.6	2.5
Long-term Trends:			
1970–80	–1.3	2.1	1.0
1980–89	1.0	2.3	1.8

[a]Includes Nassau, Putnam, Rockland, Suffolk, and Westchester counties.

[b]Projections for New York State and New York City area are based on projected growth rates for nonfarm employment for 1983 to 1990 and 1990 to 2000 by the U.S. Bureau of Economic Analysis. Projected employment is distributed among New York City suburbs and the rest of the state based on past employment distribution.

[c]These are only rough approximations of the business cycles because they are based on annual averages.

Source: U.S. Department of Labor, Bureau of Labor Statistics, *Employment, Hours and Earnings, States and Areas;* and U.S. Department of Commerce, Bureau of Economic Analysis, *1985 OBERS BEA Regional Projections.*

FIGURE 4

Employment Trends and Unemployment Rates (1970–1989)

EMPLOYMENT TRENDS (1970–1989)
NEW YORK CITY, SUBURBS, AND OTHER NEW YORK STATE

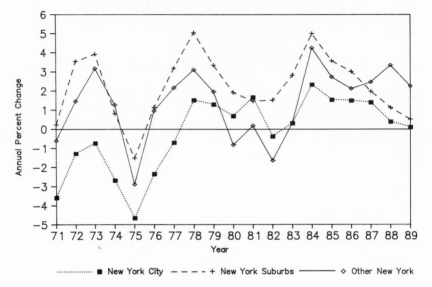

UNEMPLOYMENT RATES (1970–1989)
NEW YORK CITY AND THE REST OF NEW YORK STATE

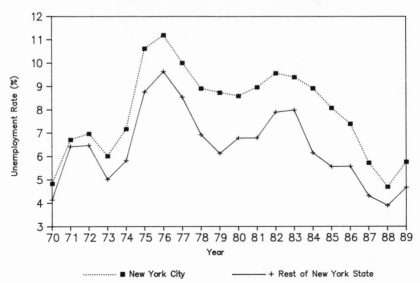

Sources: New York State Department of Labor; U.S. Bureau of Labor Statistics

City. Employment in these areas has increased faster than during the 1970s, grew even during the 1981–82 recession, and has increased by 2.6 percent per year since 1982. Rapid growth has also occurred in the nearby mid-Hudson region, suggesting a "spreading out" of the New York City gains to the immediate region.[10] Although growth in these suburban areas is expected to slow during the 1990s, it should still exceed the national growth rate (see Table 9).

Within the regions of upstate New York, employment growth was slow during the 1970s in the traditional manufacturing centers of Buffalo, Binghamton, Elmira, and Utica. In contrast, the more diversified economies of Albany, Rochester, and Syracuse fared better. These patterns appear to have continued during the 1980s. Employment in the Albany, Rochester, and Syracuse metropolitan areas (and regions) has grown at or above the statewide average rate. In contrast, Buffalo, Elmira, and Utica have experienced slow employment growth (or even absolute decline) since 1980. However, employment growth in these areas has rebounded since the 1981–82 recession as they continue to restructure their economies.[11] These areas are forecast to continue their slow employment growth during the 1990s.

Composition of Employment Growth

Although most areas in New York State appear to have faced an improved employment picture during the 1980s, not all population groups within the state have benefited equally. Based on information from the *Current Population Survey*,[12] it is possible to identify which occupations and which demographic groups appear not to have shared in New York's growth in the 1980s.[13]

As is clear from Table 10, there are significant differences in occupational distribution between white and nonwhite employees. More than 30 percent of whites hold professional, technical, and managerial positions compared to 20 percent or less for nonwhites. Eleven percent of whites in New York State hold higher skill blue-collar jobs compared to 8.5 percent for nonwhites. Within New York State, this disparity appears to have widened since 1980 for professional/managerial jobs and to have narrowed somewhat for skilled blue-collar jobs.

Nonwhite employees continue to be disproportionately concentrated in service and lower skilled blue-collar jobs. These data suggest

TABLE 10

Demographic and Occupational Distribution of Employment
For New York State, New York City, and the Nation

	1980			1986		
	United States	New York State	New York City	United States	New York State	New York City
White:						
Percent of Population	87.5	85.0	70.8	86.1	83.2	68.9
Percent of Population Employed:	60.1	56.3	51.4	61.5	58.5	51.8
Distribution of Employment by Occupation (Percent):[a]						
Professional/Manager	28.5	30.4	32.1	28.3	32.2	35.9
Clerical/Sales	25.4	28.6	32.3	28.8	30.3	30.9
Blue Collar:	31.3	26.8	23.2	27.4	23.0	19.7
Precision/Craft	13.3	11.1	8.8	12.7	11.0	8.7
Other	18.0	15.7	14.4	14.7	12.0	11.0
Service Workers	12.1	13.0	12.4	12.2	12.8	12.9
Nonwhite:						
Percent of Population:	12.5	15.0	29.2	13.9	16.8	31.1
Percent of Population Employed:	53.2	51.0	49.4	54.1	50.4	49.0
Distribution of Employment by Occupation (Percent):[a]						
Professional/Manager	17.9	19.5	19.1	17.3	19.3	18.2
Clerical/Sales	21.3	28.6	31.4	24.5	31.9	34.5
Blue Collar:	35.9	26.8	25.1	33.2	24.2	23.4
Precision/Craft	9.6	7.2	7.1	9.7	8.5	8.9
Other	26.3	19.6	18.0	23.5	15.7	14.5
Service Workers	23.1	25.1	24.4	23.8	20.3	23.8

[a]Percentages will not add to 100 since some minor occupational categories were not included.

Source: U.S. Department of Labor, Bureau of Labor Statistics, *Geographic Profile of Employment and Unemployment*, 1980 and 1986.

that the concern that minorities are concentrated in low-paying, dead-end jobs is well justified. This, combined with recent research showing that the "working poor" are an increasing percentage of those below the poverty line and that low earnings is the major cause,[14] indicates that many nonwhite households would remain poor even if they were able to find full-time employment.

Recent national projections show that two of the three occupational categories that are most likely to employ minorities—clerical and low-skill blue-collar occupations—are anticipated to experience below-average growth during the 1990s.[15] Only service occupations are projected to grow faster than average. The highest growth is expected to be in occupations requiring the most education. As summarized by Silvestri and Lukasiewicz, "Blacks and Hispanics, who traditionally have had lower educational attainment than whites, are likely to continue to be at a disadvantage in the job market unless their educational attainment improves."[16] Since New York State and especially New York City have a higher percentage of nonwhite residents, such occupational disparities may be particularly important.

It is well documented that unemployment rates have been much higher among nonwhites, and such differences appear to have widened during the 1980s.[17] Since lower skill occupations generally have higher unemployment rates, minorities have been especially hurt. Although undoubtedly a portion of this unemployment is transitory, there is evidence that much of it is structural, particularly among nonwhite teenagers.[18] In addition, labor force participation rates have been significantly lower among the poor, with the "increase in the proportion of poor families headed by women" as the major reason.[19] A growing economy will not necessarily help such disadvantaged workers, that is, there is a case for more targeted assistance.

Changes in Employment Structure

The major change in employment structure that has taken place over the last several decades, from goods to service production, has received significant attention. However, the implications of these structural changes remain a matter of great controversy. Is America deindustrializing, and what does this imply for long-run competitiveness and economic growth? What effect will the strong growth in services have on income distribution and cyclical fluctuations in employment? How serious is the displaced worker problem? Will they ever be absorbed by the growing service sectors?

It is beyond the scope of this study to review the extensive literature in this area and try to answer these questions for New York State. Instead, we summarize the structural changes that took place during the 1980s, with a focus on pinpointing the growing and declining industries (Box 3).

Box 3. Employment Estimates

Ideally, research should utilize employment estimates that provide both the most complete coverage of employees and the greatest disaggregation by industry and geographic area. Unfortunately, no one source meets all of these criteria. The most generally accepted employment estimate is the "Current Employment Statistics" or "Establishment Survey" produced jointly by state labor departments and the U.S. Bureau of Labor Statistics. (This is the basic source used in chapter 2.) It is based on an extensive survey of establishments and provides a consistent time series over the last several decades. However, it does not cover proprietors, self-employed, or agricultural workers and has limited geographic and industry disaggregation.

There are several other sources of employment data but none are able to meet all of these criteria. As parts of the research for this chapter, an extensive comparison was made of these different employment estimates for New York State.[a] Not surprisingly, it was found that there is significant variation in the coverage between these sources, both by sector and geographic area. Although it is clear that these estimates should not be mixed, the key question is whether they produce different answers about employment trends. Despite the major differences in coverage, the trends in employment in the BLS Establishment Survey, Bureau of Economic Analysis estimates, and census *County Business Patterns* appear to be quite similar.[b] This gives us some confidence in using these other two sources to supplement the basic employment data from the BLS.

---

[a] The other sources examined include employment estimates by the U.S. Bureau of Economic Analysis (BEA), which provide the most complete coverage but lack detailed industry estimates; the "Insured Employment Statistics" (ES-202) published by the U.S. Bureau of Labor Statistics (BLS), which provides county level data but is not revised for consistency; and U.S. Bureau of the Census, *County Business Patterns*, which provides detailed geographic and industry disaggregation but is not current and revised for consistency.

[b] This does not appear to be the case for the BLS ES-202 data that show significant differences in growth rates for services and government employment. The results of this comparison are available from the authors upon request.

Goods-producing Sectors

For the purposes of presenting information on employment trends, industries are divided according to whether they produce goods or services. Although there are always gray areas whenever such divisions are made, we will use this classification throughout this presentation. The goods-producing sector includes agriculture, mining, construction, and manufacturing. Since manufacturing has dominated employment in the goods-producing sector, this is where most of the attention is focused.

New York State has followed national trends, with a sharp drop in the relative importance of manufacturing employment. From more than 30 percent of nonagricultural employees in 1960, manufacturing employment decreased to 14 percent in 1989 (Table 11). However, unlike the rest of the country, New York State has experienced an *absolute* decline in manufacturing employment since 1960. The decline during the 1980s (2.1 percent per year) was on par with that of the 1970s. Both durable and nondurable manufacturing employment declined sharply since 1980, compared to the last half of the 1970s, when only nondurable manufacturing employment declined (Table 12).

These trends are similar to those experienced by the other northeastern states, with a decrease of 2.1 percent in manufacturing employment. The major industrial states—Connecticut, Massachusetts, New Jersey, and Pennsylvania—all lost more than 2 percent per year of their manufacturing employment during the 1980s. The losses were also spread evenly between durable and nondurable industries.

New York City has consistently experienced the sharpest decrease in manufacturing employment (4 percent per year since 1970), with a loss of more than 40 percent of jobs in heavy industry since 1975. It is possible that some of this decrease is the result of migration of firms and jobs to the New York City suburbs, which is the only area of the state experiencing manufacturing employment growth since 1975.[20]

In upstate New York, manufacturing employment has continued to decline. Although manufacturing employment fell during the early 1970s, growth resumed during the recovery in the second half of that decade. This has not carried over to the 1980s. Manufacturing employment dropped sharply during the two recessions early in the

TABLE 11

Percent Distribution of Employment by Industry Class[a]: New York and Total United States

	United States		New York State		New York City		New York City Suburbs[b]		Rest of New York State	
	1975	1989	1975	1989	1975	1989	1975	1989	1975	1989
Total Employment	100.0	100.0	100.0	100.0	100.0	100.0	100.0	100.0	100.0	100.0
Goods-producing Sectors:	29.4	23.6	24.0	18.6	18.8	13.3	23.0	19.8	31.8	24.0
Mining	1.0	0.7	0.1	0.1	0.0	0.0	0.0	0.0	0.2	0.2
Construction	4.6	4.9	3.1	4.1	2.4	3.3	4.4	5.5	3.4	3.9
Total Manufacturing	23.8	18.1	20.8	14.4	16.3	10.0	18.6	14.3	28.2	19.9
Durable	13.9	10.6	11.2	7.9	4.9	2.6	11.6	8.8	19.9	13.7
Nondurable	9.9	7.4	9.6	6.6	11.5	7.4	7.0	5.4	8.3	6.2
Service-producing Sectors:	70.6	76.4	76.0	81.4	81.2	86.7	77.0	80.2	68.2	76.0
Distributive Services:	11.6	11.0	12.7	10.8	15.9	12.3	10.7	11.5	9.1	8.5
Transportation and Public Utilities	5.9	5.3	6.4	4.9	8.2	5.9	4.8	4.3	4.6	4.1
Wholesale Trade	5.7	5.7	6.3	5.8	7.7	6.4	5.9	7.2	4.5	4.5
Retail Trade	16.4	18.0	14.2	15.2	11.5	11.2	19.4	18.3	15.4	18.2
Consumer Services:	6.4	7.1	6.1	7.3	6.1	7.6	7.9	10.1	7.0	8.5
Lodging/Amusement	1.9	2.4	1.7	2.2	1.4	2.2	1.9	2.0	2.0	2.3
Other	4.5	4.8	4.4	5.2	4.6	5.4	6.0	8.1	5.0	6.3

Producer Services:	10.3	15.4	15.8	20.6	22.6	29.3	10.8	14.3	7.0	10.5
FIRE	5.4	6.3	8.5	9.6	12.8	14.7	5.2	7.2	4.1	4.8
Business Services	2.7	5.3	4.1	5.4	5.7	7.4	4.2	5.3	1.8	3.1
Other	2.3	3.8	3.3	5.6	4.2	7.2	1.4	1.8	1.2	2.6
Nonprofit Services:	6.7	8.5	7.7	10.1	7.5	9.7	7.9	10.3	7.9	10.5
Health Services	5.4	7.0	5.7	7.3	5.6	6.9	6.0	8.1	5.6	7.4
Educational Services	1.3	1.5	2.1	2.7	1.9	2.8	1.8	2.2	2.4	3.0
Government	19.1	16.3	19.5	17.5	17.5	16.7	20.4	15.9	21.7	19.4

[a] The classification methodology is available from the authors upon request. The subcategories may not add to the total due to rounding.

[b] Includes Nassau, Putnam, Rockland, Suffolk, and Westchester counties.

Source: U.S. Department of Labor, Bureau of Labor Statistics, *Employment and Earnings*, May 1985–89, March 1990, and *Employment, Hours and Earnings, States and Areas.*

TABLE 12

Annual Percent Change in Employment by Industry Class[a]:
New York and Total United States

	United States		New York State		New York City		New York City Suburbs[b]		Rest of New York State	
	1975-80	1980-89	1975-80	1980-89	1975-80	1980-89	1975-80	1980-89	1975-80	1980-89
Total Employment	3.3	2.1	1.1	1.5	0.1	1.0	2.9	2.3	1.5	1.8
Goods-producing Sectors:	2.6	0.0	0.2	-0.9	-1.5	-1.9	2.9	0.6	0.6	-0.9
Mining	6.4	-3.8	-3.8	-0.8	-4.1	-12.3	8.4	1.7	-4.9	0.8
Construction	4.3	2.2	-0.2	5.4	-0.8	5.1	1.0	6.0	-0.5	4.7
Total Manufacturing	2.1	-0.4	0.3	-2.1	-1.6	-3.5	3.3	-0.9	0.7	-1.7
Durable	2.7	-0.6	0.9	-2.3	-2.0	-4.7	4.0	-1.2	0.9	-2.1
Nondurable	1.2	0.0	-0.4	-1.9	-1.4	-3.0	2.3	-0.2	0.3	-0.8
Service-producing Sectors:	3.6	2.8	1.3	2.2	0.4	1.5	2.9	2.8	1.9	2.8
Distributive Services:	3.1	1.5	0.4	0.1	-0.8	-1.4	3.8	2.7	1.1	1.3
Transportation and Public Utilities	2.5	1.2	-0.1	-0.7	-0.9	-2.1	1.8	1.7	0.8	0.8
Wholesale Trade	3.6	1.9	0.9	0.8	-0.7	-0.8	5.4	3.3	1.4	1.8
Retail Trade	3.5	3.0	0.9	2.4	-0.7	1.1	2.0	2.2	1.7	3.6

Consumer Services:	3.0	3.4	1.4	3.5	1.3	2.8	3.6	4.8	1.3	4.1
Lodging/Amusement	4.2	3.8	2.0	3.7	3.1	4.1	1.4	3.8	1.2	3.2
Other	2.5	3.1	1.2	3.4	0.8	2.3	4.3	5.0	1.3	4.4
Producer Services:	6.5	4.9	3.6	3.1	3.0	2.3	4.9	4.5	4.8	4.5
FIRE	4.4	3.1	1.6	2.7	1.3	1.9	3.6	5.6	1.8	3.6
Business Services	8.7	7.2	5.7	2.2	5.3	1.2	6.6	3.0	6.5	5.2
Other	8.4	5.0	5.6	5.0	4.5	4.8	4.4	4.8	11.2	5.5
Nonprofit Services:	4.6	4.2	2.6	3.7	1.6	3.0	4.3	4.7	3.2	4.0
Health Services	5.0	4.2	2.3	3.8	1.0	2.9	3.7	5.3	3.3	4.0
Educational Services	2.6	4.1	3.5	3.4	3.3	3.2	6.3	2.7	2.7	3.9
Government	2.0	1.0	-0.2	1.1	-2.1	1.7	1.4	0.4	1.0	0.8

[a]The classification methodology is available from the authors upon request.

[b]Includes Nassau, Putnam, Rockland, Suffolk, and Westchester counties.

Source: U.S. Department of Labor, Bureau of Labor Statistics, *Employment and Earnings*, May 1985–89, March 1990, and *Employment, Hours and Earnings, States and Areas.*

decade and has not recovered during the present expansion. Especially hard hit were the Albany, Buffalo, Elmira, and Utica metropolitan areas, declining by more than 2 percent per year since 1980.[21]

The declines were particularly sharp in durable goods industries, which represent the majority of upstate manufacturing employment. The durable manufacturing industries where most of the decline occurred were primary metal products and transportation (Buffalo), machinery (Syracuse and Rochester), fabricated metal products (Buffalo, Rochester, and Binghamton), and instruments (Rochester). Among nondurable manufacturing, most employment decline occurred in apparel and textile products (New York City and its suburbs), food and kindred products (Albany, New York City, and Rochester), and chemicals (New York City).[22]

Based on recent Bureau of Labor Statistics (BLS) projections for national employment by sector, it appears that employment in most of these industries will continue to decline to the end of the century. The success of U.S. manufacturing industries in the 1990s, according to the BLS, will depend on their ability to generate foreign exports. According to Personick, "Most of the export growth will be concentrated in capital goods industries, in particular, computers."[23]

What does the declining importance of manufacturing imply for the state and national economy in the long run? Advocates of the deindustrialization hypothesis point to the declining employment and stagnant productivity in manufacturing and are concerned about the loss of whole parts of the manufacturing base to foreign competition.[24] This loss of manufacturing employment will displace many blue-collar workers who will be forced to take lower paying service jobs or who will drop out of the work force entirely.[25] Their emphasis has been on the human and social cost of deindustrialization.

On the other side of this debate are those who view deindustrialization as either an inaccurate characterization of what has occurred in the U.S. economy or as a part of a healthy transformation of the U.S. economy.[26] It is emphasized that absolute manufacturing employment at the national level has not declined and that the stagnant employment trends have been accompanied by productivity improvements. Manufacturing output has maintained its share (in constant dollars) of gross national product (GNP) over the last several decades.[27] Although certain manufacturing industries have not fared well, as a whole, the manufacturing sector is not in bad shape. The transition that has occurred to financial and high-technology services is a natural response to the changing comparative advantage of this country.[28]

These structural transformations appear to have occurred more rapidly in New York State than in the rest of the nation. Unlike the country as a whole, New York has actually lost manufacturing jobs, one-third since 1960. Given the recent record, it is likely that such declines will continue in the near future. Understanding the effects of this structural change, particularly on vulnerable groups, takes on a special urgency in New York State.

Service-producing Sectors

In contrast to the goods-producing sectors, the service-producing sectors have been the primary source of employment growth over the last several decades. These sectors in New York State have grown from 71.5 percent of employment in 1970 to 81.4 percent today (see Table 11). While the goods-producing sector has experienced an absolute decline in employment since 1980, service employment has grown by 21 percent. This employment growth has occurred over all parts of the state and has been especially rapid since 1983, growing by 2.6 percent per year. Despite this rapid growth in New York, service-sector employment growth has lagged behind that for the rest of the region and nation.[29]

However, the service sectors are far from a homogeneous group of industries, and no one industry clearly dominates. Even defining goods versus services is a matter of controversy (Box 4). There are significant differences in the relative importance of the various parts of the service sector (see Table 11) and striking differences in the growth rates (see Table 12).

Consistently, the fastest growing service sector, both nationally and in New York State, has been producer services. Statewide employment in producer services has grown by more than 3.0 percent per year since 1980, compared to a national rate of 4.9 percent per year. This rapid growth appears to have taken place throughout the state despite the wide variation in the relative importance of this sector to total employment.[30] Certain industries in producer services have consistently been among the fastest growing industries in the state and nation during the 1980s (see Table 12).

The largest part of producer services is the finance, insurance, and real estate (FIRE) sector.[31] As the name implies, this is a diverse

---

Box 4. Defining the Service Sector

The service-producing sector has often been defined as a residual category, that is, all those industries not involved primarily in the production of goods. For analytic purposes, this definition is less useful than it would appear. The distinction between goods and services can become particularly difficult within the transportation, communications, and public utility sectors.[a] The division appears even more arbitrary when the many service functions performed within a manufacturing firm are considered. If the firm chooses to provide the services itself, the resulting employment would be classified as goods producing under the residual method.[b]

Another alternative, defining the components of services by the division (1 digit) level of standard industrial classification (SIC), is also inadequate, in our view, because the service sector (SIC 7 and 8) is too broad to be meaningful. A third approach, and the one we have chosen, is to reclassify the industries in the service according to end use (final demand versus intermediate use) and type of provider (private, nonprofit, and government).[c]

---

[a] For example, Stanback, in his first book on the service sector, classified transportation, communications, and public utilities as goods rather than services. In his later work, he appears to have revised this definition, placing these industries in services. See Thomas Stanback, *Understanding the Service Economy* (Baltimore: Johns Hopkins University Press, 1979); and Stanback, *Services: The New Economy* (Totowa, NJ: Allenheld, Osmun & Co., 1981).

[b] The U.S. Bureau of the Census, in its publication *County Business Patterns*, does attempt to break out separately "administrative and auxiliary" employment in manufacturing. However, our view is that coverage below the state level is too spotty to be usable.

[c] This classification borrows heavily from that developed by Stanback in *Services: The New Economy*. Due to data limitations, some modifications were made to his scheme, and it was not possible to carry out this disaggregation for upstate metropolitan areas or regions. Employment for these areas is presented by major industry classification (Tables C-4 and C-5 in Appendix C).

---

sector that provides many consumer as well as producer services.[32] FIRE employment growth was relatively strong in all parts of the state during the 1980s, averaging 2.0 percent per year in New York City, 5.6 percent in its suburbs, and 3.6 percent in the rest of the state (see Table 12). With the exception of a few areas (Binghamton and Glens Falls), employment growth was 2.5 percent or greater in all MSAs and regions in upstate New York.[33]

Not surprisingly, New York City accounts for the largest share of FIRE employment in the state (two-thirds in 1989). From 1980 to

1987, FIRE employment grew by close to 3.0 percent per year, only slightly below the national rate of 3.5 percent. Since 1987, employment has declined by 2 percent per year. Especially affected have been the security and commodity broker and banking sectors. This decline was undoubtedly due in part to the stock market "crash" of October 1987 (Box 5). The long-term effects of the crash on FIRE employment in New York City are unclear, but nationally, employment growth is projected to be strong for security and commodity

---

Box 5. October 1987 Crash

One employment issue receiving significant attention in the New York City area over the last several years is the effect of the October 1987 stock market "collapse." There has been disagreement over the short-term and long-term impact on the local and state economy.[a] Although it is too early to assess long-term trends, the short-run effects appear to be concentrated in certain sectors of the economy.

From October 1987 to October 1988, New York City lost thirteen thousand jobs in the FIRE (finance, insurance, and real estate) sector (a 2.3 percent loss compared to a 2.6 percent annual growth from October 1982 to October 1987). FIRE employment continued to decline in New York City by more than 2.0 percent during 1989, with the losses concentrated in banking (3.3 percent) and security and commodity brokers (4.6 percent). This appears to have led to stagnant employment growth from 1987 to 1989 for the FIRE sector for New York State as a whole. However, FIRE employment in the rest of New York State continued to grow by more than 4 percent per year during this period. The rest of the country also experienced slower growth in FIRE employment after the crash (2.3 percent per year growth from 1987 to 1989 compared to 3.5 percent from 1980 to 1987).

The one other service sector that might have been affected by the crash was business services. Employment grew by 3.1 percent per year in New York City and 6.3 percent in the rest of the state from 1980 to 1987 but dropped by 5.2 percent and 3.4 percent per year, respectively, from 1987 to 1989. It would not appear that there has been a "ripple" effect to other services since growth rates from 1987 to 1989 remained at levels similar to those from 1980 to 1987. The overall effect on employment appears to have been primarily a dampening of growth rates in New York City but a relatively small impact on the rest of the state or nation.

---

[a] See, for example, *New York Times* articles on December 12, 1987 ("Job Outlook After Stock Collapse Rated Cloudy in New York"), and January 22, 1988 ("Big Drop in Jobs in New York City Is Predicted by Its Budget Director").

brokers (3.0 percent per year) but weak in banking employment (0.7 percent).[34]

In upstate New York, retail services, such as insurance and real estate agencies, grew the fastest.[35] Despite the recent growth, there is some indication that employment growth in this sector may begin to slow outside the New York City area. The deregulation of the banking industry, automation of banking and security industries, and the increased use of mutual funds may result in a slowdown in the growth of branch banks and brokerage services.[36] Whether the rapid growth in insurance and real estate can continue in upstate New York without sustained growth in other sectors is an open question. Nationally, annual employment growth in the 1990s for insurance and real estate agents is projected to be 1.8 percent and 0.8 percent per year, respectively.[37]

The other major component of producer services is the business service sector. These services range in importance from 3 percent of employment in upstate New York to 7 percent in New York City. They have grown by more than 2.0 percent per year since 1980, well below the national rate of 7.2 percent. Employment growth was strong in this sector in New York from 1980 to 1987 (more than 4 percent per year). Since then, business service employment has decreased by 4.5 percent per year, with the decline spread throughout the state. This appears to be the other service sector affected by the crash of October 1987 (see Box 5). The majority of new business service jobs continue to be in the New York City area. Of every one hundred new jobs in the business service sector during the 1980s, thirty-three were in New York City and twenty-six were in the downstate suburbs. Despite the recent declines in this sector in New York, it is projected to be one of the fastest growing sectors in the country during the 1990s (3.4 percent per year).[38]

This sector is quite diverse, ranging from lower skill "services to buildings" (mainly janitorial) to high-tech computer and data processing.[39] By far the most rapid growth in this sector has been in the computer and data processing industry, with growth rates of 10 percent or higher not uncommon. While the growth in the data processing part of this industry has been hurt by the rapid expansion of minicomputers, this has been offset by the programming and software services industries, which have benefited from this change. Over the last three business cycles, this industry appears to have been recession-proof.[40]

Employment growth in this sector is expected to approach 5 percent per year in the 1990s.[41]

This does not appear to be the case for the other major industries in this sector, including building services, personnel supply, and credit collection. These industries have experienced significant fluctuations during the last several business cycles. They also appear to be major employers of low-paid clerical and custodial employees, primarily women. Although rapid growth of the business service sector is expected to continue,[42] the lower skilled employees in this sector may be adversely affected by cyclical fluctuations.

The other sector that has experienced consistently rapid growth has been nonprofit services. This is composed of health and education services and represents between 8 and 11 percent of total nonagricultural employment. Employment growth statewide has been 3.7 percent per year since 1980, slightly below the national average (see Tables 11 and 12). As with producer services, growth has been widespread, with industries in this sector consistently ranked as the top growth industries both upstate and in the New York City area. In health services, the highest growth has been in physicians' offices, nursing homes, and hospitals. Educational services are dominated by private schools and universities.

Although composed of private organizations, these sectors clearly depend on government expenditures for a portion of their revenues. For example, the health service sector is dependent on changes in Medicare funding.[43] Private universities often receive a significant portion of their funding from federal and state sources. While this sector has expanded, government employment growth has been relatively slow. Only in New York City has public employment growth been above the national average.[44] Employment growth in health services is expected to continue to grow rapidly in the 1990s (3.0 percent per year) while growth in educational services is expected to slow down (1.1 percent).[45]

Consumer services and retail trade also experienced strong growth during the 1980s but with significant variation among industries and geographic areas. Statewide, employment in retail trade grew by 2.4 percent per year since 1980, but this is less than the growth rate for the nation or most other northeastern states. Employment growth was especially slow in New York City. Retail trade includes some of the most rapidly growing industries (food stores and eating and drinking places) and a major declining industry (general merchandise).

Consumer service growth in New York has been on par with the rest of the country and has been strong statewide. The fastest growing industries have been primarily concentrated in the lodging and recreation industries. Employment growth nationally is expected to slow down to less than 2 percent per year for most of these services in the 1990s.

The services most like the goods-producing sectors in terms of structure and capital intensity—transportation, communications, public utilities, and wholesale trade—experienced slow growth or even declining employment during the 1980s. Compared to a national growth rate of 1.5 percent, employment in distributive services stagnated in New York, due largely to a 1.4 percent per year decline in New York City. Particularly hard hit were the railroad and communications sectors, as slackening demand, reorganization, and automation have dampened employment growth.

In summary, the service-producing sectors have, as a whole, been *the* source of employment growth in New York State. However, these sectors are quite diverse, with most of the growth concentrated in producer and nonprofit services. There seems to be a dichotomy in the producer service sector between more technically advanced industries with a high percentage of professional and technical personnel and low-skill support services. Both have experienced high growth, but the latter has been much more sensitive to business cycle fluctuations. Nonprofit services have also been a major source of employment growth; this growth, though, is at least partially dependent on government funding.

The service sectors have been and will continue to be the major source of employment growth in New York State, but growth in services may be a mixed blessing. Although the most rapid growth has been in the more technically advanced and higher paying service sectors, it is questionable how well the jobs demanded in these industries fit the skills available, especially among minority, central-city residents.[46] It is possible that a majority of these higher paying jobs will go to suburban rather than central-city residents. There has been strong growth in lower skill occupations, particularly in retail trade and consumer services, but these jobs appear to be vulnerable to business cycle fluctuations and are likely to be lower paying than the manufacturing jobs they have "replaced."

The High-technology Sector

Like most states, New York would like to support its transition from manufacturing to services with the attraction of high-paying, white-collar, nonpolluting firms. High-tech was the buzzword of the late 1970s and early 1980s, and the promotion of high-tech industry has received significant attention in the public policy arena.[47] The rapid employment and income growth in California's Silicon Valley and Massachusetts's Route 128 are held up as models of what high-tech industries can do for a state and local economy. The growth of new high-tech centers in places as diverse as the Research Triangle in North Carolina, Austin, and Phoenix has reinforced the view that high-tech industries are desirable and their growth can be promoted.[48]

Recent BLS projections that the major growth in manufacturing employment and output in the 1990s will be in high-tech (particularly computer) industries geared for the export market[49] suggest that promotion of high-tech and export-oriented firms will continue to be a high priority for state policymakers. Whether it is feasible (and even desirable) for state and local governments to successfully duplicate such high-tech centers is still a matter of significant controversy.[50] It is not possible in this report to review and evaluate the extensive literature on the high-tech sector and firm location.[51] Instead, this section will provide some limited evidence on how high-tech industries have fared in New York State during the 1980s (Box 6).

The level of employment in New York State that is in high-tech industries varies widely from 2.6 percent to 10.9 percent (in 1985), depending on the definition used (Table 13). The proportion of high-tech employment in New York is presently around the national average. Although New York ranks in the top five states in total high-tech employment, in terms of relative employment (as a percent of total employment), it is not in the top ten states.[52] New York appears to have lost ground compared to the rest of the nation in attracting high-tech employment from 1978 to 1985.

The claim that high-tech industries tend to experience faster and more stable employment growth does appear to be borne out during the 1978 to 1985 period. For all of the definitions used, employment grew faster during the expansions (1978 to 1980 and 1983 to 1985) and declined less (or even increased) during the recessions compared to manufacturing employment as a whole. However, high-tech employment growth in New York State lagged behind that of the

Box 6. Definitions of High Tech

The first difficulty in addressing this issue is defining high-technology industries. There seem to be as many definitions as there are studies of this sector. Generally, industries have been classified as "high tech" based either on their heavy utilization of scientific and technical workers, high research and development (R & D) expenditures, or because of the "technical sophistication" of their product. Studies have varied not only in the definitions used but in the sources of data on occupational distribution or R & D expenditures and the "cutoff" point selected. We have chosen to present a range of definitions that vary significantly in criteria used and the level of employment covered.[a] Detailed annual employment data were used (from *County Business Patterns*) for the period 1978 to 1985 to examine high-tech employment growth in New York State (Table 13).[b]

---

[a] Three of the definitions were based on those defined in Richard Riche, Daniel Hecker, and John Burgan, "High Technology Today and Tomorrow: A Small Slice of the Employment Pie," *Monthly Labor Review* 106 (November 1983): 50–58; and the fourth from Brian Smith, "An Investigation of the High Technology Sector: Prospects for New York State and Syracuse," Master's thesis (Syracuse: Syracuse University, December 1983).

[b] Due to disclosure restrictions with these data, it was not possible to provide estimates for individual metropolitan areas in New York State.

---

nation. Although high-tech industries fared better than the manufacturing sector in terms of employment growth, they still generated fewer jobs than many of the service sector industries.[53]

There was substantial variation in the growth rates, depending on the definition of high-tech industry used. Generally, the broader the definition, the slower the growth. Except for the narrowest definition (see Table 13, number 2), more than half of the industries classified as high-tech actually experienced employment declines from 1980 to 1985. There was also variation across time periods as to which were the fastest growing high-tech industries. This would indicate that targeting assistance and subsidies to particular high-tech industries may be difficult.

The Foreign Trade Sector

The international economy has become an increasingly important influence on the New York economy. At the same time it raises great opportunities for job and income generation,[54] it creates more uncertainty about future economic growth and leaves the economy more vulnerable to uncontrollable, external influences. The impact of the international economy on New York is something about which we need to know more because the increased uncertainty and vulnerability place a higher premium on economic and fiscal planning.

To begin thinking about this issue, it is useful to ask two questions: (1) What is New York's competitive position in the market for "world goods"? and (2) How is the New York economy affected by changes in the international economy? In the first case, the question is whether New York offers something more or less unique that can lead to employment generation in the state. The second question is how these various activities are potentially affected by a changing value of the U.S. dollar on world currency markets or by worldwide recession.

New York's Competitive Advantage

New York-manufactured products do not appear to hold any special advantage on world markets. Despite the lack of current data (Box 7), it is possible to give some estimate of the importance of foreign trade to the New York economy (Table 14). The following stylized facts summarize New York's position:

- Total export-related output and employment have accounted for approximately 10 percent of total manufacturing, both in New York State and nationwide.
- New York has maintained a 6 percent share of national export-related output and a 7 percent share of employment.
- New York State accounts for 9 percent of the national product[55] but only 6 percent of the value of all exports.
- During the 1970s, New York and national export industries tended to grow faster both in terms of output and employment than the manufacturing sector in total. This applied to both direct exports and those industries supporting export industries.
- During the 1980s, New York followed national trends, with export-related shipments and employment declining sharply from 1981 to 1983 but rebounding during the 1983 to 1986 period. These fluctuations appear to be tied directly to changes in the strength of the U.S. dollar.

TABLE 13

Growth of High-technology Industries
for New York and the United States

High-tech Estimate	Percent of 1985 Total Employment	Percent of U.S. Employment[a]		Annual Percent Change			
		1978	1985	1978–80	1980–83	1983–85	1980–85
New York State:							
Total Employment	100.0	8.2	8.0	2.3	–0.1	3.9	1.5
Manufacturing Employment	20.8	7.5	7.0	–0.1	–4.7	0.9	–2.5
(1) Employment of Technical Workers	10.9	7.6	7.1	2.5	–2.5	2.9	–0.4
(2) R & D Expenditures[b] (Narrow)	2.6	9.8	8.3	7.0	0.5	1.6	1.0
(3) R & D Expenditures[b] (Broad)	4.6	9.3	8.1	4.3	–0.1	0.6	0.2
(4) Nature of Product	6.6	8.5	7.6	2.6	–2.3	1.8	–0.7

United States:

Total Employment	100.0	3.2	-0.8	5.4	1.6
Manufacturing Employment	24.0	1.3	-4.8	3.2	-1.7
(1) Employment of Technical Workers	12.3	4.4	-2.7	4.4	0.1
(2) R & D Expenditures[b] (Narrow)	2.5	11.9	0.6	5.8	2.7
(3) R & D Expenditures[b] (Broad)	4.5	7.8	-0.1	4.4	1.7
(4) Nature of Product	6.9	4.0	-2.0	5.5	0.9

[a] Percent of U.S. employment in each category. For example, New York accounts for 8 percent of total U.S. employment, 7 percent of U.S. manufacturing employment, and between 8 and 10 percent of high-tech employment depending on the definition used.

[b] Research and development expenditures.

Source: Employment data are from U.S. Bureau of the Census, *County Business Patterns*, various years. High-tech definitions (1), (2), and (4) are from Riche, Hecker, and Burgan, "High Technology Today and Tomorrow: A Small Slice of the Employment Pie," *Monthly Labor Review*, November 1983. High-technology definition (3) is from Brian Smith, "An Investigation of the High Technology Sector: Prospects for New York State and Syracuse," master's thesis in economics, Syracuse University, December 1983. Due to lack of availability of data in a few categories, modifications and estimates were made by the authors. See authors for full description of methodology.

Box 7. Foreign Trade Statistics by Sample
The major difficulty in examining the effects of foreign trade on state economics is the lack of good data. The only source of export data by state is the U.S. Bureau of the Census, *Annual Survey of Manufactures*. These estimates are made on an irregular basis (latest, at the time of this writing, are for 1986) for both the value of exported goods and employment in manufacturing either directly or indirectly related to exports. The year 1987 is the first year that information on total imports by states became available. There is still no published information on imports by industrial sector by state.

- In New York State, the top seven export industries provided close to 80 percent of output and employment directly related to exports. These industries included chemicals, printing and publishing, machinery, electrical equipment, instruments, transportation equipment, and fabricated metal products. Six out of seven of these correspond to the top export industries in the total United States and five out of seven of these industries are classified as high tech.

Services, on the other hand, would appear to be New York's competitive advantage in world markets. This, of course, is primarily a New York City advantage. Drennan has done an excellent job of organizing some facts to illustrate this importance.[56]

- Of the one-hundred largest multinational corporations in the United States (ranked by foreign revenues), twenty-four had headquarters in New York City and another sixteen in its suburbs. These multinationals accounted for 36 percent of the foreign revenues of the one-hundred largest corporations (55 percent if the New York suburbs are included).
- New York City has six of the nation's ten largest banks, and these banks account for 85 percent of all foreign deposits in large U.S. banks.
- In 1985, 191 foreign-owned banks were located in New York City, with assets of $238 billion and employment of 27,000.
- One-half of the nation's large law firms with foreign branches are located in New York City.
- Six of the Big Eight accounting firms are headquartered in New York (with 44 percent of worldwide gross revenues from

foreign work). Seven of the largest management consulting firms in the United States are headquartered in New York City. Twelve of the twenty-five leading management consulting firms in New York had a total of seventy-three foreign offices.

- New York's thirty largest advertising agencies earned 68 percent of total advertising agency gross income in the United States.
- More than 60 percent of all international air passengers in the United States were on flights to or from the three major New York airports. Twenty percent of the national overseas message units in the United States were attributable to the 212 (New York City) area code.

There is some evidence that New York State has begun to search for a better understanding of the effects of foreign trade on the state economy. A recent report examines both the relative success of industries in this state in exporting goods and the effect of import penetration on New York State industries.[57] There is also a belief that states can take an aggressive and effective role in stimulating growth in the export sector.[58] This is particularly important in the manufacturing sector, where New York does not appear to have a strong comparative advantage.

Vulnerability to External Shocks

Changes in the strength of the U.S. dollar can have a significant and two-edged effect on the New York economy. On the one hand, a strong dollar dampens the demand for U.S.-manufactured exports. On the other hand, it attracts foreign capital and benefits certain traders by lowering the relative price of imports.

For example, with the strengthening of the U.S. dollar in the early 1980s, that part of the manufacturing sector based on export activity was significantly hurt. Between 1981 and 1983, there was a substantial drop in output and employment directly (or indirectly) related to exports—more than 11 percent per year at both the state and the national level (see Table 14). The top seven industries in New York State seemed to fare a little better but still dropped by more than 7 percent per year. This performance was far worse than that of the manufacturing sector as a whole.

In contrast, export-related employment and shipments rebounded from 1983 to 1986. While total manufacturing shipments

TABLE 14

Annual Percent Change in Value of and Employment Related to Manufacturing Exports:
New York Compared to the Total United States

	New York				United States			
	1972–77[a]	1977–81	1981–83	1983–86	1972–77[a]	1977–81	1981–83	1983–86
Value of Manufacturing Shipments (in Constant 1982 Dollars)[b]:								
Total Shipments	0.6	-0.2	-2.3	0.0	4.7	1.5	-4.0	0.1
Total Export Related	NA	5.3	-7.7	2.9	NA	8.1	-9.4	2.9
Direct Exports	7.1	5.7	-12.1	-0.3	10.1	8.2	-11.7	0.9
Supporting Exports[c]	NA	4.5	0.6	7.3	NA	8.0	-6.0	5.5
Percent of Total Shipments[d]	10.3	12.8	11.4	12.4	10.5	13.5	12.0	13.0
Percent of Total United States[e]	6.2	5.6	5.8	5.8				

Manufacturing Employment:

Annual Growth Rates:								
Total Employment	-1.9	-0.1	-4.0	-2.9	1.0	0.8	-3.9	-0.6
Total Export Related	NA	5.1	-11.0	5.7	NA	6.9	-11.8	4.6
Direct Exports	5.3	4.8	-10.8	-1.3	7.5	7.7	-13.0	-1.9
Supporting Exports[c]	NA	5.5	-11.2	13.8	NA	6.0	-10.2	11.7
Percent of Total Employment[d]	9.4	11.5	9.9	12.7	10.2	12.8	10.8	12.6
Percent of Total United States[e]	7.1	6.6	6.7	6.9				

[a] Data for 1972 are not strictly comparable to estimates for later years due to changes in methodology.

[b] Value of shipments deflated using the implicit GNP deflator.

[c] This category includes shipments of components, supplies, and so forth, used by plants producing exports.

[d] Based on the last year of the given period, 1977, 1981, 1983, and 1986. Percent of total manufacturing shipments and employment that are related to exports in New York and total United States.

[e] Based on the last year of the given period, 1977, 1981, 1983, and 1986. Export-related shipments or employment in New York as a percent of export-related shipments and employment for total United States.

Source: U.S. Department of Commerce, Bureau of the Census, *Annual Survey of Manufacturers, Origin of Exports of Manufactured Products*, Nos. AR86-1, M84(AS)-5, M83(AS)-5, M81(AS)-5, and MC77-SR-12; and *1972 Origin of Exports of Manufacturing Establishments.*

were stagnating and employment declining, export-related shipments grew by 2.9 percent per year and employment by around 5.0 percent per year in New York and the nation. This drastic change in fortunes for these industries indicates how sensitive they are to changes in the world economy and to U.S. policy. The U.S. dollar appreciated by close to 30 percent relative to the European currencies from 1981 to 1983 while it depreciated by the same amount from 1983 to 1986.[59]

The financial and services sector in New York City grew with the strong dollar in the first half of the 1980s. The largest New York banks increased their national share of foreign deposits, the number of foreign banks and their asset values increased, and the foreign share of gross revenues of large accounting and management consulting firms increased.[60] The New York region's position in the United States with respect to dominance in this sector has declined only slightly. In 1985, the New York metropolitan region held 35.8 percent of the assets of the top two-hundred financial firms as compared to 36.0 percent in 1979. With respect to the assets of the top one-hundred bank holding corporations, the corresponding figures were 33.8 percent in 1986 and 36.2 percent in 1979.[61]

With the weaker dollar in the late 1980s, it is not clear what effect this has had on the New York City economy. As discussed previously, FIRE and business service employment has declined and overall employment has stagnated since 1987. It is likely that this economic slowdown is both related to the stock market crash and the changing international economy.

Although there is no detailed data on imports by state, the Port Authority reports that the port of New York and New Jersey handled approximately $50 billion worth of cargo in 1986, with about four-fifths of the volume of cargo imported. This trade activity is an important job generator in the region. The Regional Plan Association estimated that in the early 1980s, the port alone was generating about 3 percent of the region's jobs and output. The air cargo industry was generating an additional 1 percent of gross regional product.[62]

Conclusions

The 1980s brought stronger employment growth to New York, especially in New York City in the early 1980s and in the downstate suburban counties during the entire decade. The pattern of deconcentration of employment to nonmetropolitan areas, which occurred in the 1970s, ended as employment in metropolitan areas grew slightly faster than that in nonmetropolitan areas.[63] However, employment appears to have further deconcentrated *within* metropolitan areas.

Although New York State enjoyed unemployment rates below the national average during most of the 1980s, employment growth continues to lag behind that of the Northeast and the country as a whole. Some parts of the state, particularly western and central New York, have experienced stagnant or even declining employment. Some segments of the state population do not appear to have benefited from the economic growth that has occurred. Nonwhite residents, heavily concentrated in the central cities, have suffered from significantly higher unemployment rates and lower labor force participation rates. Nonwhite employment is heavily concentrated in lower paying jobs, and these workers are most likely to belong to the working poor segment of the population.

The state is still losing manufacturing jobs, more than 250,000 since 1980, as the economic structure continues to shift toward services and trade. The shift is in step with what is happening in the rest of the nation, but it does pose some problems for state policy. In particular, the overall effect of this structural shift on income distribution is unclear. There is concern that in the long run, service employment will be lower paying and provide less job security than the jobs lost in manufacturing. The service sector is divided between high-paying professional and technical jobs and low-paying, more cyclically sensitive, clerical, maintenance, and trade occupations. The shift in economic activity to the service sector also may have a dampening effect on the taxpaying capacity of the economic base. Many parts of the service sector are either nontaxable (for example, the government, or certain nonprofit organizations) or are given preferential treatment. It follows that a job in the service sector, even if it pays the same wage, may not have the same taxpaying power as a job in the manufacturing sector.[64]

New York's lagging employment growth has led the state government to take a more active role in the promotion of new industry. High-technology industry has been a high-profile part of this effort, but, in fact, the dependence on high-tech employment in New York is presently at about the national average. Moreover, New York appears not to have gained any ground compared to the rest of the nation in attracting high-tech employment during the 1980s. While high-tech firms do show some promise of increasing manufacturing employment in New York State and reducing some of its cyclical sensitivity, these industries have not done as well as many of the service sectors, especially producer services. There also has been considerable variation in growth rates among these high-tech firms. This would indicate that even if it is possible to successfully attract high-tech firms, it will be difficult to effectively target such assistance. Using even the broadest definition of high-tech industries, they presently provide jobs for only 10 percent of nonagricultural employees.

The foreign trade sector has been a two-edged sword for New York. When the dollar is strong, New York's manufacturing export industry has been hurt severely. On the other hand, New York City has a strong comparative advantage in international financial and business services, and employment growth in this sector has flourished with the strong dollar. As the dollar weakened in the late 1980s, export-related manufacturing grew strongly in New York; however, employment in financial and business services, particularly in New York City, began to decline. The downside of the "internationalization" of the New York economy is that the city and state economies are more vulnerable than ever to the influence of external events, such as U.S. budget and trade policy, the macroeconomic policy decisions of other countries, and the general performance of the world economy.

In summary, employment in New York State in the 1980s began growing again and the state has enjoyed unemployment rates below the national average. Growth has been concentrated in certain geographic areas, industrial sectors, and economic groups. Of particular concern for state and local governments in New York are the effects of the changing employment structure on taxable capacity and on the income position of low-income residents. It is not clear that the employment trends of the 1980s indicate a full recovery from the decline of the 1970s.

Notes

1. For a review of employment trends in the 1970s, see Roy Bahl, "The New York Economy: 1960–1978 and the Outlook," Metropolitan Studies Program Occasional Paper, No. 37 (Syracuse: Maxwell School, Syracuse University, October 1979).

2. The concept of an employment "growth gap" is a shorthand way of describing the difference between the national growth rate in employment and the state growth rate. For example, the New York State growth gap between 1983 and 1989 is 538,600, which means that if New York State had grown at the national average rate between 1983 and 1989, it would have gained an *additional* 538,600 jobs. See Table C-1 in Appendix C for more details.

3. This reversal has been due entirely to a sharp drop in the number of unemployed since 1980. The labor force has actually grown at a slower rate in New York than for the country as a whole.

4. New York State defines dislocated workers as those (1) out of work due to a permanent closing, (2) unlikely to return to their previous industry or occupation, and (3) unemployed more than fifteen weeks.

5. Glenn Yago and Richard McGahey, "Can the Empire State Strike Back? The Limits of Cyclical Recovery in New York," *New York Affairs* 8 (1984): 23–25.

6. Samuel Ehrenhalt, "Looking to the 1990s: Continuity and Change." Paper presented at the 20th Annual Institute of Challenges of the Changing Economy of New York City, sponsored by the New York City Council of Economic Education, July 1987, p. 5.

7. For more detailed substate employment, see Table C-2 in Appendix C. See Appendix A for the definitions of substate areas used in this report.

8. This stagnant employment growth was predicted by the Port Authority of New York and New Jersey in early 1989. See their publication "The Regional Economy: Review 1988, Outlook 1989 for the New York–New Jersey Metropolitan Region" (March 1989).

9. Unemployment trends for substate areas are available from the authors upon request. New York City continues to lag behind the rest of the nation in the percentage of its population in the labor force and employed. However, there does not appear to have been any further deterioration since 1980. See U.S. Bureau of Labor Statistics, *Geographic Profiles of Employment and Unemployment* (Washington, D.C.: U.S. Department of Labor, 1986).

10. See Table C-2 in Appendix C.

11. See Table C-2 in Appendix C. For a review of changes in the Buffalo labor market, see Fred Doolittle, "Adjustments in Buffalo's Labor Market," *Federal Reserve Bank of New York Quarterly Review* 10 (Winter 1985–86): 28–37.

12. The *Current Population Survey* (CPS) is a regular monthly survey carried out by the U.S. Bureau of the Census of approximately sixty thousand households. The results of this survey are summarized in the annual publication, *Geographic Profiles of Employment and Unemployment.*

13. Ideally, it would be desirable to compare the 1970s to the present.

However, due to changes in published data, it is possible to go back only as far as 1980 (see Tables 10 and C-3).

14. See Sheldon Danziger and Peter Gottschalk, "Work, Poverty, and the Working Poor: A Multifaceted Problem," *Monthly Labor Review* 109 (September 1986): 17–21; and Bruce Klein and Philip Rones, "A Profile of the Working Poor," *Monthly Labor Review* 112 (October 1989): 3–13.

15. George Silvestri and John Lukasiewicz, "Projections of Occupational Employment, 1988–2000," *Monthly Labor Review* 112 (November 1989): 42–65.

16. Ibid., p. 65.

17. For evidence for New York State and the nation, see Table C-3 in Appendix C.

18. Gerald Lynch and Thomas Hyclak, "Cyclical and Noncyclical Unemployment Differences among Demographic Groups," *Growth and Change* 15 (January 1984): 9–17.

19. In 1986, 40 percent of poor women heading households worked compared to 75 percent for the nonpoor counterparts. See Mark Littman, "Reasons for Not Working: Poor and Nonpoor Householders," *Monthly Labor Review* 112 (August 1989): 16–21.

20. It is beyond the scope of this study to review the literature on firm location. Generally, the data on changes in firm employment and location are either prohibitively expensive to gather or of dubious accuracy if they are readily available. Until good data sources are developed, research in this area will be difficult.

21. See Tables C-4 and C-5 in Appendix C for employment trends by major industrial sectors for substate areas. For good reviews of structural changes in the Buffalo labor market, see Doolittle, "Adjustments in Buffalo's Labor Market"; and Mark Goldman, *High Hopes: The Rise and Decline of Buffalo, New York* (Albany: State University of New York Press, 1983).

22. Detailed information on declining industries in New York State is available from the authors upon request.

23. Valerie Personick, "Industry Output and Employment: A Slower Trend for the Nineties," *Monthly Labor Review* 112 (November 1989): 25–41.

24. For advocates of this argument, see Barry Bluestone and Bennett Harrison, *The Deindustrialization of America* (New York: Basic Books, 1982); Paul Krugman and George Hatsopoulos, "The Problem of U.S. Competitiveness in Manufacturing," *New England Economic Review* (January/February 1987): 18–29; and Norman Perna, "The Shift from Manufacturing to Services: A Concerned View," *New England Economic Review* (January/February 1987): 30–38.

25. A survey by the U.S. Bureau of Labor Statistics provides mixed evidence on the displaced worker problem. Most of those who were unem-

ployed in 1981 had found employment by 1986, the majority with earnings at least as high as before. However, close to 50 percent had been unemployed for at least a half year, and lower skilled or minority workers appeared to have a much lower probability of reemployment. See Francis Horvath, "The Pulse of Economic Change; Displaced Workers of 1981–85," *Monthly Labor Review* 110 (June 1987): 3–12.

26. See, for example, Robert Lawrence, *Can America Compete?* (Washington, D.C.: Brookings Institution, 1984); Molly McUsic, "U.S. Manufacturing: Any Cause for Alarm?" *New England Economic Review* (January/February 1987): 3–17; and Ronald Kutscher and Valerie Personick, "Deindustrialization and the Shift to Services," *Monthly Labor Review* 109 (June 1986): 3–13.

27. This has not been the case for the current dollar share of manufacturing output, which has consistently declined over the last several decades. For a review of the differences between these measures, see Perna, "The Shift from Manufacturing to Services."

28. See David Birch, "Who Creates Jobs?" *The Public Interest* 65 (Fall 1981): 3–14.

29. Due to data limitations, it was not possible to develop a sectoral analysis, such as Tables 11 and 12, for all other northeastern states. Employment growth for the service category (standard industrial classification: SIC 7 and 8) averaged 4.8 percent per year for the rest of the Northeast compared to 3.8 percent for New York and 5.3 percent nationally. Growth was higher in this category and in the FIRE (finance, insurance, and real estate) sector in every other northeastern state than it was in New York.

30. For example, producer services have ranged from 11 percent of employment in upstate New York to 29 percent in New York City. See Table C-5 in Appendix C for distribution of employment by sector for substate areas.

31. For a comprehensive review of this sector in New York through 1985, see New York State Department of Commerce, *Financial Services Industries in New York State: A Statistical Profile* (Albany: New York State Department of Commerce, May 1986).

32. In fact, the majority of employment in this sector tends to be in the retail rather than wholesale sector (for example, real estate and insurance agents, branch banks, and stock brokers). See Aaron Gurwitz and Julie Rappaport, "Structural Change and Slower Employment Growth in the Financial Services Sector," *Federal Reserve Bank of New York Quarterly Review* 9 (Winter 1984–85): 39–45.

33. See Table C-4 in Appendix C for growth rates by major industry in substate areas in New York.

34. Personick, "Industry Output and Employment: A Slower Trend for the Nineties," Table 6.

35.   Information on substate trends for the major increasing industries in New York is available from the authors upon request.

36.   See Gurwitz and Rappaport, "Structural Change and Slower Employment Growth in the Financial Services Sector."

37.   Personick, "Industry Output and Employment: A Slower Trend for the Nineties," Table 6.

38.   Ibid.

39.   For a good review of employment trends in this sector, see Wayne Howe, "The Business Services Industry Sets Pace in Employment Growth," *Monthly Labor Review* 109 (April 1986): 29–36.

40.   Robert Kirk, "Are Business Services Immune to the Business Cycle?" *Growth and Change* 18 (Spring 1987): 15–23.

41.   Personick, "Industry Output and Employment: A Slower Trend for the Nineties," Table 6.

42.   Annual employment growth rates in these three sectors in the 1990s are projected to be 2.3 percent for building services, 4.1 percent for personal supply, and 3.2 percent for credit reporting. Ibid.

43.   See Albert Eckstein and Dale Heien, "Causes and Consequences of Service Sector Growth," *Growth and Change* 16 (April 1985): 12–17.

44.   Changes in public employment and compensation are addressed in more detail in chapters 4 and 5.

45.   Personick, "Industry Output and Employment: A Slower Trend for the Nineties." Table 6.

46.   For a review of the skills mismatch issue, see Daniel Chall, "New York City's 'Skills Mismatch,'" *Federal Reserve Bank of New York Quarterly Review* 10 (Spring 1985): 20–27, and Thomas Bailey and Roger Waldinger, "A Skills Mismatch in New York's Labor Market?" *New York Affairs* 8 (1984): 3–29.

47.   Governor Mario Cuomo, in his 1989 Message to the Legislature, stressed the importance of high-technology and export promotion in his discussion of the state economic development strategy. Governor Mario M. Cuomo, "Message to the Legislature" (Albany: State of New York, January 4, 1989), pp. 83–87.

48.   There are many differences between these new growth centers and the original high-tech centers. It is still a matter of debate whether these new centers can ever achieve the self-sustaining growth of Silicon Valley and Route 128. For an interesting review of these centers, see Edward Malecki, "Research and Development and the Geography of High-Technology Complexes," in *Technology, Regions and Policy*, ed. J. Rees (Totowa, NJ: Rowman & Littlefield, 1986), pp. 51–74.

49.   Personick, "Industry Output and Employment: A Slower Trend for the Nineties," Table 6.

50.   For several recent studies of high-tech industry in New York State, see New York State Department of Labor, *High-Technology Industries in New York State* (Albany: New York State Department of Labor, 1988); and Battelle-Columbus Division, *Development of High Technology Industries in New York State* (Albany: New York State Science and Technology Foundation, 1982).

51.   For a review of the literature on regional growth and firm location, see John Rees and Howard Stafford, "Theories of Regional Growth and Industrial Location: Their Relevance for Understanding High-Technology Complexes," in *Technology, Regions and Policy*, pp. 23–50; and Ann Markusen, Peter Hall, and Amy Glasmeier, *High Tech America* (Boston: Allen & Unwin, 1986).

52.   See Richard Riche, Daniel Hecker, and John Burgan, "High Technology Today and Tomorrow: A Small Slice of the Employment Pie," *Monthly Labor Review* 106 (November 1983): 50–58.

53.   All but definition (2) in Table 13 included a few industries from the service sector, particularly business services. These were among the fastest growing of the high-tech industries. For a review of this relationship, see Lynn Browne, "High Technology and Business Services," *New England Economic Review* (July/August 1983): 5–17.

54.   See Gabriel Manrique, "Foreign Export Orientation and Regional Growth in the U.S.," *Growth and Change* 18 (Winter 1987): 1–12.

55.   Based on gross state product estimates made by the U.S. Bureau of Economic Analysis. See Vernon Renshaw, Edward Trott, Jr., and Howard Freidenberg, "Gross State Product by Industry, 1963–86," *Survey of Current Business* 68 (May 1988): 30–46.

56.   Matthew Drennan, "Local Economy and Local Revenues," in *Setting Municipal Priorities, 1988*, eds. Charles Brecher and Raymond Horton (New York: New York University Press, 1988), chapter 1.

57.   Governor's Project on Trade and Competitiveness, *The Impact of the National Trade Deficit on New York State Employment* (Albany: New York State Industrial Cooperation Council, June 1987).

58.   See Cletus Coughlin and Phillip Cartwright, "An Examination of State Foreign Export Promotion and Manufacturing Exports," *Journal of Regional Science* 27 (August 1987): 439–449.

59.   Relative to the value of the European Currency Unit, which is based on a weighted average of currencies of the countries in the European Common Market. See International Monetary Fund, *International Finance Statistics, 1989 Yearbook* (Washington, D.C.: International Monetary Fund, 1989).

60.   Drennan, "Local Economy and Local Revenues," chapter 1.

61.   Regional Planning Association, *The Region in the Global Economy*

(New York: New York University Press, May 1988), p. 11.

62. Ibid., p. 17.

63. This runs counter to the conclusions of recent research that would suggest that industry is becoming less dependent on urban locations. See Ruth Young, "Industrial Location and Regional Change: The United States and New York State," *Regional Studies* 20 (August 1986): 341–369.

64. Roy Bahl and David Greytak, "The Response of City Government Revenues to Changes in Employment Structures," *Land Economics* 52 (November 1976): 415–434.

3

Personal Income

The recovery in real income growth that occurred in New York State during the 1980s had been even stronger than that for employment. Total income grew at a rate on par with the rest of the Northeast region and the nation. New York City went from declining real income to more than 3 percent per year growth. Per capita income is now 17 percent higher in New York State than the national average (15 percent if transfer payments are removed). This is a major reversal. As with employment and population, the 1970s was a decade of relative decline in real income for New York State. While income stagnated in New York State and declined by 1 percent a year in New York City, it grew by more than 3 percent a year in the rest of the country. Per capita income dropped from 20 percent above the national average in 1970 to only 7 percent above in 1979 (4 percent if transfer payments are removed).

Not surprisingly, the newfound income growth of the 1980s has been unbalanced. Some regions and industrial sectors, and some population groups, have benefited more than others. Another imbalance, and a very important puzzle to solve in explaining this trend, is why personal income grew so rapidly while employment and population growth lagged behind national rates. Understanding these imbalances is crucial to gaining a proper assessment of the extent to which the strong income growth in New York State implies a new underlying strength in the economy (Box 8).

General Trends

Real personal income in New York State grew by more than 3 percent per year from 1980 to 1989, which was above the national growth rate

75

Box 8. Sources of Income Data

Ideally, this analysis should utilize some measure of disposable income (after taxes and social insurance contributions) that allows disaggregation by source, industry, geographic area, and socioeconomic status. Unfortunately, there are no sources that provide such information.

This chapter utilizes the personal income estimates prepared by the U.S. Bureau of Economic Analysis. This includes income from wages and salaries, dividends, rents, interest, transfer payments, other labor income, and income of small proprietors. Social insurance contributions are removed, but not taxes, so this is an incomplete measure of disposable income. Resident adjustments are made to earnings by place of work to estimate income by place of residence. The primary benefit of this income estimate is that it is disaggregated by source, industry (two-digit SIC), and geographic area (county level) on an annual basis. However, this is not a microlevel survey so it does not permit estimates by socioeconomic group.

The personal income estimates were recently revised at both the state and county levels to be consistent with the 1986 revisions of the *National Income and Product Accounts*.[a] The major changes involved the inclusion of Medicaid and several other new transfer payment categories and an updating of estimates using more recent data. Particularly important was the revision of the "resident adjustment factor" that is used to convert earnings from place of work to place of residence (the new estimates used "journey to work" data from the *1980 Census of Population*, whereas the previous estimates used the 1970 journey to work data).

There are several other sources of income that have been frequently used in the literature. The U.S. Bureau of the Census makes annual estimates of money income based on both survey data (*Current Population Survey*) and IRS and BEA income estimates. The definition of money income is similar to personal income but does not include imputed income or remove social insurance contributions. The Bureau of the Census does estimate "after-tax money income" on a periodic basis but not below the regional level. Money income (before taxes) is available for small geographic areas (villages and townships) but provides no disaggregation by industry or source. Most of the research that has attempted to examine income distribution has used the *Current Population Survey* data on money income. However, due to small sample size, such estimates would have dubious accuracy below the regional level.

The IRS has detailed individual income tax records that contain information on "adjusted gross income" and income after taxes. This concept of income does not include imputed income and most transfer payments and, of course, covers only those who file tax returns. The IRS does provide to the public a small sample from this information; however, it is generally nonrepresentative at the state level.

---

[a] For a review of these revisions, see U.S. Bureau of Economic Analysis, "State Personal Income, 1969–85: Revised Estimates," *Survey of Current Business* 66 (August 1986): 21–23.

(Figure 5).[1] Real income even grew moderately during the 1981–82 recession (compared to declining income for the nation as a whole), and since 1982, income has increased by close to 4 percent per year.

By 1989, New York State had regained much of its lost relative share of national income (Table 15). This performance is remarkable given the dismal economic position of the state just fifteen years ago.[2] Real income in New York declined sharply during the 1973–75 recession (2 percent per year) and grew only slightly during the early stages of the ensuing expansion.

Despite the strong income growth in New York, real per capita personal income grew even faster in most other northeastern states (Table 16). Connecticut, Massachusetts, and New Jersey, in particular, had growth rates exceeding 3.5 percent during the 1980s. Only Pennsylvania had income growth (2.0 percent per year) that significantly lagged behind that in New York. For the first time, the other northeastern states had, on average, per capita income that was equal to that of New York.

FIGURE 5
Personal Income Trends (1970–1989)
New York, Other Northeast Region, and Total United States

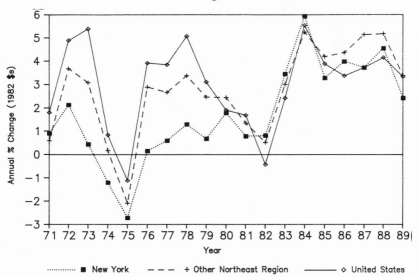

Source: U.S. Bureau of Economic Analysis

TABLE 15

Real Per Capita Personal Income Trends and Projections: For New York,
the Northeast Region, and the United States
(Constant 1982 Dollars)[a]

| | New York State | | | | Other Northeast Region[b] | | | | United States | |
| | | | —Percent of U.S.— | | | | —Percent of U.S.— | | | |
Year	Personal Income	Annual Percent Change	Total	Without Transfer Payments	Personal Income	Annual Percent Change	Total	Without Transfer Payments	Personal Income	Annual Percent Change
1970	11,579		119.9	118.4	10,436		108.0	108.0	9,668	
1975	11,672	0.2	113.8	110.2	10,798	0.7	105.4	104.4	10,241	1.2
1980	12,515	1.4	108.1	105.0	12,312	2.7	106.2	105.7	11,610	2.5
1983	13,071	1.5	112.3	109.9	12,808	1.3	110.0	109.8	11,644	0.1
1987	15,283	4.0	116.0	114.0	15,125	4.2	114.8	115.8	13,178	3.1
1988	15,915	4.1	117.1	115.2	15,799	4.5	116.2	117.4	13,593	3.1
1989	16,263	2.2	116.9	NA	16,264	2.9	116.9	NA	13,909	2.3

Business Cycles[c]:			
Expansion 1971–73	1.8	3.0	4.0
Contraction 1973–75	–1.5	–1.0	–1.1
Expansion 1975–79	1.2	2.7	2.9
1980–81	0.8	1.1	0.6
Contraction 1981–82	0.7	0.4	–1.4
Expansion 1982–89	3.6	3.9	2.8
Long-term Trends:			
1970–80	0.8	1.7	1.8
1980–89	3.0	3.2	2.1
BEA Projections:			
1988–2000	1.2	1.1	1.2

[a]Personal income is deflated using the implicit GNP deflator.

[b]Includes New York, Connecticut, Maine, Massachusetts, New Hampshire, New Jersey, Pennsylvania, Rhode Island, and Vermont.

[c]These are only rough approximations of the business cycles because these estimates are based on annual averages.

Source: U.S. Department of Commerce, Bureau of Economic Analysis, unpublished personal income data; and *Survey of Current Business*, May 1990, for projections.

TABLE 16

Real Per Capita Personal Income Trends[a]:
New York Compared to Other Northeast States
and High- and Low-income Regions of the Country

| | Annual Percent Change | | Percent of United States | | |
	1970–80	1980–89	1970	1980	1989
High-Income Regions[b]:	1.6	2.3	109.3	107.0	108.9
New York	0.8	3.0	119.9	108.1	116.9
Connecticut	1.7	3.6	124.3	122.1	140.1
Maine	1.7	3.4	84.1	82.9	92.8
Massachusetts	1.4	4.0	111.4	107.0	126.4
New Hampshire	2.1	3.8	96.0	98.7	115.3
New Jersey	1.7	3.8	118.6	116.7	135.3
Pennsylvania	1.8	2.0	99.8	99.7	99.2
Rhode Island	1.4	2.8	100.0	96.0	102.8
Vermont	1.6	2.9	89.0	86.5	93.4
Other Northeast	1.7	3.2	108.0	106.2	116.9
East North Central	1.8	1.8	102.5	101.6	99.0
Pacific	1.9	1.5	113.9	114.4	109.1
Low-income Regions[b]:	2.3	1.9	87.7	91.7	90.0
West North Central	2.1	1.6	93.6	96.1	92.4
South Atlantic	2.0	2.7	91.2	92.5	97.8
East South Central	2.4	2.1	74.0	78.2	78.2
West South Central	2.9	0.8	84.4	94.0	83.7
Mountain	2.2	1.2	92.0	95.2	88.3

[a]Personal income is deflated using the implicit GNP deflator.

[b]Regions as defined by the U.S. Bureau of the Census. The Northeast region used in this book includes the New England and Middle Atlantic regions from the census.

Source: U.S. Department of Commerce, Bureau of Economic Analysis, unpublished personal income data.

The strong growth in per capita personal income in most northeastern states led to a reversal in the 1980s of the long-standing trend of "convergence" in per capita income between the high- and low-income regions of the country.[3] Real per capita income grew in the 1980s by 2.3 percent per year in the high-income regions compared to 1.8 percent in the low-income regions. This is almost an exact reversal of the trends during the 1970s. Among high-income regions, the Northeast gained while the East North Central and Pacific regions declined relative to the rest of the country. All the low-income regions, except the South Atlantic, either grew at the same rate or slower than the national average. Especially hard hit were the energy-based economies of the West South Central and Mountain regions. A key question from the standpoint of this study is whether this signals a new resurgence in the economies of the Northeast and New York, in particular, or a short-term aberration to long-term "convergence."

Almost all areas of the state experienced more rapid personal income growth during the 1980s than in the 1970s, but New York City appears to be the major reason for the reversal in aggregate income growth for New York State. Real personal income declined by 1 percent per year during the 1970s and was hit hard by the 1973–75 recession (declining close to 3 percent per year).[4] This compares to a real growth of more than 3 percent per year from 1980 to 1988, with an annual rate of 4.1 percent per year since 1982 (Figure 6). Real income per capita grew from 10 percent above the national average in 1980 to 17 percent above in 1988 (Table 17).

The fastest growth in real income in the state continues to be in the suburbs surrounding New York City. Growth was 4 percent a year during the 1980s and 5 percent per year since 1982. Based on real per capita income, these areas continue to be much more affluent than the rest of the country. Per capita income has grown from 26 percent above the national average in 1978 to 52 percent higher in 1988, 56 percent higher if transfer payments are removed (see Table 17).

Growth in the rest of the state, 2.7 percent per year, lags behind regional and national growth rates and there is considerable variation among areas. Some of the patterns of the 1970s carried forward to the 1980s. The slowest growth in income (1 percent per year) continues to be in the primary manufacturing centers of Buffalo and Elmira. These rates are on par with the slow employment growth that occurred in these areas.

FIGURE 6

Personal Income Trends (1970–1988)
New York City, Suburbs, and Other New York State

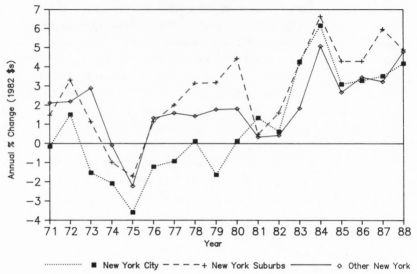

Source: U.S. Bureau of Economic Analysis

Most of the other areas of the state showed substantially higher real income growth during the 1980s than in the previous decade. Only one-third of New York State counties experienced real income growth exceeding 2 percent per year in the 1970s compared with two-thirds of all counties in the 1980s. One-third of the counties had growth of 3 percent or higher. Growth was particularly rapid in the mid-Hudson region, where the highest growth rates in the state occurred.

Such aggregate figures do not permit analysis of how low-income families fared during the 1980s. In fact, despite the recent strong income growth in many upstate counties, real income per capita in the upstate area still lags behind the national average, especially if transfer payments are removed (see Table 17). Per capita income remains well below the state and national average in many of the nonmetropolitan areas in the Southern Tier and North Country regions.

Sources of Income Growth

While New York's real income and employment grew at about the same pace during the 1970s, this was not the case during the 1980s. Growth in real income was more than twice as fast as that of employment in New York and the rest of the Northeast region. This was true in New York City and even in many of the metropolitan areas of upstate New York that continued to experience slow employment growth.[5] What are the possible reasons for this discrepancy? What does it imply for the future economic health in the state and for fiscal condition?

Cost of Living and Inflation

One possible explanation for this difference is that it is purely a result of the higher rate of increase in the cost of living in New York State. What is important in this discussion is not absolute costs but how price levels changed during the 1980s. The only price index that provides subnational estimates is the Consumer Price Index developed by the U.S. Bureau of Labor Statistics. For New York, estimates are made only for the New York City/Northeast New Jersey area and Buffalo. From 1980 to 1989, by this index, inflation averaged 4.7 percent for the nation, 5.1 percent in the Northeast region, 5.3 percent in the New York City area, and 4.2 percent in Buffalo.[6] Although higher inflation may account for a portion of the higher rate of income growth in New York City, this would not appear to be as important in other areas of the state.

Since the New York City region accounted for so much of the strong income growth in New York in the 1980s, it is worth looking more closely at inflation as an explanation. Ehrenhalt reports that between 1981 and 1987, consumer prices in the New York City region were up 23 percent as compared to 18 percent nationally. In the prior six years, the local increase was 55 percent as compared to 69 percent nationally.[7] The trend continued through 1987, and for the 1985–87 period, the inflation rate was higher in the region than in the nation in each major consumption category except energy.[8] Real estate prices were also affected. A New York City study commission reported that commercial rents for small retailers increased by an average of 32 percent over the 1984–86 period,[9] and the median price of a

TABLE 17

Real Per Capita Personal Income Trends: In New York City,
New York City Suburbs, and the Rest of the State
(Constant 1982 Dollars)[a]

Year	New York City				New York City Suburbs[b]				Rest of New York State			
	Personal Income	Annual Percent Change	Percent of U.S.— Total	Percent of U.S.— Without Transfer Payments	Personal Income	Annual Percent Change	Percent of U.S.— Total	Percent of U.S.— Without Transfer Payments	Personal Income	Annual Percent Change	Percent of U.S.— Total	Percent of U.S.— Without Transfer Payments
1970	12,523		129.8	126.1	13,107		135.9	139.4	9,536		98.9	97.5
1975	12,437	−0.1	121.4	114.0	13,373	0.4	130.6	133.7	9,820	0.6	95.9	92.9
1980	12,709	0.4	109.8	102.5	15,239	2.6	131.7	136.1	10,743	1.8	92.8	90.0
1983	13,340	1.6	114.6	108.5	16,096	1.8	138.2	144.0	11,059	1.0	95.0	91.9
1987	15,233	3.4	115.6	110.6	19,753	5.3	149.9	156.0	12,758	3.6	96.8	93.7
1988	15,852	4.1	116.6	NA	20,648	4.5	151.9	NA	13,263	4.0	97.6	NA

Business Cycles[c]:			
Expansion 1971–73	1.4	2.0	2.3
Contraction 1973–75	–1.6	–1.5	–1.3
Expansion 1975–79	0.4	2.2	1.6
1980–81	1.2	0.6	0.5
Contraction 1981–82	0.4	1.5	0.5
Expansion 1982–88	3.5	4.8	3.4
Long-term Trends:			
1970–80	0.1	1.5	1.2
1980–88	2.8	3.9	2.7
BEA Projections[d]:			
1983–90	1.6	2.3	2.7
1990–2000	1.2	1.4	1.3

[a]Personal income is deflated using the implicit GNP deflator.

[b]Includes Nassau, Putnam, Rockland, Suffolk, and Westchester counties.

[c]These are only rough approximations of the business cycles because these estimates are based on annual averages.

[d]Personal income projections for New York State and New York City area are based on projected growth rates for 1983 to 1990 and 1990 to 2000 by the U.S. Bureau of Economic Analysis. Distributed between substate areas based on past shares. Population projections are based on those made by the New York State Data Center.

Source: U.S. Department of Commerce, Bureau of Economic Analysis, unpublished personal income data; *Survey of Current Business,* April 1990, and *1985 OBERS BEA Regional Projections;* and New York State Data Center, *Official Population Projections for New York State Counties, 1980–2010,* April 1985.

single-family home increased from $70,500 in 1982 (approximately the national median) to $183,000 in 1987–highest in the nation and more than double the nationwide median.[10] In light of this evidence, the very high rate of growth in personal income in New York City may not suggest the great improvement in comparative living standards and productivity that many might believe.

Transfer Payments

Unlike the 1970s, when they were by far the fastest growing source of income, transfer payments were one of the slower growing sources during the 1980s.[11] Transfer payments grew by 2.4 percent per year from 1980 to 1988 compared to a 4.4 percent annual growth rate in the 1970s (Table 18). For every $1 increase in personal income in the 1970s, transfer payments increased by $1.35, whereas the comparable figure in the 1980s was $0.12. The slowdown in transfer payment growth was even more dramatic for the rest of the Northeast region and the nation.

Most of the slower growth appears to have occurred in income maintenance, veterans, retirement, and unemployment insurance programs due in part to changes in eligibility standards and to the generally improved economic picture during much of the 1980s. The most rapid growth in transfer payments continues to be in medical payments (more than 6 percent per year), primarily Medicare and Medicaid payments.[12] Rising medical costs, not higher enrollments, would appear to explain much of this growth.

The consumer price index for medical costs in the United States grew by 8.2 percent compared to a 4.7 percent growth for all items from 1980 to 1987. While the number of recipients of Medicare (1980 to 1984) and Medicaid (1980 to 1986) increased by 4 and 1 percent per year, respectively, the amount reimbursed grew by 14 and 10 percent, respectively, in the United States.[13] Based on information in the *Statistical Supplement* of the New York State Department of Social Services, such trends would appear to apply to Medicaid expenditures in New York State as well.[14]

Wages and Salaries

The growth in total wages and salary income has rebounded strongly after declining in the 1970s (see Table 18). After falling by 0.6 percent per year during the previous decade, wages and salaries experienced real growth in excess of 3.5 percent per year during the 1980s, which was well above the national growth rate. Except for Buffalo, Elmira, and Utica, growth was strong throughout the state. The growth rate in New York City was 3.9 percent in the 1980s (compared to a sharp drop in the 1970s) and more than 4 percent per year in the New York City suburbs and mid-Hudson region.

The key issue is why wage and salary growth had been so rapid given moderate growth in employment. Possible explanations include an above-average growth in real wage rates or a shifting of employment toward high-wage sectors. Unfortunately, except for manufacturing, the only compensation data available are total payrolls for all employees in an industry. For production workers in manufacturing, the BLS does estimate average weekly (and hourly) earnings by industry for substate areas.[15] We compared real average earnings growth in New York State with the nation. Earnings grew by 0.4 percent per year in New York compared to 0.2 percent for the country as a whole from 1980 to 1988. Average real earnings in manufacturing within New York State remained at around the national average.

Using information from the U.S. Bureau of Economic Analysis, it is possible to calculate average annual earnings per employee (Table 19). Although this is only a rough approximation of actual annual salaries,[16] it should be adequate to describe trends. The comparison shows that aggregate salaries in New York grew significantly faster from 1980 to 1988 than for the Northeast and the nation as a whole. If it is assumed that these rates approximate wage and salary trends, then the real wage growth of 2 percent a year appears to account for the gap between personal income and employment growth.

As illustrated in Table 19, this above-average wage growth held true for almost all sectors of the economy but particularly in the service sector. Wages and salaries in the service sector grew by 2.3 percent per year in New York compared to 1.9 for other Northeast states and 1.0 percent for the country. The most rapid salary growth was in producer services, especially FIRE, where earnings grew twice as fast as those in the nation or Northeast region. Since this sector has higher than average salaries, this rapid growth has added impact.

A key issue for the state is whether these increases in real wages were accompanied by productivity improvements. Using the value-added estimates for manufacturing made by the U.S. Bureau of the Census in its *Census of Manufactures* and its annual *Survey of Manufac-*

TABLE 18

Personal Income Trends by Source:
New York Compared to Other Northeast States
(Annual Percent Change—Constant 1982 Dollars)[a]

| | Income by Place of Work | | | | Income by Place of Residence | | | |
| | Wages and Salaries | | Proprietor's Income | | Transfer Payments | | Dividends, Etc. | |
	1970–80	1980–88	1970–80	1980–88	1970–80	1980–88	1970–80	1980–88
New York	-0.6	3.7	-0.9	4.8	4.4	2.4	1.2	4.0
Connecticut	1.3	4.7	0.1	3.6	4.9	3.1	2.4	5.0
Maine	1.7	4.0	1.3	4.6	6.9	2.4	3.4	6.6
Massachusetts	0.7	4.9	1.0	5.9	4.8	2.3	1.5	6.0
New Hampshire	3.4	6.3	3.4	7.7	7.1	3.2	4.7	7.7
New Jersey	1.1	4.5	0.1	4.9	5.9	2.3	3.2	5.9
Pennsylvania	0.6	1.4	0.1	2.4	5.9	2.3	3.1	4.8
Rhode Island	0.1	3.5	0.4	4.5	5.3	2.3	2.6	5.1
Vermont	1.6	4.5	2.1	1.9	6.0	2.0	3.9	5.7
Other Northeast	0.9	3.6	0.4	4.0	5.6	2.4	2.7	5.5
Total United States	2.1	2.8	1.0	3.0	6.4	3.0	4.0	4.9

(Percent of Total Personal Income)[b]

	Wages and Salaries		Proprietor's Income		Transfer Payments		Dividends, Etc.	
	1970	1988	1970	1988	1970	1988	1970	1988
New York	68.6	64.3	7.5	7.4	11.5	15.8	15.3	17.6
Connecticut	62.6	60.8	7.3	5.8	8.3	10.2	16.3	18.2
Maine	63.8	55.9	10.6	9.3	12.6	16.1	13.1	16.5
Massachusetts	66.1	63.2	6.7	7.1	11.3	13.2	15.3	17.0
New Hampshire	59.6	53.6	8.2	8.2	9.8	9.8	14.6	16.5
New Jersey	60.9	56.5	6.9	6.0	8.7	10.9	14.0	17.8
Pennsylvania	67.3	56.8	8.8	7.6	11.5	17.3	12.3	17.1
Rhode Island	66.3	58.3	6.5	6.3	12.4	16.4	13.5	16.4
Vermont	63.2	57.3	12.2	9.5	11.7	13.5	14.2	17.7
Other Northeast	64.6	58.4	7.8	6.9	10.4	13.6	13.9	17.4
Total United States	66.1	59.7	9.7	8.0	10.4	14.4	13.3	17.0

[a]Personal income is deflated using the implicit GNP deflator.

[b]These percentages will not generally sum to 100 since there are adjustments made to income by place of work, and there are other sources of income not included ("Other Labor Income").

Source: U.S. Department of Commerce, Bureau of Economic Analysis, unpublished personal income data.

TABLE 19

Earnings Per Employee for New York, Northeast Region, and Total United States[a]
(Constant 1982 Dollars Per Employee)

Industry	New York State			Other Northeast Region[b]			Total United States		
	Earnings 1988	Annual % Change 1975–80	1980–88	Earnings 1988	Annual % Change 1975–80	1980–88	Earnings 1988	Annual % Change 1975–80	1980–88
Total Nonagricultural Earnings	22,723	−0.4	1.9	20,023	0.1	1.4	18,755	0.3	0.6
Goods-producing Sectors:	26,761	0.6	1.2	25,880	0.9	1.3	24,275	1.2	0.3
Mining	27,111	6.0	−11.8	28,984	2.3	−5.5	25,985	0.3	−2.8
Construction	25,449	−0.3	0.9	25,032	0.1	1.0	22,179	0.5	−0.6
Manufacturing:	27,223	0.6	1.5	26,107	1.0	1.6	24,936	1.3	0.9
Nondurable Goods	25,736	0.5	1.9	24,553	1.0	2.3	22,566	1.2	1.1
Durable Goods	28,456	0.6	1.3	27,161	0.9	1.2	26,581	1.3	0.7
Service-producing Sectors:	21,842	−0.7	2.3	18,235	−0.3	1.9	17,208	0.0	1.0

	28,525	0.3	0.8	26,293	0.6	0.9	25,405	0.8	0.3
Distributive Services:									
Transportation and Public Utilities	28,841	0.8	-0.1	26,123	1.0	0.0	26,059	1.1	-0.2
Wholesale Trade	28,248	-0.2	1.6	26,443	0.3	1.9	24,765	0.5	0.8
Retail Trade	11,755	-2.2	0.7	11,550	-1.9	1.1	10,653	-1.6	-0.3
Consumer Services:	12,634	-0.2	1.6	11,987	1.4	1.9	11,045	1.9	0.8
Lodging/Amusement	15,967	-0.7	2.2	11,648	1.2	2.9	11,736	0.4	1.5
Other	10,592	0.0	1.0	12,181	1.6	1.4	10,662	2.7	0.4
Producer Services:	28,031	-0.2	3.9	20,007	-0.3	2.7	18,676	-0.1	2.0
FIRE	33,306	-0.2	5.4	19,559	-1.0	2.7	17,852	-0.8	2.1
Business Services	20,853	-0.5	2.3	19,269	0.8	2.5	16,896	1.0	1.0
Other	27,652	0.4	3.3	21,459	0.0	3.1	21,784	0.3	2.8
Nonprofit Services:	20,570	-1.9	1.5	20,108	-0.8	2.5	20,201	-0.2	1.7
Health Services	22,790	-1.5	1.2	22,032	-0.3	2.5	21,865	0.2	1.6
Educational Services	14,554	-3.9	2.3	14,188	-3.2	1.9	13,064	-3.4	1.7
Government	22,257	-1.3	2.6	19,698	-0.2	2.2	18,826	-0.2	1.7

[a]Total earnings by place of work divided by full-time and part-time employees. For comparison with employment data, only nonagricultural earnings were used (minus farm and agricultural services). The classification methodology is available from the authors upon request. Personal income is deflated using the implicit GNP deflator.

[b]Includes Connecticut, Maine, Massachusetts, New Hampshire, New Jersey, Pennsylvania, Rhode Island, and Vermont.

Source: U.S. Department of Commerce, Bureau of Economic Analysis, unpublished personal income and employment data.

tures, some simple productivity comparisons can be made. Based on these measures, productivity growth in New York manufacturing appears to have exceeded that in the rest of the nation from 1982 to 1986.[17]

Although these productivity measures are too crude to draw strong conclusions, they do suggest that wage increases have been at least partially due to productivity improvements. Similar information is not available for the service sectors, many of which experienced the most rapid wage growth. One study, however, notes the wide difference in national inflation rates between the service and manufacturing sectors and concludes that "the principal source of wage and price differentials between services and manufacturing seems to be the growth of demand for services against a background of low labor mobility between manufacturing and services."[18] This suggests that the high growth rate in wages in the service sector was not primarily due to differential productivity growth but to a demand explanation of rapidly rising wages in the service sector that have put upward pressure on prices.

Another possible explanation for rising real wages is the strong position of organized labor in New York State. Although the relationship between unions and productivity is controversial,[19] there seems to be general agreement that unions are associated with higher wages.[20] Unfortunately, there is no consistent data series on union membership by state available since 1982.[21] New York State has consistently had higher levels of unionization than the national average and in 1982 had the highest percent of public and private employment organized in the country (third highest for private workers alone).

Due to data limitations, it is difficult to draw strong conclusions on the reasons for rapid growth in real wages and salaries. Since employment growth was strong in both high-wage (producer services) and low-wage (consumer services, retail trade) industries, it is unlikely that changes in the "industry mix" were the major factors. Rising real wage rates appear to have accounted for the majority of this growth. This recent growth in real wages was associated with comparable productivity growth, at least in manufacturing, and continued high levels of unionization within the state. Finally, inflation in the New York City area may partially explain income growth in this region.

Capital and Proprietor Income

The fastest growing sources of income have been capital (dividends, etc.) and proprietor income, with annual rates of income 4.0

and 4.8 percent, respectively, since 1980 (see Table 18).[22] Both of these categories experienced little growth (or even decline) during the 1970s. The growth in capital income was concentrated in 1981, 1984, and 1988, with real growth of 10 percent or more per year. Proprietor income has exhibited strong growth since 1982, increasing by 10 percent per year in New York State. Growth in capital income in New York State continues to lag behind the rest of the Northeast region and nation while proprietor's income has grown more rapidly.

The data used for this analysis do not permit disaggregation of capital income to determine what accounts for the rapid growth in the 1980s. Clearly, one of the priorities of former President Ronald Reagan's administration was to stimulate the productivity and growth of the private sector with an increased after-tax rate of return to capital as the primary lure. The policy instruments to achieve this goal included, at one time or another, anti-inflation measures, income tax reductions, investment tax credits, and accelerated depreciation. It is likely that these policies, combined with the strong economic recovery beginning in 1983, accounted for much of the recent growth in capital income.

New York State experienced significantly faster growth in proprietor income than the nation as a whole (4.8 versus 3.0 percent per year, respectively, since 1980). This growth was primarily due to employment growth (versus growth in earnings per employee). Most of the growth since 1980 has been in the service sectors, particularly producer and consumer services. Proprietor income in FIRE and lodging and amusement services in New York State grew much faster than in the rest of the country. Producer services accounted for close to 40 percent of proprietor (and other labor) income in 1986.[23]

Since proprietor income generally comes from self-employed individuals, this growth would indicate expansion of small businesses in these sectors. In the producer service sector, this may have been the result of rapid growth in specialized financial, computer, or other business services in which New York City has a comparative advantage. Consumer services have been led by the lodging and amusement sectors, with New York City accounting for most of this growth. This may explain why proprietor income grew by 7 percent per year from 1980 to 1988 in New York City.

It would appear that many of these small firms are providing support services to the corporate sector. Whether growth in proprietor income in the New York City area can continue to outpace the nation will depend on how broad the market is for these services. Assuming that they are heavily dependent on corporations in the New York City area, the linkage between the corporate and small business sectors in New York is an important area for future research. Especially important is understanding how changes in the finance sector affect small proprietors in the New York City area.

Structural Change and Income Distribution

Ideally, this chapter would conclude with an analysis of what has happened to income distribution with the strong growth in personal income during the 1980s. It is important to understand whether low-income groups benefited equally from this growth. Much of the recent interest in the issue of industrial transformation has been due to its potential effect on income distribution. Those expressing concern over "deindustrialization" point to the loss of higher paying manufacturing jobs as leading to greater income inequality.[24] The issues of whether the middle class is shrinking and if these effects are structural or transitory have become quite controversial.[25]

Research on income distribution has generally employed surveys of individual households, most commonly the *Current Population Survey* from the U.S. Bureau of the Census. Since the small sample size limits the reliability of these data below the regional level, it was not possible to carry out similar research for New York State. This section will instead take on the more modest task of describing changes in real earnings by industrial sector and how this may have affected income distribution in the state.

As with employment, the goods-producing sectors have generally experienced the slowest growth in total real earnings. Since 1980, earnings have grown by 0.6 percent per year compared to 4.3 percent growth for the service sectors in New York State.[26] Earnings in manufacturing declined at a faster rate in New York than in the rest of the Northeast region and the country. The most rapid growth in total earnings during the 1980s occurred in the service sectors, growing by more than 4 percent per year, which was well above the rate of growth for the rest of the country. Growth appears to have extended to most parts of the state, with growth in the New York City area particularly rapid.

To highlight the possible effects of structural changes in the economy on income distribution, it is necessary to compare growth in real wages between high-paying and low-paying sectors. Annual earnings per employee were calculated (see Table 19) indicating the relative salary differential between sectors of the economy and where salary growth has been the most rapid. The "shrinking middle class" hypothesis would suggest that low-paying service sectors have been the primary source of employment growth and that wage growth in these sectors continues to lag behind the higher paying goods-producing sectors.[27] The evidence for New York is mixed.

As identified in the employment section, the most rapid employment growth during the 1980s in New York was in service sectors, especially FIRE—finance, insurance, and real estate—business services, nonprofit services, and consumer services. Earnings per employee in FIRE and some other producer service sectors are on par with (or exceed) that in manufacturing. However, the other high-growth service sectors tend to pay below-average salaries. This contrasts with manufacturing and distributive services that have higher salary levels but that have experienced slow employment growth. In other words, the strongest employment growth has not necessarily been in the lowest paid sectors, as the "shrinking middle class" hypothesis would suggest.

The evidence on whether wage growth in the low-wage sectors lags behind other sectors also appears mixed. The fastest growth in earnings per employee has been in the producer service sectors, particularly FIRE and legal services, while manufacturing and distributive services, which also tend to have higher than average earnings, have experienced slow to moderate growth in earnings per employee. Employee earnings growth in some lower paying sectors, such as retail trade, has been slow as well. However, growth has been fairly rapid in educational, lodging, and amusement services, which are low-paying sectors.

While not overwhelming, this analysis would lend some support to the hypothesis of widening income inequality, especially in New York State, where the structural transformation has occurred more rapidly. Much of the employment growth was in low-paying service sectors, which continue to experience slow wage growth. Since it is likely that many of these jobs are concentrated in central cities, the demands for social services in these cities are likely to increase as the industrial transformation continues.

It is important to understand how low-income families fared during the 1980s. Recent evidence would suggest that nationally the position of the poor worsened somewhat during the past decade.[28] A recent estimate for 1985 to 1987 shows that 15.2 percent of persons in New York and 14.0 percent nationally are below the poverty line.[29] This compares to rates of 13.4 percent for New York and 12.4 percent for the nation in 1980.[30]

Using the available information on national poverty rates by type of household, race, and age and state estimates on racial composition and age structure, we have developed poverty estimates for New York (Table 20). The total poverty rate for New York is estimated to be 15.0 percent in 1990 and will be 15.6 percent at the end of the century. This compares to national rates of 13.5 and 13.8 percent, respectively. The increase in poverty in New York and nationally is driven by a rising poverty rate among female-headed households (more than 42 percent in 1990 in New York) and rapid growth of population in such households (1.7 percent per year from 1980 to 1990 in New York). Population in such households is estimated to account for 15 percent of total population in 1990 and 47 percent of persons below the poverty line. Particularly hard hit are minority households headed by women, which are estimated to have poverty rates of 55 percent in 1990.

Conclusions

Personal income growth appears to provide the strongest evidence that the New York State economy "turned around" in the 1980s. Real income rebounded from little growth in the 1970s to annual real growth of more than 3 percent per year since 1980—above the national average. Per capita income in New York has again risen to 17 percent above the national average. With the exception of a few manufacturing centers in western New York, strong income growth has occurred statewide.

This pattern raises several issues. First, what explains a strong growth in personal income alongside a below-average growth in employment and population? The most obvious explanations— inflation and transfer payments—were clearly not the whole story. The growth was broad-based. Transfer payments, which were the major source of income growth in the 1970s, experienced slower

TABLE 20

Estimate of Poverty Rates by Age, Race, and Type of Household[a]
(Percent of Each Category Below the Official Poverty Line)

	New York State			Total United States		
	1980	1990	2000	1980	1990	2000
Total Population						
Total	13.4	15.0	15.6	12.4	13.5	13.8
Under 5	22.6	27.9	28.9	18.1	22.2	22.4
5–17	17.9	23.0	23.5	15.3	19.0	19.3
18–24	16.2	19.2	20.5	16.0	15.3	15.7
25–64	10.1	12.3	12.6	8.7	10.3	10.6
Over 65	11.6	9.2	10.4	14.8	12.2	12.1
White	9.4	10.7	10.7	9.4	10.5	10.5
Black and Others	34.0	33.1	33.1	30.8	29.4	29.4
Persons in						
Female-headed Households:						
Total	38.0	42.4	43.2	34.4	38.3	38.9
Under 5	67.8	76.8	77.1	60.0	66.0	66.2
5–17	50.8	58.4	58.8	44.2	50.6	51.0
18–24	32.6	43.7	46.7	29.5	32.0	32.9
25–64	27.8	30.8	31.1	25.4	28.4	29.3
Over 65	8.6	7.8	9.7	11.8	11.5	11.4
White	26.9	32.1	32.1	24.7	29.5	29.5
Black and Others	52.8	55.2	55.2	51.0	53.4	53.4
Persons in Other						
Households:						
Total	9.3	9.6	9.8	9.6	9.8	9.9
Under 5	11.4	13.7	14.3	11.0	12.7	12.8
5–17	8.3	9.6	9.7	8.9	10.1	10.2
18–24	12.9	11.3	11.4	14.1	11.8	11.9
25–64	8.0	9.6	9.8	7.1	8.3	8.4
Over 65	11.9	9.3	10.5	15.1	12.3	12.2
White	7.5	7.9	7.9	8.0	8.4	8.4
Black and Others	22.7	19.5	19.5	22.1	19.0	19.0

[a]The estimation methodology is available from the authors upon request.

Source: U.S. Department of Commerce, Bureau of the Census, *1980 Census of Population, Current Population Reports,* Series P-25, No. 1017, October 1988, Series P-60, No. 163, February 1989, and No. 166, October 1989.

growth in the 1980s. The one exception has been medical payments, which continued to expand rapidly due to rising costs.

Proprietor income grew rapidly in the 1980s in New York State after a sharp decline in the previous decade. Most of this growth was in the New York City area in certain producer and consumer services. Whether these small businesses depend on the local corporate sector or have a broader market for their services is unclear.

The major source of income growth has been in wages and salaries, which rebounded from real decline in the 1970s to grow by more than 3 percent per year since 1980. Since this growth has been more than twice that of total employment, it raises the question of what has driven this increase. Based on the analysis in this chapter, it would appear that most of this discrepancy can be accounted for by a high rate of growth in average real wages in most sectors of the economy. Both productivity growth and union influence may be elements in this explanation. A more comprehensive analysis of the causes of wage growth will be important for assessing changes to the competitiveness of New York during the 1980s.

The strong growth in earnings per employee in New York and other northeastern states appears to be the major factor explaining the widening of the income gap between high- and low-income states in the 1980s. This earnings growth was the result not of a change in "industry mix" toward high-wage sectors but was due to strong growth in almost all sectors.[31] The key issue for state policymakers is whether this signals a new resurgence in northeastern economies.

As discussed by Browne, the 1970s and 1980s seem to indicate two different patterns of regional development. In the 1970s and the decades before it, the "convergence" of regional incomes was consistent with the view that "capital and labor movements tend to eliminate cost disparities" and the "earnings differences are self-correcting." In other words, factor mobility in the long run will level out factor prices. The 1980s, on the other hand, suggested that regional economic growth is most strongly affected by "shocks to a region's export industries [which] have powerful multiplier effects."[32] The "shocks" in the 1980s were the major recessions early in the decade and the resulting decline in mineral and energy prices.

Are these two patterns of regional economic development incompatible? We concur with Browne that "Economic shocks that affect regions differentially may occur against a backdrop of cost equalization and wage convergence. In the 1980s, economic shocks overwhelmed any tendencies toward convergence; in the 1970s, they may have reinforced such tendencies."[33] This suggests that the strong earnings growth in the Northeast during the 1980s may be primarily transitory. Barring similar "shocks" in the future, it is not unreasonable to expect that per capita income differentials will continue their long-term pattern of convergence in the 1990s.

Finally, there is the question of the impact of structural change on income distribution. Although the data to assess changes in disposable income among socioeconomic groups are not available, aggregate data on earnings per employee do shed light on this issue. There appears to be mixed support for the view that the middle class is shrinking, that is, income inequality is worsening. With the exception of some producer services, the most rapid employment growth occurred in lower paid service sectors that experienced slow income growth. This would suggest that there is a significant group of low-income workers, the "working poor," who may have benefited little from the rapid income growth in the state. This, plus the higher unemployment and poverty rates among minorities, suggests that local governments, particularly central cities, may be faced with an increasing demand for social services.

Notes

1.   For real income trends in New York and its substate areas, see Tables D-1 to D-3 in Appendix D.

2.   These rapid growth rates appear to have caught the U.S. Bureau of Economic Analysis (BEA) off guard when it made its projections of personal income growth to 1990 (using 1983 data). The growth rates in New York State during the 1980s have far exceeded those anticipated by the BEA. See U.S. Bureau of Economic Analysis, *1985 OBERS BEA Regional Projections* (Washington, D.C.: U.S. Government Printing Office, 1985).

3.   For two recent analyses of regional income trends, see Daniel Garnick, "Accounting for Regional Differences in Per Capita Personal Income Growth: An Update and Extension," *Survey of Current Business* 70 (January 1990): 29–40; and Lynne Browne, "Shifting Regional Fortunes: The Wheel Turns," *New England Economic Review* (May/June 1989): 29–40.

4.   See Tables D-2 and D-3 in Appendix D for detailed personal income trends for substate areas. See Appendix A for the definitions of substate areas used in this book.

5. For a comparison of personal income and employment trends for substate areas, see Table D-3 in Appendix D.

6. For a review of methodology, see U.S. Bureau of Labor Statistics, *CPI Detailed Report* (Washington, D.C.: U.S. Department of Labor, October 1986).

7. Samuel Ehrenhalt, "Looking to the 1990s: Continuity and Change." Paper presented at the 20th Annual Institute of Challenges of the Changing Economy of New York City, sponsored by the New York City Council of Economic Education, July 1987, p. 19.

8. The Port Authority of New York and New Jersey, *Regional Perspectives: The Regional Economy* (New York: Port Authority of New York and New Jersey, September 1987), p. 14.

9. New York City, *Small Retail Business Study Commission: Final Report* (New York: Small Retail Business Study Commission, June 1986), pp. i–vi.

10. The Port Authority, *Regional Perspectives*, p. 11.

11. For a good review of transfer payment trends, see Thomas Holloway and Jane Reed, "Sources of Changes in Federal Transfer Payments to Persons: An Update," *Survey of Current Business* 66 (June 1986): 21–25.

12. One of the major recent revisions in personal income data is the inclusion for the first time of Medicaid payments.

13. Social Security Administration, *Social Security Bulletin, Annual Statistical Supplement, 1987* (Washington, D.C.: U.S. Department of Health and Human Services, 1987).

14. New York Department of Social Services, *Statistical Supplement to the Annual Report* (Albany: New York State Department of Social Services, various years).

15. Because of differences in industry mix among areas, comparisons of wage growth should be made at the lowest industry classification level feasible. It has not been possible to carry out such a disaggregated analysis for this chapter.

16. Defined as total earnings divided by total full- and part-time employment. Since it is not possible to break out full- and part-time earnings or employment, variations in earnings per employee may represent different salary levels or different relative levels of part-time employment.

17. Real value added per production hour grew by 8.6 percent per year in New York compared to 2.9 percent for the nation from 1982 to 1986. Based on data in U.S. Bureau of the Census, *1982 Census of Manufactures* (Washington, D.C.: U.S. Government Printing Office, 1984); and *1986 Survey of Manufactures* (Washington, D.C.: U.S. Government Printing Office, 1988).

18. Peter Rappaport, "Inflation in the Service Sector," *Federal Reserve Bank of New York Quarterly Review* 12 (Winter 1987): 35–45.

19. The most commonly cited study showing that unions increase productivity is R. L. Freeman and J. L. Medoff, *What Do Unions Do?* (New York: Basic Books, 1984). For a study showing generally no relationship, see Steven Allen, "Productivity Levels and Productivity Change Under Unionism," NBER Working Paper No. 2304 (Cambridge: National Bureau of Economic Research, July 1987).

20. The classic work in this area is Gregg Lewis, *Unionism and Relative Wages in the United States: An Empirical Inquiry* (Chicago: University of Chicago Press, 1963). For recent work confirming many of his conclusions, see John Pencavel and Catherine Hartsog, "A Reconsideration of the Effects of Unionism on Relative Wages and Employment in the United States, 1920–80," NBER Working Paper No. 1316 (Cambridge: National Bureau of Economic Research, March 1984).

21. Recent research on unionization in New York State uses data from the *Current Population Survey* to estimate the level of unionism from 1984 to 1986. However, these estimates are not compatible with previous research and the small sample size makes accuracy of these estimates questionable. See New York State Industrial Cooperation Council, "New York is Working This Labor Day: New Data on Business and Labor Growth in NY" (Albany: New York State Industrial Cooperation Council, August 1987). The data used in this chapter are based on the actual financial statements unions are required to file, which are compiled in the work of Leo Troy and Neil Sheflin, *Union Sourcebook: Membership, Structure, Finance, Directory* (West Orange, NJ: Industrial Relations Data and Information Service, 1985).

22. Proprietor's income includes that from unincorporated sole proprietorships, partnerships, and nonprofit cooperatives. Capital income includes income from personal dividends and interest, rental income (including imputed rent), and royalties. See U.S. Bureau of Economic Analysis, *Local Area Personal Income: 1978-83, Methodology* (Washington, D.C.: U.S. Government Printing Office, 1985), for a detailed definition of these terms.

23. The conclusions in this section are based on an analysis of trends for proprietor and other labor earnings per employee from 1980 to 1986. In 1986, proprietor income accounted for 58 percent of both sources in New York State and 59 percent nationwide.

24. See Barry Bluestone and Bennett Harrison, *The Deindustrialization of America* (New York: Basic Books, 1982); and recently Bennett Harrison, Chris Tilly, and Barry Bluestone, "Wage Inequality Takes a Great U-Turn," *Challenge* 29 (March/April 1986): 26–32.

25. Studies examining this issue have differed in the unit of analysis, measures of economic class, and time period studied. For a good review of much of this research, see Gary W. Loveman and Chris Tilly, "Good Jobs or Bad Jobs: What Does the Evidence Say?" *New England Economic Review* (January/February 1988): 46–65.

26.   See Table D-4 in Appendix D for earnings trends in New York and the Northeast region.

27.   See Loveman and Tilly, "Good Jobs or Bad Jobs," for a good review of the evidence on this hypothesis.

28.   The gap (per family member) between the average income of families below the poverty line and the poverty line increased from $1,041 in 1980 to $1,086 in 1986 (in 1986 dollars). The increase was considerably more for families headed by women. In addition, the percent of poor persons below 50 percent of the poverty line grew from 33.5 percent in 1980 to 39.2 percent in 1986. See Mark Littman, "Poverty in the 1980s: Are the Poor Getting Poorer?" *Monthly Labor Review* 112 (July 1989): 13–18.

29.   See Robert Plotnick, "How Much Poverty Is Reduced by State Income Transfers?" *Monthly Labor Review* 112 (July 1989): 21–26.

30.   The poverty rate in New York City, by contrast, was 20 percent in 1980. See U.S. Bureau of the Census, *1980 Census of Population* (Washington, D.C.: U.S. Government Printing Office, 1983 and 1984).

31.   Garnick, "Accounting for Regional Differences in Per Capita Personal Income Growth: An Update and Extension"; and Browne, "Shifting Regional Fortunes: The Wheel Turns."

32.   Browne, "Shifting Regional Fortunes: The Wheel Turns," p. 37.

33.   Ibid.

PART II

New York's Fiscal Performance and Health

4

The Public Sector in New York in the 1980s

There is no question but that the New York State economy performed better during the 1980s than during the previous decade. This economic growth presented the state with the opportunity to carefully review its fiscal policies and to make significant changes with minimum disruption. In particular, it gave the governor, the state legislature, and some local governments an opportunity to reexamine the proper role and size of the public sector in New York State. This opportunity also presented a dilemma. On the one hand, the new economic growth was accompanied by changing demographics and employment structure, which imply an increased demand for public services. On the other hand, state and local leaders were faced with the possible adverse consequences of a large public sector for economic growth.

In this chapter, we examine the growth and relative size of New York's public sector during the 1980s. The comparatives used are the entire United States and the neighboring states of New Jersey, Pennsylvania, Massachusetts, and Connecticut. The conclusion of this analysis is that the growth in public expenditures continued strong in the 1980s and that the government share in the New York economy remains among the highest in the nation. The last section of this chapter examines the implications of this public sector size and growth for economic development in the 1990s.

Explaining and Measuring Government Growth

Since the late 1970s, there has been a renewed interest in the issue of government growth and size. The overwhelming election victory of President Reagan in 1980 was interpreted as a mandate to reduce the size and reach of the public sector in this country, but was this the right mandate to give? The central question, whether high taxes retard economic growth, has led to a new round of research studies on some old questions about government expenditures: What has driven the strong postwar growth of government relative to the private sector? What are the proper measures of government's impact on society? When does government become so large that it leads to declining economic growth and living standards?

It is valuable to review the growth in New York's public sector in a context of the common theories of government growth and size.[1] There have been numerous studies of the growth in the public sector in the United States and comparisons of public sector size for different countries.[2] Despite the national focus of most of this research, many of the theories of government growth are also applicable to explaining the growth of state and local governments.[3] Although categorizing this diverse literature is difficult, most of the studies may be grouped into those emphasizing revenue versus expenditure growth and, among expenditure theories, those that focus on demand versus supply factors.

The research on revenue growth has stressed the "hidden" nature of some revenue sources. As stated by Lowery and Berry, "This explanation of the growth in government is based on the premise that there are certain characteristics of a government's tax system that lead citizens to underestimate the true cost of public goods and services and thus demand more of these goods and services than they would otherwise."[4] Some of these "fiscal illusions" include debt financing, hidden taxes, such as a sales tax, and tax withholding for the income tax. Based on these explanations, we should expect that government growth would be associated with increasing use of these sources of revenue.

Another hidden growth factor is a high built-in elasticity of the tax system. This makes it possible for taxes, and therefore expenditures, to increase at a greater rate than total income without the voters having a direct say. Progressive rate income taxes, broad-based sales taxes, and property taxes characterized by updated valuations are features of tax systems that promote a greater rate of growth in the government sector.[5]

The demand side theories stress that voters' desire for public services is what fuels government expenditure growth. What lies behind much of this demand literature is the argument, originally advanced by Adolph Wagner in 1877, that increasing income and industrialization are associated with public sector growth.[6] Researchers since then have tried to develop and test "Wagner's law" as an explanation of government growth. Explanations of this empirical relationship include: that public services are income elastic, that is, the demand for public services rises faster than total income; that the increasing urbanization accompanying industrialization has led to externalities that are best handled by government; and that industrialization requires parallel investment by government in physical and human capital.[7] According to these demand theories, government expenditure growth should be greatest for functions with a high income elasticity; functions that address the externalities of industrialization (such as the environment, housing, and social services); or functions that promote infrastructure and educational services.[8]

Supply side theories stress that there are institutional or service-related factors that lead to an expansion of the public sector and generally inefficient service provision. Because many public services are relatively labor-intensive by nature, there is concern that lagging productivity is endemic in the public sector. If government agencies are forced to keep their wages competitive with the private sector, then the cost of public services will continue to rise and an increasing portion of society's resources will be diverted to the public sector, the so-called "Baumol's disease."[9] This explanation of government growth implies that it will occur primarily in personnel compensation, particularly in labor-intensive services, such as police, fire, and education.

Another body of literature stresses that public officials or civil servants have the incentive and influence to expand the public sector. The "bureaucratic" theories stress that public agencies act as monopoly suppliers of public services and that this gives public administrators (bureaucrats) significant power to pursue their own personal objectives. Much of this research has assumed that bureaucrats attempt to expand their income and power by maximizing their budgets, staffs, and "discretionary funds."[10] In line with this, some research has focused on the power of public employees as voters.[11] These theories would imply that rapid government growth comes with an expansion in public employment and wages and salaries.[12]

Other theorists focus on the relationship between elected officials and interest groups. Legislative committees are supposedly dominated by "high demanders" for different types of public services, and legislative rules tend to promote cooperation rather than competition in passing appropriations legislation.[13] The type of government expenditure that will grow will depend on the dominant interest groups in a legislature.

Size and Growth of the Government Sector

New York has long been known for its large and expansionary public sector. This reputation continues to be deserved. This analysis shows that the public sector in New York expanded in the 1980s and that the size of government has grown relative to the nation and most neighboring states.

In the early 1970s, New York state and local governments did not curtail their expenditure growth when real personal income ceased to grow and total employment turned down. As may be seen from Table 21, real state and local government expenditures grew as fast in New York as in the rest of the nation despite the fact that the economic growth to support these expenditures was not present in New York. Real tax revenue in New York grew by more than 1 percent per year from 1970 to 1975 while real personal income and employment declined.[14] By 1975, per capita expenditures of New York state and local governments were 51 percent above the national average and taxes had climbed to 15 cents per dollar of personal income—nearly 37 percent above the U.S. average (Table 22).

New York was not alone in its expansionary policies in the early 1970s. Massachusetts and New Jersey also had growth in tax revenues well above that for employment and personal income. However, among New York's neighbors, only Massachusetts had tax and expenditure burdens well above the national average. The disparity would have been even worse had it not been for the above-average growth in federal aid in New York (and most of its neighbors).

TABLE 21

Average Annual Percent Change in Selected Indicators
of Economic and Fiscal Activity[a]:
New York, Neighboring States, and the Total United States

	New York			*Total United States*		
	1970– 75	*1975– 80*	*1980– 88*	*1970– 75*	*1975– 80*	*1980– 88*
Real Federal Aid	9.0	2.7	–0.5	7.9	3.6	–1.0
Real Tax Revenue	1.2	–0.9	3.4	2.1	1.3	3.0
Real Expenditures[b]	3.5	–2.2	3.0	3.5	1.6	2.8
Real Personal Income	–0.1	0.9	3.3	2.3	3.6	3.0
Employment	–0.9	1.1	1.6	1.7	3.3	2.0
	Connecticut			*Massachusetts*		
Real Federal Aid	9.3	2.3	0.2	7.8	7.2	–2.6
Real Tax Revenue	0.0	0.9	4.7	2.7	0.4	1.9
Real Expenditures[b]	1.6	0.3	4.3	3.7	0.2	2.5
Real Personal Income	0.3	3.5	4.3	0.5	2.5	4.5
Employment	0.4	3.1	2.0	0.3	3.1	2.1
	New Jersey			*Pennsylvania*		
Real Federal Aid	12.2	2.0	0.9	10.0	0.9	–0.6
Real Tax Revenue	2.4	1.3	3.6	1.6	0.9	1.1
Real Expenditures[b]	4.9	0.8	3.6	2.9	–0.2	1.5
Real Personal Income	1.0	2.8	4.3	1.5	2.3	2.0
Employment	0.7	2.5	2.3	0.4	1.4	0.7

[a]All monetary data are deflated using the implicit GNP deflator for state and local government purchases except personal income, which is deflated by the implicit GNP deflator for total GNP.

[b]Direct general expenditures. Deflated using the implicit GNP deflator for state and local government purchases.

Source: U.S. Department of Commerce, Bureau of Economic Analysis, unpublished personal income data, revised April 1990; Bureau of the Census, *Governmental Finances,* various years; and U.S. Department of Labor, Bureau of Labor Statistics, *Employment, Hours and Earnings, States and Areas,* on computer tape.

TABLE 22

State and Local Revenues and Expenditures in New York State
As a Percent of United States Average[a]

	Real Per Capita Amounts				Amounts Per $1,000 of Personal Income			
	1970	1975	1980	1988	1970	1975	1980	1988
General Revenue	137.5	145.4	137.1	149.2	115.2	127.3	127.7	128.0
Own-source Revenue	142.5	150.3	138.8	149.9	119.4	131.6	129.3	128.6
Total Taxes	151.9	156.2	150.8	165.2	127.3	136.8	140.5	141.6
Property Taxes	140.9	154.3	164.7	159.5	118.0	135.2	153.5	136.8
Income Taxes	NA	230.6	202.0	241.5	NA	202.0	188.2	207.1
General Sales Tax	NA	142.0	127.9	132.9	NA	124.4	119.2	114.0
Federal Aid	112.3	126.5	131.0	145.7	94.0	110.8	122.0	125.0

Total Expenditures	141.5	151.3	135.2	146.7	118.5	132.5	126.0	125.8
By Object:								
Operating Expenditures	147.8	154.7	142.9	151.6	123.8	135.5	133.2	130.0
Total Payroll	138.7	143.8	124.1	148.1	116.2	126.0	115.6	127.1
Employment[b]	121.7	120.7	111.6	127.4	NA	NA	NA	NA
Payroll/Employee	114.4	119.2	111.1	116.3	NA	NA	NA	NA
Capital Expenditures	117.6	135.5	89.2	113.3	98.5	118.7	83.2	97.1
Long-term Debt Outstanding	162.4	181.6	174.1	142.0	136.0	159.0	162.2	121.8
By Function:								
Education	117.2	121.3	113.5	122.6	98.2	106.3	105.7	105.2
Health	202.4	219.0	138.0	172.1	169.5	191.8	128.6	147.6
Highways	86.9	81.7	83.7	97.9	72.6	71.7	77.6	83.6
Public Safety	NA	NA	142.5	159.2	NA	NA	132.2	135.9
Public Welfare	185.7	183.6	177.2	200.6	155.5	160.8	165.1	172.1

[a]Expenditures are direct general expenditures. Per capita amounts deflated using the implicit GNP deflator for state and local government purchases except payroll, which is deflated by the implicit GNP deflator for state and local government compensation.

[b]Full-time equivalent employment.

Source: U.S. Department of Commerce, Bureau of the Census, *Governmental Finances* and *Public Employment*, various years.

The well-known events of this period in New York's economic history included a continued slow growth in economic activity in the late 1970s, the fiscal collapse of New York City in 1975, and real expenditure reductions in the latter half of the 1970s.[15] Many observers thought this would be a major turning point in the way New York governments would view the role of the public sector. Based on the analysis in this chapter, however, the New York City fiscal crisis of 1975 turned out to be more of a minor blip than a major turnabout in fiscal philosophy.

These fiscal and economic problems and the tax and expenditure limitation movements clearly had an impact on New York governments in the short run. Between 1975 and 1980, there actually was expenditure retrenchment relative to the rest of the region and the nation, with real expenditures declining by 2.2 percent per year compared to 1.6 percent growth in the nation (and slow growth in Connecticut, Massachusetts, and New Jersey). Even with this new fiscal conservatism, New York was unable to bring its tax burden per dollar of income more in line with the rest of the country. The rate of growth in personal income was so much greater in other states that New York's share of taxes on personal income actually rose from 36.8 percent above the national average in 1975 to 40.5 percent in 1980.[16]

By 1980, the economic and fiscal picture had improved. The state and most local governments were beginning to show revenue growth, New York City had a Financial Control Board, and the state and city economies were in an upswing. In 1981, the city entered the long-term bond market for the first time since 1975. In the next sections, we explore the revenue and expenditure patterns that accompanied this upswing of the 1980s.

Revenues

Real tax revenues in New York grew at a higher rate than in the rest of the United States in the 1980s and well above the real growth rates of the 1970s (see Table 21). This disparity is amplified when revenues are adjusted for population: real per capita taxes grew by 3.1 percent per year in New York compared to 2.0 percent for the nation. Despite the above-average income growth in New York, the tax share of personal income, relative to the rest of the nation, actually increased between 1980 and 1988 (see Table 22).

New York's taxes relative to personal income grew faster than those of all its neighboring states during the 1980s except for Connecticut. New York is now the *only* large northeastern state with tax burdens above the national average. Taxes relative to income are close to 50 percent higher (or more) in New York compared to those in all of New York's principal neighbors.[17]

Most of New York's tax and revenue growth has occurred since 1983. Between 1980 and 1983, taxes per dollar of personal income actually dropped in New York by more than the decline nationally (Table 23). Since 1983, the growth in New York taxes has accelerated and the gap with the rest of the nation and with the region has widened.

Was the financing of New York's public expenditure programs different in the 1980s than in the 1970s? In particular, we might ask whether the tax system was more consistent with the traditional goals of industrial policy, for example, whether the state began to rely less on those taxes that are said to be most offensive to the business sector. These include company income taxes, progressive rate individual income taxes, and nonresidential property taxes. A comparison of the New York tax structure in 1975, 1980, and 1988 (Table 24) shows that there has been a continued increase in the reliance on the income tax. This contrasts with the rest of the country, where the income tax has not increased in relative importance since 1980. New York also relies more heavily on the property tax than does the rest of the country, although this reliance has decreased significantly in recent years. General sales taxes make up a smaller share of revenues in New York than in other states, and there was no significant change in this pattern in the 1980s. By comparison with other states, New York does not raise as much general revenue from user charges and licenses.

Personal and corporate income taxes were the fastest growing major revenue sources in New York State during the 1980s. The increase was especially rapid after 1983 and was twice the national rate of increase (see Table 23). Compared to its neighbors, New York's income tax grew faster than all but New Jersey's.[18] The growth in income tax revenues came without major discretionary increases. In fact, the state has been engaged in a long-run program of reduction in income tax rates.[19] Instead, the rapid increase in personal income, especially in the higher brackets, and the progressivity of the individual income tax structure were the reasons for the revenue growth.

TABLE 23

Annual Percent Change in Revenues[a]:
New York and Total United States

	Real Per Capita Amounts				Amounts Per $1,000 of Personal Income			
	1970–80	1980–83	1983–88	1980–88	1970–80	1980–83	1983–88	1980–88
New York:								
General Revenue	1.9	0.3	4.2	2.7	1.9	-0.8	1.3	0.5
Own-source Revenue	1.0	1.4	4.8	3.5	1.0	0.3	1.9	1.3
Total Taxes	0.6	0.5	4.8	3.1	0.6	-0.6	1.8	0.9
Property Taxes	-0.3	-0.8	2.8	1.4	-0.3	-1.9	-0.1	-0.7
Income Taxes	NA	3.1	5.8	4.8	NA	2.0	2.8	2.5
General Sales Taxes	NA	0.1	5.0	3.1	NA	-1.0	2.0	0.9
Federal Aid	6.2	-4.3	1.5	-0.7	6.2	-5.3	-1.3	-2.8
Total United States:								
General Revenue	1.9	-0.5	2.9	1.7	0.8	-0.3	1.0	0.5
Own-source Revenue	1.3	0.9	3.5	2.5	0.2	1.1	1.5	1.4
Total Taxes	0.6	-0.5	3.5	2.0	-0.4	-0.3	1.5	0.8
Property Taxes	-1.8	0.3	2.8	1.8	-2.9	0.5	0.8	0.7
Income Taxes	4.7	-1.0	4.6	2.4	3.5	-0.8	2.6	1.3
General Sales Taxes	2.8	-0.7	4.6	2.6	1.7	-0.5	2.6	1.5
Federal Aid	4.6	-5.7	0.2	-2.0	3.5	-5.5	-1.7	-3.1

[a]Per capita amounts deflated using the implicit GNP deflator for state and local government purchases.

Source: U.S. Department of Commerce, Bureau of the Census, *Governmental Finances*, various years.

TABLE 24

Percent Distribution of Revenues[a]:
New York State and the United States

	New York State			*Total United States*		
	1975	*1980*	*1988*	*1975*	*1980*	*1988*
Own Source Revenue:						
Income Taxes	23.8	26.9	29.6	15.5	18.5	18.4
Sales Taxes	NA	18.4	16.8	NA	22.2	21.7
General	15.2	15.8	15.3	16.1	17.1	17.3
Motor Vehicles	NA	2.6	1.5	NA	5.1	4.5
Property Tax	29.2	27.2	23.1	28.4	22.9	21.7
Other Taxes	NA	8.6	9.3	NA	11.1	9.7
User Charges	NA	10.8	11.6	NA	14.8	15.5
Other Revenues	NA	8.1	9.7	NA	10.5	13.0
Total	100.0	100.0	100.0	100.0	100.0	100.0
Exhibit: Federal Aid as a Percent of Own-source Revenues	21.9	26.2	18.8	26.0	27.7	19.3

[a]Percentages may not add to 100 due to rounding.

Source: U.S. Department of Commerce, Bureau of the Census, *Governmental Finances*, various years.

Despite the rate reductions of the 1980s, a 1.0 percent increase in personal income in New York was associated, on average, with a 2.5 percent increase in income taxes (by comparison with 1.3 percent for the whole country). New York's income tax burden relative to income grew from 88 percent above the national average in 1980 to 107 percent above in 1988 (see Table 22). Its income tax burden was 38 percent higher than that in Massachusetts and more than 100 percent above its other neighbors.

The other major outlier is the local property tax. Property taxes relative to income actually declined 0.7 percent per year in New York in the 1980s compared to a 0.7 percent annual increase nationally.

Although the gap between New York and the nation narrowed in the 1980s, the per capita property tax burden in New York State is still 60 percent higher than in the rest of the country and 37 percent higher relative to personal income (see Table 22). With the sharp drop in property taxes in Massachusetts due to Proposition 2 1/2 (a 5.7 percent per year decrease from 1980 to 1988 relative to income), New York now has a higher property tax burden (relative to income) than any of its neighboring states. Despite the fact that effective property tax rates in New York State and the nation as a whole have dropped sharply since the late 1970s, New York State still has one of the highest effective rates (ranked fifth) in the country, 80 percent above the national average.[20]

Relative to personal income, general sales tax revenue actually grew more slowly in New York State than in the rest of the country (see Table 23). Most of this growth was due to the performance of the economy because New York State, unlike many other states, did not make major changes in the state sales tax rates during the 1980s.[21] Even so, the combined state and local sales tax rate in New York State was equal to or higher than that in all but eight states in 1989.[22] In per capita terms, the total sales tax burden was 33 percent above the national average in 1988, and relative to personal income was 14 percent above. The sales tax burden was higher in New York than in any of its neighbors, although the gap narrowed during the 1980s.

As a cross-check on the conclusion from this simple ratio analysis—that New York's tax burden is high—the tax effort estimates prepared by the U.S. Advisory Commission on Intergovernmental Relations (ACIR) are presented in Table 25. The ACIR attempts to improve on income or population ratios by taking into account the structure of income, consumption, and production within the state (Box 9).[23] They pose the following question: If every state levied a "representative tax system" at national average rates, how much could they raise? Their results show that for fiscal year 1988, New York State had a fiscal capacity index of 109, that is, New York's fiscal capacity is approximately 9 percent above the national average. However, New York makes a fiscal effort that is 52 percent above the national average. In other words, the ratio of the actual level of taxes raised to the estimated level of fiscal capacity was 52 percent higher in New York than in the average state. New York's tax effort ranked second only to that of Washington, D.C., and was well above that of its neigh-

> ## Box 9. The Yield of a Representative Tax System in New York
>
> The ACIR periodically estimates the amount of revenue that a representative tax system (RTS) would yield if applied in every state.[a] The first step is to estimate the overall taxable capacity in each state based on the size of those bases that could be taxed. Then, average national use of these bases (average effective rates) is assumed and a "taxable capacity" is estimated. The quotient of this taxable capacity and actual taxes raised is tax effort.
>
> Estimated taxable capacity of New York state and local governments by this method in 1988 was $34.6 billion. Actual revenues raised were $52.5 billion; hence, New York's tax effort index was 152. Among the neighboring states, Massachusetts was 94, Pennsylvania 97, New Jersey 101, Connecticut 90, and Ohio 97.
>
> There has been some improvement in New York's tax effort position largely due to its improved taxable capacity, as described in the graph below.
>
>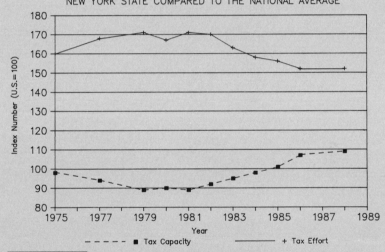
>
> ### TOTAL TAX CAPACITY AND EFFORT
> ACIR'S REPRESENTATIVE TAX SYSTEM (RTS)
> NEW YORK STATE COMPARED TO THE NATIONAL AVERAGE
>
> [a] Advisory Commission on Intergovernmental Relations, *1986 State Fiscal Capacity and Effort*, Information Report M-165 (Washington, D.C.: ACIR, 1989); and unpublished estimates for 1988.

boring states. Interestingly, New York's tax effort by ACIR calculations dropped significantly from 1979 to 1988, particularly for the property and income taxes (see Table 25). This decrease was due to a rapid growth in taxable capacity.[24]

TABLE 25

ACIR Tax Effort Index for New York and Neighboring States[a]:
Selected Years

	Total Taxes	Personal Income Taxes	Corporate Income Taxes	General Sales Taxes	Selective Sales Taxes	Property Taxes
New York:						
1979	172	194	197	140	108	221
1982	170	214	191	138	109	197
1986	152	175	196	136	104	159
1988	152	177	198	127	100	151
Connecticut:						
1979	103	13	137	126	140	131
1982	99	14	164	121	144	121
1986	94	19	175	111	146	108
1988	90	18	128	112	139	106
Massachusetts:						
1979	145	170	185	64	94	221
1982	119	166	164	57	92	144
1986	103	146	200	61	79	99
1988	94	131	143	65	74	89
New Jersey:						
1979	117	65	99	72	126	180
1982	113	67	127	73	138	152
1986	103	63	113	78	144	135
1988	101	66	104	78	135	136
Pennsylvania:						
1979	105	128	128	84	119	87
1982	106	123	112	80	122	95
1986	101	121	100	79	100	96
1988	97	109	116	76	102	89

[a]Average for the United States equals 100.

Source: Advisory Commission on Intergovernmental Relations, *Tax Capacity of the Fifty States: Methodology and Estimates*, Report M-134, March 1982, *Tax Capacity of the Fifty States*, Report M-142, May 1985, *1986 State Fiscal Capacity and Effort*, Report M-165, March 1989, and unpublished data for 1988 provided by ACIR.

As may be seen in Figure 7, New York's tax effort was high relative to the rest of the country in 1988, primarily because of the higher rates for individual income and property taxes. For example, 40 percent of New York's above-average tax effort was due to its high

FIGURE 7
Why New York's Tax Effort
Was 52 Percent Above the National Average in 1988
(Percent Distribution by Tax Type)

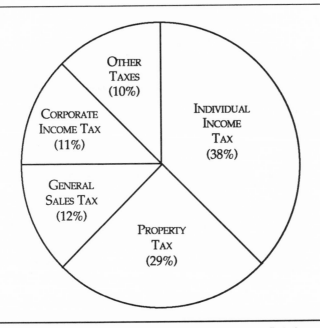

Source: U.S. Advisory Commission on Intergovernmental Relations

effective rate of personal income tax. Only in the case of user charges and licenses did New York not appear to make as much use of its capacity as does the average state. With respect to those taxes that may affect business investment and location, New York ranked high in intensity of use: a property tax effort 50 percent above the national average, sixth highest in the United States;[25] a corporate income tax effort twice the national average, highest in the country; and a personal income tax effort 77 percent above the national average and second highest in the nation.

New York continues to be more successful than most other states in the competition for federal aid dollars. This favorable position is illustrated vividly in the following statistics: per capita federal grants to state and local governments in the United States averaged $435 compared to $623 for all state and local governments in New York and

$752 in New York City.[26] While real per capita (and per dollar of income) federal aid declined in New York during the 1980s, it declined even faster in the rest of the nation. The share of total federal aid distributed to New York State and local governments rose from 10.3 percent in 1970 to 11.0 percent in 1988; New York City's share of federal aid to local governments increased from 6.9 to 7.2 percent in 1986.[27] These relative gains occurred despite an increase in New York's per capita income relative to the national average and a decrease in its share of the nation's total population.

One reason why New York governments fared relatively well in the competition for declining federal aid was the concentration of their aid in federal welfare grants. While real federal grants to the New York State government increased 1.1 percent a year between 1980 and 1988, its welfare grants rose almost 4.0 percent a year.[28] By 1988, New York State's share of all federal welfare assistance reached 16.1 percent, and these funds comprised 70.0 percent of New York State's federal aid (compared to 48.0 percent of aid to all states).[29] New York City, because of its large welfare population, also did relatively well in the competition for aid dollars from both the state and federal governments. New York City received 72 percent of state welfare grants;[30] 46 percent of the city's federal aid was devoted to social services.[31]

In summary, the story of the 1980s seems to be that New York state and local governments did not significantly reduce their tax burdens relative to the rest of the country, at least by the measures used here. New York taxes still are half again as large as those in other states, even if differences in taxable capacity are accounted for. The main reason for this high effort appears to be the heavy use of income and property taxes. Despite discretionary rate reductions in the individual income tax, revenues have increased because of the progressive structure of the tax and because of the rate of increase in the incomes of middle and higher income New Yorkers.

Expenditures

Real per capita state and local government expenditures rose during the 1980s. Real per capita expenditures grew by 2.8 percent per year from 1980 to 1988, significantly faster than the national growth rate of 1.7 percent (Table 26). However, when expenditures are weighted by personal income, expenditure growth in New York was on par with the nation and with most of its neighbors.

The level of expenditures in New York remains well above that in the rest of the country. The gap between per capita expenditures in New York State and the average of all states widened from 35 percent in 1980 to 47 percent by 1988 (see Table 22). When the expenditure burden is measured relative to personal income, the finding is that New York continued to be 26 percent higher during the 1980s. Expenditures relative to income were close to 40 percent higher in New York compared to surrounding states, and the "gap" has widened with all states but Connecticut.[32]

Were the expenditure increases really necessary? We cannot answer this subjective question—it depends on whether higher public expenditures bought a faster rate of job creation and a better quality of life for New Yorkers than would have been bought by lower taxes. It also depends on whether future generations of New Yorkers will be asked to pay for the higher quality of life that present residents are enjoying. We can learn something by studying the composition of this growth in expenditures.

OBJECTS OF EXPENDITURES. Expenditures can be disaggregated into current and capital, with the latter generally representing purchases of equipment or construction of facilities with a "useful life" of more than one year. Since 1983, capital expenditures relative to population or personal income have grown much faster in New York than in the rest of the nation (see Table 26); however, capital expenditures by most other states in the region grew even faster. Per capita expenditures for capital purposes in New York increased from below the national average in 1980 to 13 percent above in 1988. New York still spends a smaller share of its expenditures on capital than does the average state.[33] Relative to its income level, New York spends slightly less than the national average but more than its neighbors. These trends would suggest that New York in the 1980s made a concerted effort to "catch up" in the rebuilding of its infrastructure. Interestingly, this increase in capital expenditures did not appear to have been funded primarily with long-term debt. Long-term debt relative to population or income grew much slower in New York than in the rest of the nation or region. Whether this was an attempt to consciously reduce the high debt burdens in the state is unclear, but per capita debt dropped from 74 percent above the national average in 1980 to only 42 percent above in 1988.

TABLE 26
Annual Percent Change in Expenditures[a]: New York and Total United States

	Real Per Capita Amounts				Amounts Per $1,000 of Personal Income			
	1970–80	1980–83	1983–88	1980–88	1970–80	1980–83	1983–88	1980–88
New York:								
Total Expenditures	1.0	0.6	4.1	2.8	1.0	-0.5	1.2	0.6
By Object:								
Operating Expenditures	1.9	0.7	4.0	2.7	1.9	-0.4	1.1	0.5
Total Payroll	-0.2	1.6	3.0	2.5	-0.6	1.1	1.3	1.2
Employment[b]	1.0	0.3	2.5	1.7	NA	NA	NA	NA
Payroll/Employee	-1.2	1.2	0.7	0.9	NA	NA	NA	NA
Capital Expenditures	-4.8	-0.4	5.4	3.2	-4.8	-1.5	2.5	1.0
Long-term Debt Outstanding	0.9	-3.2	4.3	1.4	0.8	-4.2	1.4	-0.7
By Function:								
Education	0.1	-0.3	3.6	2.1	0.1	-1.4	0.7	-0.1
Health	-1.1	5.5	4.8	5.0	-0.6	3.4	1.8	2.4
Highways	-2.2	2.6	2.2	2.4	-2.3	1.1	-0.7	0.0
Public Safety	NA	3.5	6.5	5.4	NA	2.0	3.5	2.9
Public Welfare	2.1	-0.2	5.3	3.2	2.0	-1.3	2.4	1.0

United States:								
Total Expenditures	1.5	-0.7	3.2	1.7	0.4	-0.5	1.2	0.6
By Object:								
Operating Expenditures	2.3	0.3	3.0	2.0	1.2	0.5	1.0	0.8
Total Payroll	0.9	-0.7	0.8	0.2	-0.6	0.1	0.0	0.0
Employment[b]	1.9	-1.4	0.6	-0.2	NA	NA	NA	NA
Payroll/Employee	-0.9	0.6	0.2	0.3	NA	NA	NA	NA
Capital Expenditures	-2.1	-6.9	4.7	0.2	-3.2	-6.8	2.7	-1.0
Long-term Debt Outstanding	-0.4	2.5	5.6	4.4	-0.9	1.7	3.6	2.9
By Function:								
Education	0.4	-1.6	2.8	1.1	-0.6	-1.4	0.8	0.0
Health	3.3	2.0	1.7	1.8	2.2	2.2	-0.3	0.7
Highways	-1.9	-4.3	3.3	0.4	-2.9	-4.4	1.2	-0.9
Public Safety	NA	2.9	4.6	3.9	NA	2.8	2.4	2.6
Public Welfare	2.5	0.0	2.7	1.6	1.4	0.1	0.7	0.5

[a]Expenditures are direct general expenditures. Per capita amounts deflated using the implicit GNP deflator for state and local government purchases except payroll, which is deflated by the implicit GNP deflator for state and local government compensation.

[b]Full-time equivalent employment.

Source: U.S. Department of Commerce, Bureau of the Census, *Governmental Finances* and *Public Employment*, various years.

The major form of current expenditures is wages and salaries, and real payroll expenditures in New York increased at a much higher rate than those in the rest of the nation (see Table 26). The growth in New York was much stronger than for all of its neighboring states, with payroll per dollar of personal income growing by 1.2 percent in New York while it stagnated or declined in the other states.

A crucial issue for assessing the causes and consequences of payroll growth is determining whether it was driven by growth in employment or wages. Employment growth, although possibly a contributor to a "bloated bureaucracy," may also indicate an improvement in state services. Wage growth, on the other hand, unless accompanied by commensurate productivity improvements, implies rising costs, that is, the case of "Baumol's disease."

Payroll growth in New York seems to have been driven by both factors. New York state and local government employment per capita grew by 1.7 percent per year from 1980 to 1988 compared to a slight decline in the rest of the nation (see Table 26). This was a higher employment growth rate than in all New York's neighbors except Pennsylvania. The result was that the number of state and local government employees per ten thousand population in New York increased from 542 to 610. This increase is important. By 1988, the level of government employment per capita in New York had risen to nearly 27 percent above the national average, an even higher figure than had been attained before the fiscal crisis of 1975. This was well above the level of per capita public employment in New York's neighboring states.

Public employee compensation[34] in New York State also increased above the national growth rate, but the disparity is much less severe than in the case of employment. State and local government compensation grew at three times the national rate and exceeded that for all neighboring states but Connecticut. New York City and certain upstate cities (for example, Buffalo) had compensation growth significantly above the state and national rates.[35] By 1988, payroll per employee for all New York state and local governments combined was 16 percent above the national average (see Table 22), roughly on a par with the 17 percent per capita personal income advantage in New York.

EXPENDITURE BY FUNCTION.   Another possible explanation for the high rate of expenditure growth in New York State is the continued growth in the entitlement programs, generally public welfare and health. Growth above the national average in these categories implies that New York State either chose to provide higher benefit standards (than nationally mandated standards) or had a larger than average growth in recipient population. In fact, health and welfare expenditures experienced strong growth in the 1980s. Real welfare spending per capita has gone up by 3.2 percent per year since 1980, twice the national rate (see Table 26). On a real per capita basis, state and local government welfare expenditures went from 77 to 101 percent above the national average from 1980 to 1988, respectively (see Table 22) and were at least 25 percent higher than all of New York's neighbors.[36] Even if New York's higher income and therefore greater ability to pay for welfare services are taken into account, there was a growing disparity with the rest of the nation.

The detailed breakdown and analysis of public welfare and welfare-related expenditures provided in chapter 5 indicate that most of this growth was in Medicaid. Medical—not public assistance—payments were the main source of growth in transfer payments. This is consistent with evidence that New York State provides one of the "best" Medicaid coverages in the country.[37] There is evidence that public assistance recipients and benefit levels in New York (and the nation) have not grown during the 1980s, although New York State remains near the top in terms of the level of Aid to Families with Dependent Children and food stamp benefits provided.

The problems of extreme poverty presently claim a small share of state and local government fiscal resources, but this claim is likely to increase. Ten percent of New York City residents are estimated to live in persistent poverty, and there is a growing awareness of the homeless problem. The Citizens Budget Commission estimates that "the cost of providing shelters for adults and families [in New York City] increased by four times between 1983 and 1988. The average number of persons sheltered each night rose from 4,359 in 1983 to 9,682 in 1988 (individuals) and from 1,309 to 5,164 (families). Although the amount spent is only about 1 percent of the city budget, the constant dollar increase of more than 300 percent is dramatic."[38]

Another area of rapid expenditure growth in the 1980s was in health expenditures. Real per capita expenditures in New York grew by more than two and a half times the national growth rate and above that for all neighboring states but Connecticut. Relative to personal income, health expenditures rose from 29 percent above the national average in 1980 to 48 percent above in 1988. The health expenditure "gap" was more than 100 percent relative to most of New York's neighbors in 1988.

The most rapid growth in public expenditures among major functions occurred in the public safety category. Public safety expenditures include fire protection, police services, and corrections. Per capita expenditures in New York grew by more than 5 percent per year in the 1980s, faster than for the nation and New York's neighbors. The fastest growth occurred in corrections, with the annual growth in real per capita expenditures exceeding 10 percent (compared to 7 percent nationally). Not surprisingly, New York spent in 1988 60 percent more per capita on public safety than the national average and 80 percent more for corrections. Its expenditures are well above those of other states in the region.

Many would argue that the two areas of public expenditure most likely to encourage firm (and individual) migration to a state are education and highways. How has New York fared with respect to these two functions? Real per capita education expenditures grew faster in New York than in the rest of the nation. Relative to personal income growth, however, education expenditures in New York and in the whole United States stagnated. Education expenditures relative to income actually declined in all neighboring states except Pennsylvania. As for New York, the per capita level of education expenditures was more than 20 percent above the national average in 1988—35 percent for primary and secondary education. The expenditure level compared to income, though, was only 5 percent above the nation in 1988. The story, then, is that New York spends at a high rate on a per person basis for education but is not so big a spender if its income level is taken into account.

Highway expenditures per capita in New York grew by 2.4 percent per year compared to a much slower national growth (0.4 percent). Still, this expenditure growth is low by comparison with many states in the region. Relative to personal income there has been no growth in highway expenditures. New York continues to spend less on highways per capita or per dollar of income than the national average and less than all neighboring states but Massachusetts.

These simple expenditure effort measures can be compared with those developed by Robert Rafuse of the ACIR. He estimates "expenditure needs" based on work loads and the average state fiscal response to these work load measures.[39] He estimates that in 1986 to

1987, New York state and local governments actually spent 53 percent more than they "needed" based on the average practice in the rest of the country (up from 47.5 percent in 1983 and 1984). New York was above the national average and most of its neighbors in all the major expenditure categories. These results are consistent with our findings.

Government Size and Economic Growth

Relative to the rest of the country, New York has a large government sector. Per capita expenditures of the state and local governments in New York are 47 percent higher than those in the rest of the country. New York employs 131 more workers per ten thousand population than does the average state and pays the average worker 16 percent more (Table 27). How does a state with a per capita income only 17 percent above the national average manage to spend at a rate nearly 50 percent above the national average? The answer is that it imposes a very high tax effort (second only to Washington, D.C.) and receives a high level of federal aid (fourth in the United States in per capita terms). How New York has managed to support such a large budget is not as difficult to sort out as is the question of whether big government helps or harms the state's economic growth prospects.

One should not jump immediately to the negative aspects of big government in New York. There are perfectly valid reasons why a large government sector can be good public policy. The size of the public sector reflects the preferences of voters. Interstate variations in the size of government may tell us that there are different strategies for achieving the standard of living and income distribution goals a state has set for itself and that there are different voter preferences concerning the importance of these goals. The greater level of expenditures could be used to create a more productive labor force and a better infrastructure. These advantages attract industry to the state. Second, the larger public sector gives the state more opportunity to redistribute income and deal directly with the problems of the poor. New York may not have solved the problem of low-income families but it has probably allocated more resources to dealing with their problems than have other states.

The other side of the story is that a large public sector may in fact indicate bad public policy decisions, or at least it may indicate that state and local governments in New York have chosen an expansive

TABLE 27

Relative Fiscal Position of New York
State and Local Governments in 1988[a]

Variable	New York	United States	New York's Rank
Per Capita Expenditures	3,343	2,279	4
Per Capita Taxes	2,335	1,414	4
Taxes as a Percent of Income	16	11	4
ACIR Tax Effort Index (1988)	152	100	2
Per Capita Federal Aid	556	382	3
Employees per 10,000 Population[b]	610	479	4
Average Employee Compensation	1,807	1,553	4

[a]Expenditures are direct general expenditures. All monetary data are deflated using the implicit GNP deflator for state and local government purchases except compensation, which is deflated by the implicit GNP deflator for state and local government compensation.

[b]Full-time equivalent employment.

Source: U.S. Department of Commerce, Bureau of the Census, *Governmental Finances* and *Public Employment*, various years; and Advisory Commission on Intergovernmental Relations, unpublished tax effort estimates for 1988.

public sector without carefully considering the costs that are implied. Two issues are important here. First, big government implies the creation of a larger bureaucracy. The larger bureaucracy and the higher expenditure levels that accompany it do not necessarily tell us that public services are better.[40] It may tell us only that public employee salaries are high or that it costs more to provide the same level of services in a particular state or even that the work force in some states is less productive than in others. If one associates a large public sector with a substantial rate of unionization and relatively high public (versus private) employee benefit levels, then the additional expenditure dollars in a large public sector may not purchase proportionately more public services.

The second disadvantage of a large government sector, and the one we will concentrate on in this section, is the possibility that it may compromise the economic development objectives of the state. This is a subject of much debate, and the many studies on this subject have not given us a firm conclusion about the extent to which taxes are a primary determinant of plant location decisions. Research on the influence of fiscal variables on firm location has involved three types of studies: (1) surveys of business firms; (2) microstudies of business firm migration, expansion, and contraction; and (3) aggregate studies of employment or income growth.[41] The surveys and microstudies seem to show less support for the influence of taxes and expenditures on firm location than do the aggregate studies.

Despite the significant variation between studies, there are a few conclusions that can be drawn from this literature. Fiscal factors by themselves are not usually the most important influence on industry location decisions. Wage rates and access to markets and suppliers appear to be much more important determinants. However, in the second stage of a firm's location decision, when it is trying to narrow down its selection to metropolitan areas within a region, fiscal variables can be important. Especially significant for a good "business climate" in a state are low levels of business taxes (corporate income and nonresidential property taxes), low personal income taxes, and high levels of primary and secondary education expenditures. Recent evidence suggests that interstate differentials in personal income taxes are reflected in wages,[42] which implies that they may indirectly affect business location through wages.

In addition, industry is concerned about fiscal certainty—will there be large changes in tax rates and service quality in the future? One-time tax reductions or incentive programs are not as important as a long-term commitment to maintain reasonable and stable tax burdens.

Finally, the significance of fiscal variables depends on how far out of line a state is. As summarized by Wasylenko:

> Briefly stated, researchers generally conclude that for most states fiscal variables have at best secondary effects on the location of new plants and on employment growth. But states whose taxation levels are very much out-of-line with those in their neighboring states will have lower employment growth. . . . the few states that are out-of-line are probably at a significant disadvantage for attracting industry.[43]

New York, with tax and expenditure levels well above the national average and its neighbors, may be too far out of line. Particularly significant are the high income and property taxes, with per capita levels of 142 and 60 percent, respectively, above the national average. Education expenditures are also above the national average, but only by 20 percent. New York State has chosen to focus its economic development strategy on tax incentives for specially targeted areas. Specifically, New York State offers targeted assistance to certain firms, local governments, and geographic areas (for example, "economic development zones"). This assistance includes tax incentives, low-cost loans, project grants, and technical or management assistance.[44] Although limited, the available research would suggest that special targeted assistance, such as tax and expenditure incentives and industrial revenue bonds, is not very effective in stimulating new employment.[45] New York State might be better off eliminating such programs and using these resources to reduce the effective rates for its major taxes.

Conclusions

The 1980s were not the time of fiscal retrenchment that was foreseen in the latter half of the 1970s. New York's tax and expenditure growth has been on par with or exceeded that of other states in the nation and in its region. Accordingly, the public sector remained 25 to 50 percent above the national average, depending on the measure used. Particularly significant was the rapid growth in income taxes and health and welfare expenditures.

One can evaluate this public sector growth in two ways. The first, a positive evaluation, would hold that the above-average expenditure increases were necessary to keep the state competitive as an industry location choice and to protect the level of public services for citizens. After all, these expenditure increases came on the heels of a decline in real expenditures during the 1975–80 period. It also may be argued that the expenditure increases in the 1980s were not really out of line with the rest of the country. There is some merit to this argument. The growth rate in total expenditures between 1980 and 1988 was 3.0 percent per year in New York and 2.8 percent in the rest of the country—a difference that is about commensurate with the differential growth in personal income. Moreover, the biggest disparities with the rest of the nation were for capital outlays and health expenditures.

The other view is less positive and holds that New York had a golden opportunity to bring the level of government expenditures into line with the ability of the state economy to support those expenditures and it passed on this opportunity. Personal income growth was above the national average during 1980 to 1988, and even federal grant reductions have not been as severe in New York as elsewhere. The evidence for 1988 and 1989 suggests that New York spent these windfall gains, perhaps even to a greater extent than has been widely recognized. Rather than using these gains to reduce the accumulated deficit, the spring borrowing has been increased. Moreover, a special windfall gain in the form of increased capital gains taxes in 1987 was placed into an infrastructure fund to finance increased capital expenditures (and was eventually drawn on to finance the 1988–89 deficit). There has been extensive borrowing from other fund balances within the state. Finally, the tax share of personal income increased. Quite clearly, New York has been spending at a rate that even its admirable recent income growth cannot support without bringing pressure for increased taxes.

Notes

1. This section is based on the valuable literature reviews on government growth by William Berry and David Lowery, *Understanding United States Government Growth: An Empirical Analysis of the Post-War Era* (New York: Praeger, 1987); Patrick Larkey, Chandler Stolp, and Mark Winer, "Theorizing About Government Growth: A Research Assessment," *Journal of Public Policy* 1 (May 1981): 157–220; and Richard Musgrave, "Leviathan Cometh—Or Does He?" in *Tax and Expenditure Limitations*, eds. Helen F. Ladd and T. Nicholas Tideman (Washington, D.C.: Urban Institute Press, 1981), pp. 77–120.

2. See, for example, David Cameron, "The Expansion of the Public Economy: A Comparative Analysis," *American Political Science Review* 72 (December 1978): 1243–1261; Frank Gould, "The Growth of Public Expenditures: Theory and Evidence from Six Advanced Democracies," in *Why Governments Grow: Measuring Public Sector Size*, ed. Charles Taylor (Beverly Hills: Sage Publications, 1983); David Lowery and William Berry, "The Growth of Government in the United States: An Empirical Assessment of Competing Explanations," *American Journal of Political Science* 27 (November 1983): 665–691; and Rati Ram, "Government Size and Economic Growth: A New Framework and Some Evidence from Cross-Section and Time-Series Data," *American Economic Review* 76 (May 1986): 191–203.

3. Lowery and Berry, "The Growth of Government in the United States: An Empirical Assessment of Competing Explanations," pp. 688–691.

4. Ibid., p. 673.

5. Of course, the voters will eventually see the elasticity effect, especially if the rate of inflation causes the real tax rate to rise dramatically. The Proposition 13 debacle in California is exactly an example of this.

6. Adolph Wagner, *Finanzwissenschaft* (Leipzig: C. F. Winter, 1977).

7. For a good explanation of these theories, see Lowery and Berry, "The Growth of Government in the United States: An Empirical Assessment of Competing Explanations," pp. 668–669.

8. Another version of demand theory stresses that there is a basic disparity between the distribution of voters and income. Specifically, the median voter has less than the mean level of income, so the majority of voters have an incentive to vote for income redistribution through the government. This would imply that government growth should be primarily in public welfare and social service areas. See Alan Meltzer and Scott Richard, "A Rational Theory of the Size of Government," *Journal of Political Economy* 89 (October 1981): 914–927.

9. Named after William Baumol, who first examined this phenomenon. See Baumol, "Macroeconomics of Unbalanced Growth: The Anatomy of Urban Crisis," *American Economic Review* 57 (June 1967): 415–426.

10. See, for example, William Niskanen, *Bureaucracy and Representative Government* (New York: Aldine, Atherton, 1971); Jean-Luc Migue and Gerald Belanger, "Toward a General Theory of Managerial Discretion," *Public Choice* 17 (1974): 27–47; and William Orzechowski, "Economic Models of Bureaucracy: Survey, Extensions, and Evidence," in *Budgets and Bureaucrats: The Sources of Government Growth*, ed. Thomas Borcherding (Durham, N.C.: Duke University Press, 1977).

11. See, for example, Winston Bush and Arthur Denzau, "The Voting Behavior of Bureaucrats and Public Sector Growth," in *Budgets and Bureaucrats: The Sources of Government Growth*, ed. Thomas Borcherding (Durham, N.C.: Duke University Press, 1977).

12. For an analysis of the limits of bureaucratic power, see Paul Courant, Edward Gramlich, and Daniel Rubinfeld, "Public Employee Market Power and the Level of Government Spending," *American Economic Review* 69 (December 1979): 806–817.

13. See, for example, John Ferejohn, *Pork Barrel Politics* (Stanford: Stanford University Press, 1974); and Kenneth Shepsle, "Institutional Arrangements and Equilibrium in Multidimensional Voting Models," *American Journal of Political Science* 23 (February 1979): 23–57.

14. New York City alone increased taxes by 1.6 percent per year during this period while personal income was declining at an annual rate of more than 1 percent per year.

15. Peter McClelland, *Crisis in the Making: The Political Economy of New York State since 1945* (Cambridge: Cambridge University Press, 1981).

16. New York's position relative to its neighbors remained about the same, with tax burdens growing slightly relative to Connecticut and Massachusetts and declining relative to New Jersey and Pennsylvania.

17. See Tables E-1 and E-2 in Appendix E for revenue trends in New York's neighboring states.

18. The income tax in Connecticut grew the fastest among the major northeastern states; however, its personal income tax applies only to interest, dividends, and capital gains. In 1988, Connecticut's income tax burden relative to personal income was less than 50 percent of the national average.

19. The issue of automatic versus discretionary growth in New York state taxes will be analyzed in more detail in chapter 5.

20. Based on existing single-family homes with Federal Housing Administration (FHA)-insured mortgages. See Advisory Commission on Intergovernmental Relations (ACIR), *Significant Features of Fiscal Federalism, 1990*, Vol. 1 (Washington, D.C.: ACIR, 1990), Table 34.

21. During 1983 and 1984, nineteen states increased their sales tax rates. Unlike the income tax, all but one of these increases have remained in effect. For a good review of recent changes in state finances, see Steven Gold, "Developments in State Finances, 1983 to 1986," *Public Budgeting & Finance* 7 (Spring 1987): 5–23. Many counties in New York have increased their sales tax rates during the 1980s. See chapter 5 for a discussion of this issue.

22. ACIR, *Significant Features, 1990*, Vol. 1, Table 27.

23. Advisory Commission on Intergovernmental Relations, *1986 State Fiscal Capacity and Effort* (Washington, D.C.: ACIR, March 1989), and unpublished preliminary estimates for 1988 provided by the ACIR.

24. See Table E-4 in Appendix E for a detailed analysis of changes in ACIR tax capacity and effort estimates from 1979 to 1988.

25. The ACIR estimates that 34 percent of the taxable capacity for the property tax in New York is due to commercial, industrial, and utility property.

26. Sarah F. Liebschutz, "The City and the State in Washington," in *The Two New Yorks: State-City Relations in the Changing Federal System*, eds. Gerald Benjamin and Charles Brecher (New York: Russell Sage Foundation), 1988, pp. 180–187.

27. U.S. Bureau of the Census, *Governmental Finances* (Washington, D.C.: U.S. Government Printing Office, various years); *Local Government Finances in Selected Metropolitan Areas and Large Counties* (Washington, D.C.: U.S. Government Printing Office, various years); and *Local Government Finances in Major County Areas* (Washington, D.C.: U.S. Government Printing Office, various years).

28.   U.S. Bureau of the Census, *State Government Finances* (Washington, D.C.: U.S. Government Printing Office, various years). See Table E-3 in Appendix E for more detail.

29.   Federal grants for public welfare accounted for 70 percent of total federal aid to New York State in 1988 versus 57 percent in 1980. The comparable figures for all state governments are 48 and 40 percent, respectively. See Table E-3.

30.   *Governmental Finances in 1984–85*, Table 29, p. 79; and *Local Government Finances in Major County Areas 1984–85*, Table 6, p. 30.

31.   City of New York, *Comprehensive Annual Financial Report of the Comptroller for the Fiscal Year Ended June 30, 1985* (New York: City of New York, 1985), pp. 193–195. It is not possible to compare statistics presented in this source with the statistics on federal and state aid (overall and by program) in the reports of the Bureau of the Census and New York State Comptroller, because they are not consistent.

32.   Expenditure trends for New York's neighboring states are presented in Tables E-5 to E-10 in Appendix E.

33.   See Table E-7.

34.   Measured here as average payroll per employee.

35.   New York City's spending for public employees rose dramatically during the 1980s. The Citizen's Budget Commission reports that "in the 1983–88 period, average personal service expenditures per municipal worker rose nearly one-third from $39,805 to $52,439; after adjusting for inflation, the figure rose 7.1 percent. More importantly, the work force was expanded from 194,623 to 231,982, a 19.2 percent enlargement." See Citizens' Budget Commission, "Review of the City of New York's 1990 Preliminary Budget" (New York: Citizens' Budget Commission, March 1989), p. 8.

36.   See Tables E-8 and E-9 for expenditures by function in New York's neighboring states.

37.   New York's Medicaid system was ranked third behind Minnesota and Wisconsin from the perspective of a low-income consumer. Public Citizen Health Research Group, *Poor Health Care for Poor Americans: A Ranking of State Medicaid Programs* (Washington, D.C.: Public Citizen Health Research Group, 1987).

38.   Citizens' Budget Commission, "The State of Municipal Services: Hospital and Social Services between 1983 and 1988" (New York: Citizens' Budget Commission, February 1989), p. 24.

39.   For example, the work load measure for elementary and secondary education is the weighted sum of three population groups: (1) elementary school-age children (five to thirteen) net of private school enrollments; (2) children of secondary school age (fourteen to seventeen) net of private secondary enrollment; and (3) the population under eighteen living in households with incomes below the poverty line. The weights are, respectively,

0.6, 1.0, and 0.25. Each state is assigned an index and, together with actual expenditures, this is used to estimate a "normal" expenditure level. Robert Rafuse, *A Representative Expenditure Index for State and Local Governments* (Washington, D.C.: Advisory Commission on Intergovernmental Relations, unpublished, 1989); and "A Representative-Expenditure Approach to the Measurement of the Cost of the Service Responsibilities of the States," in *Federal-State-Local Fiscal Relations: Technical Papers*, Vol. 1 (Washington, D.C.: U.S. Department of the Treasury, 1986). His results are summarized in Table E-10 in Appendix E.

40. For a good statement of the relationship between service levels and expenditures in the New York City context, see Charles Brecher and Raymond Horton, "Retrenchment and Recovery: American Cities and the New York Experience," *Public Administration Review* 45 (March/April 1985): 267–274.

41. This section borrows heavily from the work of Michael Wasylenko. See, in particular, "Employment Growth and the Business Climate in New York and Neighboring States," Metropolitan Studies Program Occasional Paper No. 140 (Syracuse: Maxwell School, Syracuse University, 1990); and "Business Climate, Industry and Employment Growth: A Review of the Evidence," Metropolitan Studies Program Occasional Paper No. 98 (Syracuse: Maxwell School, Syracuse University, 1985).

42. Sally Wallace-Moore, "The Effects of Interstate Tax Differentials on Wages with an Application to Interstate Migration," doctoral dissertation (Syracuse: Maxwell School, Syracuse University, 1988).

43. Wasylenko, "Employment Growth and the Business Climate in New York and Neighboring States," p. 23.

44. For a good summary of New York's economic development programs, see New York State Department of Economic Development, "New York State: Opportunities for Business" (Albany: New York State Department of Economic Development, 1989).

45. Wasylenko, "Employment Growth and the Business Climate in New York and Neighboring States."

5

Explaining Government Growth in New York

Despite the reductions in federal aid and the tax and expenditure limitation movements of the late 1970s and early 1980s, the public sector has continued to grow rapidly in New York State. This growth is on par with national growth rates and exceeds that of most northeastern states, even when adjustment is made for the strong growth of personal income in New York. The implication is that the 1980s were not a continuation of the government retrenchment that occurred in New York in the late 1970s. New York has maintained a public sector between 25 and 50 percent above the national average and most of its neighbors.

Whether the high tax burdens have dampened and will continue to dampen economic growth in New York State in the 1990s is an open question. To form a basis for answering this question, it is necessary for those policymakers who do fiscal planning to get behind these broad measures and to examine the factors driving the tax and expenditure growth. A key issue is whether the growth in government has been fueled by an increasing revenue-raising capacity or by increasing expenditure demands, that is, which side of the budget stimulated growth in the 1980s?

Tax Revenue Growth

Real tax revenues in New York grew by 3.4 percent per year in the 1980s, well above the growth rates for the 1970s. Even adjusting for the rapid growth in total income, taxes grew faster than for the rest of

136

the nation and for most of New York's neighbors. The crucial issue from the standpoint of long-run fiscal planning is why? Has this growth been a function solely of the expanding economy in New York or has the state taken discretionary action to raise tax rates or expand tax bases? How have New York and neighboring states responded to federal income tax reforms and to interstate tax competition in the 1980s? What do these tax actions suggest for New York's competitive position in the 1990s?

Income Taxes

Income taxes are the most important source of tax revenue for the New York state government and are an important tax source for New York City (30 and 21 percent of own source revenue, respectively). As indicated in Table 28, per capita real income taxes in New York grew by close to 5 percent per year, twice the national average, during the 1980s. Compared to its neighboring states, New York was in the middle, below Connecticut's and New Jersey's growth but above that in Massachusetts and Pennsylvania. Income tax burdens in New York grew to more than 100 percent above the national average and most neighboring states. This growth occurred despite a general atmosphere nationally of income tax reductions.[1]

PERSONAL INCOME TAXES. Personal income taxes now account for about 80 percent of total income tax revenue in New York State and have grown at a rate well above that for the rest of the nation. This strong growth held even during the recessions of the early 1980s.

To gain a better understanding of this increased reliance on personal income taxes, it is useful to index revenue growth to several measures of the underlying tax base (see Table 28). For New York, Connecticut, New Jersey, and the nation as a whole, personal income tax revenue grew faster than personal income (whether transfer payments are excluded or not). For Massachusetts, revenue and revenue base growth were about the same, and for Pennsylvania, revenue growth lagged behind. By contrast, tax revenue generally grew slower than the tax capacity estimated by the ACIR.[2]

These results suggest that for New York and some of its neighbors, either the tax base and rate structure are income elastic or discretionary actions were taken. With respect to the first proposition,

TABLE 28

Annual Percent Change in Per Capita Income Tax Revenues and Tax Bases[a]: New York, Neighboring States, and Total United States

	New York			Total United States			Connecticut		
	1980–83	1983–88	1980–88	1980–83	1983–88	1980–88	1980–83	1983–88	1980–88
Total Income Taxes:	3.1	5.8	4.8	–1.0	4.6	2.4	6.9	7.1	7.0
State	3.0	5.6	4.6	–1.1	4.6	2.4	6.9	7.1	7.0
Local	3.4	6.5	5.3	0.0	4.3	2.7	NA	NA	NA
Personal Income Tax	4.8	5.5	5.3	1.2	4.5	3.2	11.9	9.3	10.3
Corporate Income Tax[b]	–2.9	6.8	3.0	–8.5	5.0	–0.3	4.8	5.9	5.5
Real Personal Income	1.5	4.0	3.1	1.0	3.1	2.0	1.8	5.0	3.8
PI (Without Transfers)	1.3	4.4	3.2	–0.3	3.4	2.0	1.4	5.4	3.9
ACIR Tax Capacity[c]:									
Personal Income Tax	NA	NA	8.9	NA	NA	4.2	NA	NA	6.5
Corporate Income Tax	NA	NA	2.7	NA	NA	0.8	NA	NA	4.3

	Massachusetts			New Jersey			Pennsylvania		
Total Income Taxes:	1.5	5.1	3.7	3.5	6.9	5.6	-2.3	1.8	0.2
State	1.5	5.1	3.7	3.5	6.9	5.6	-3.2	1.6	-0.2
Local	NA	NA	NA	NA	NA	NA	-0.3	2.2	1.3
Personal Income Tax	2.0	5.1	3.9	4.3	6.9	5.9	-0.6	2.1	1.1
Corporate Income Tax[b]	-0.3	5.2	3.1	1.9	6.9	5.0	-8.3	0.3	-3.0
Real Personal Income	2.3	5.3	4.2	2.4	4.6	3.8	-0.1	3.1	1.9
PI (Without Transfers)	2.3	5.9	4.5	2.4	5.0	4.0	-1.0	3.6	1.8
ACIR Tax Capacity[c]:									
Personal Income Tax	NA	NA	8.6	NA	NA	7.1	NA	NA	3.4
Corporate Income Tax	NA	NA	3.7	NA	NA	4.3	NA	NA	0.4

[a] Tax revenue deflated using the implicit GNP deflator for state and local government purchases. Tax base measures deflated with the implicit GNP deflator.

[b] Corporate income tax includes state taxes and for New York City the General Corporate Tax, Unincorporated Business Tax, and the Financial Corporation Tax. New York City taxes based on unpublished data provided by the Bureau of the Census and from the New York City Comptroller's annual report for 1989.

[c] The tax capacity for the personal income tax is an estimate of total federal income tax liability of state residents adjusted for deductability of state and local taxes. The base for the corporate income tax was based on distribution of national net income by industry type to individual states. Annual percent change from 1980 to 1986.

Source: U.S. Department of Commerce, Bureau of Economic Analysis, unpublished personal income data, revised April 1990; Bureau of the Census, *Governmental Finances* and *State Government Finances*, various years; Advisory Commission on Intergovernmental Relations, June 1982, and M-165, March 1989; and City of New York, *Comprehensive Annual Financial Report of the Comptroller for the Fiscal Year Ended June 30, 1989.*

New York, Connecticut, and New Jersey have a more progressive rate structure than Massachusetts and Pennsylvania, implying that rising income may push some people into higher tax brackets ("bracket creep"), explaining part of this growth. This is only part of the story about the income elasticity of the tax base, and it is difficult to draw more precise conclusions without a detailed review of each state's tax system. Since Connecticut taxes only capital income and New York and Massachusetts have taxed it at a higher rate, these states may have benefited from the slightly faster growth of capital relative to wage and salary income.[3]

Turning to the second proposition, that discretionary tax actions explain revenue growth, the 1980s were a time of major income tax changes. At the beginning of the decade, New York had one of the most progressive state income taxes in the country, with top marginal rates of 14 percent (Table 29). Neighboring states all had top rates below 10 percent (below 3 percent for New Jersey and Pennsylvania). In New York City, residents in the top bracket faced a combined tax rate of more than 18 percent. It is not surprising that New York's income tax burden was also much higher.

Income tax changes in the 1980s were driven by several factors: (1) the recessions in the early 1980s, (2) federal tax reforms, particularly in 1986, and (3) tax (economic development) competition between states. The revenue shortfalls accompanying the recessions of the early 1980s forced many states to raise sales and income tax rates in late 1982 and early 1983. As documented by Steven Gold for the National Conference of State Legislatures, sixteen states raised personal income taxes in 1983.[4] Included among them are Pennsylvania and Connecticut.[5] However, in the atmosphere of tax limitations and tax competition in the early 1980s, most of the increases were temporary, expiring in the following years.[6]

New York has been active in changing its personal income tax system. It initiated two major changes in the income tax during the 1980s. The first, a reduction in tax rates, occurred in fiscal year 1985. Both the tax rate on earned income and capital income were reduced a percentage point, to 9 and 13 percent, respectively, to take effect by fiscal year 1987. Although it is difficult to pin this change on one factor, clearly concern over promoting economic development was a major issue. An overhauling of New York's economic development programs soon followed in 1987.

The major impetus for the second change in the 1980s was the federal income tax reform in 1986. States reacted in a number of ways, depending on the nature of their legal base. For those states that based their tax directly on federal tax liability (for example, Rhode Island and Vermont), federal tax reform could have resulted in a loss of tax revenue.[7] Both Rhode Island and Vermont increased their tax rate to cover this loss. Other states have income taxes that are independent of the federal tax and thus were not affected by federal tax reform. Included are New Jersey and Pennsylvania, which did not make major changes in their income taxes after 1986.

New York, Maine, and Massachusetts use the federal adjusted gross income as the tax base. These states would have benefited from the base broadening in federal tax reform and would have enjoyed a significant "tax windfall" if they had maintained their existing rate structures. New York's and Maine's windfalls were estimated to be 9 and 12 percent, respectively.[8] Given the atmosphere of tax competition, it is not surprising that both New York and Maine undertook major tax reform to return part of the windfall.[9] New York's reform was one of the most comprehensive in the country. Tax brackets were reduced, and the top marginal rate is scheduled to decrease to 7 percent by 1991.[10] New York City also initiated a tax reform in 1987, incorporating most of the tax base changes and reducing the top marginal rate to 3.4 percent by 1990.

In summary, the rapid personal income tax revenue growth in New York in the 1980s would appear to be due primarily to strong growth in personal income and the responsiveness of New York's tax base to this growth. New York made several efforts to lower its personal tax rates and broaden its tax base. It is too early to tell how these rate reductions will affect New York's competitive position, because most occurred after 1988. However, New York's top tax rate, especially on earned income, is still above that in most of its neighboring states (see Table 29). With the exception of Pennsylvania's brief income tax increase in 1983, northeastern states have generally avoided income tax increases.[11]

CORPORATE INCOME TAX. While not nearly so important a source of revenue as personal income taxes, corporate net income taxes receive considerable attention because of their potential impact on business location. There continues to be debate on who actually

TABLE 29

Tax Rates for Major State and Local Taxes:
New York and Neighboring States

	New York	Connecticut	Massachusetts	New Jersey	Pennsylvania
Personal Income Tax (top marginal rate)[a]:					
State:					
1980 (Earned Income)	14.0 (26.8)	No Tax	5.0 (5.8)	2.5 (23.3)	2.2
(Capital Income)	14.0 (26.8)	7.0–9.0 (23.3)	9.0 (5.8)	2.5 (23.3)	2.2
1988 (Earned Income)	8.0 (10.2)	No Tax	5.0	2.0–3.5 (16–41)	2.1
(Capital Income)	8.0 (10.2)	1–12 (45–82)	10.0	2.0–3.5 (16–41)	2.1
Local					
1980	4.3	NA	NA	NA	0.25–1.0
1988	3.5	NA	NA	NA	1.0–5.0
State Corporate Income Tax[b]:					
State:					
1980	10.0	10.0	8.3	9.0	10.5
1988	9.0	11.5	NA	9.0	8.5
Local:					
1980	9.0	NA	NA	NA	NA
1988	8.85	NA	NA	NA	NA
General Sales Tax:					
State:					
1980	4.0	7.5	5.0	5.0	6.0
1988	4.0	7.5	5.0	6.0	6.0

Local:					
1980	1–3	NA	NA	NA	NA
1988	1.0–4.25	NA	NA	NA	NA
State Selective Sales Taxes[c]:					
Cigarettes ($/pack) (1980)	$0.17	$0.24	$0.24	$0.22	$0.21
(1988)	0.16	0.20	0.20	0.21	0.14
(1989)	0.24	0.30	0.19	0.20	0.13
Gasoline ($/gallon) (1980)	0.09	0.13	0.10	0.09	0.13
($/gallon) (1988)	0.06	0.16	0.09	0.08	0.09
Beer ($/gallon)	0.05–0.08	0.09–0.15	0.10–0.08	0.03–0.02	NA
Wine ($/gallon)	0.09–0.13	0.29–0.44	0.53–0.41	0.29–0.22	NA
Liquor ($/gallon)	3.91–3.92	2.87–3.33	3.87–3.00	2.67–2.07	NA
Local Property Tax (effective rate—residential)[d]:					
1980	2.8	1.6	2.5	2.6	1.6
1987	2.1	1.5	0.8	2.4	1.4

[a] Top marginal tax rate and the beginning of the top bracket in thousands of 1982 dollars (in parentheses). For several states, the range in tax rates and brackets is shown. For local taxes, includes the rates for New York City and the range of rates from Erie to Philadelphia for Pennsylvania.

[b] Estimate of corporate tax rates applied usually to net income. Tax rate may vary by type of corporation, and corporations in Massachusetts and New Jersey are subject to additional taxes imposed on value of tangible property or net worth. For local taxes, includes the rate for the General Corporation Tax in New York City.

[c] Deflated to 1982 dollars with the implicit GNP deflator for state and local government purchases. For alcohol excise taxes, includes the tax rate in 1980 and 1988.

[d] Average effective property tax rates for existing single-family homes with FHA-insured mortgages. Effective rate is equal to tax liability over full market value of house.

Source: Advisory Commission on Intergovernmental Relations, *Significant Features of Fiscal Federalism,* various years.

pays these taxes and about their impact on business decisions. In addition, it is difficult to separate the impacts of the corporate income tax from other business taxes (Box 10). Since providing separate estimates for all business taxes is difficult, the focus here is primarily on the corporate income tax.

Real per capita corporate income tax revenue in New York grew strongly during the 1980s (3 percent per year) while actually declining for the total United States (see Table 28). New York's per capita corporate income tax burden was 98 percent above the national average in 1980 and grew to 158 percent above by 1988. This is consistent with the ACIR tax effort measure, which shows New York 98 percent above the national average in 1988. Within the region, corporate income tax revenues declined in Pennsylvania but grew strongly in Connecticut, Massachusetts, and New Jersey. In 1988, New York had

---

Box 10. Defining Business Taxes

Part of the difficulty surrounding analysis of the corporate income tax is that it may be just one of a number of business taxes used by a state. For example, besides having taxes on corporate "net income," New York levies gross receipts taxes on utilities and transportation companies and property taxes on industrial and commercial property. While the corporate income tax is generally on the "net income" of corporations, for multistate corporations the allocation of taxable "net income" is based on a formula that includes the corporation's payroll, property, and sales in a state. This implies that its impact may be similar in many respects to business taxes on gross receipts, property, and payrolls. Ideally, one would segregate all the "business" taxes and analyze them separately. Unfortunately, this is not possible using government finance statistics from the Bureau of the Census.

For a comprehensive review of state corporate income tax structures and allocation formulas, see the *Multistate Corporate Income Tax Guide* published by Commerce Clearing House. For a discussion of the state allocation of corporate income taxes among multistate corporations, see Robert Carroll, "An Analysis of Corporate Income Taxation in Nebraska and Comparison with the 50 States," Metropolitan Studies Program Occasional Paper No. 123 (Syracuse: Maxwell School, Syracuse University, 1988). For analyses of tax incidence, see, for example, Charles McLure, Jr., *Economic Perspectives on State Taxation of Multijurisdictional Corporations* (Arlington: Tax Analysts, 1986); "The Elusive Incidence of the Corporate Income Tax: The State Case," *Public Finance Quarterly* 9 (October 1981): 395–413; and Peter Mieszkowski and George Zodrow, "The Incidence of a Partial State Corporate Income Tax," *National Tax Journal* 38 (December 1985): 489–496.

a higher corporate tax burden than Connecticut (111 percent above the national average), Massachusetts (105 percent above), New Jersey (73 percent above), and Pennsylvania (1 percent below).

Why the moderate growth in New York's corporate income tax revenue? The answer is that it is primarily due to an absence of discretionary changes. Revenue growth and tax capacity, as estimated by the ACIR, grew at about the same rate for all states in the region. The exception is Pennsylvania, and this is due to a significant drop in tax rates (2 percentage points). New York State and New York City also dropped rates in 1988 as part of a general business tax reform, but the base broadening measures would appear to have offset the reduction in rates.[12] In contrast, Connecticut increased its tax rates and Massachusetts and New Jersey left theirs the same.[13]

New York City is one of the few cities in the United States with a corporate income tax. In 1988, the revenue from its corporate income taxes was almost as high as that collected by the state of New York.[14] While New York State's corporate tax rate is about the median for the region, corporations in New York City face a combined corporate rate of almost 18 percent. It is not surprising, then, that corporate tax burdens in New York City continue to be among the highest in the nation.

Sales Taxes

GENERAL SALES TAX. General sales taxes are important sources of revenue for New York state and local governments. In 1988, the general sales tax accounted for 21 percent of state government tax revenue and 18 percent of local government revenues. New York has one of the more decentralized sales tax systems in the country, with revenues split evenly between the state and local levels. In fact, New York local governments generated more than a quarter of all local general sales tax revenue collected in the United States in 1988. This contrasts with New York's neighboring states, which do not have a local general sales tax. The tax revenue from local taxes actually grew faster than for state taxes due to the rising tax rates among many localities (Table 30). Twenty-two of New York's fifty-seven counties (outside of New York City) either instituted sales taxes for the first time or increased their sales tax rates from 1980 to 1988.[15]

The state sales tax rate remained the same in New York throughout the 1980s (see Table 29). Among New York's neighboring

TABLE 30

Annual Percent Change in Per Capita Sales Tax Revenues and Tax Bases[a]: New York, Neighboring States, and Total United States

	New York		Total United States		Connecticut	
	1977– 82	1982– 87	1977– 82	1982– 87	1977– 82	1982– 87
General Sales Taxes	0.1	5.1	0.9	4.0	2.4	7.3
State	–0.6	4.7	0.4	3.8	2.4	7.3
Local	1.0	5.5	3.5	5.0	NA	NA
Selective Sales Taxes[b]	–4.8	1.8	–3.7	1.8	–2.4	1.6
Selective Sales	–8.4	–0.5	–5.6	1.4	–5.7	1.5
Gross Receipts	0.9	4.2	2.3	2.6	3.0	1.7
Total Retail Sales	–0.7	3.3	–1.6	2.4	–0.2	5.2
Retail Sales						
(Without food)	–0.4	4.1	–1.8	3.1	0.2	6.2
Retail Service Sales[c]	0.5	4.3	0.7	4.8	0.5	9.1
ACIR Tax Capacity[d]:						
Retail Sales	1.0	7.1	–1.1	6.0	3.5	10.9
Selective Sales	–2.8	2.4	–4.4	2.2	–2.8	3.5
	Massachusetts		New Jersey		Pennsylvania	
General Sales Taxes	6.5	9.9	–0.2	10.4	–0.6	5.0
State	6.5	9.9	–0.2	10.4	–0.6	5.0
Local	NA	NA	NA	NA	NA	NA
Selective Sales Taxes[b]	0.6	0.7	7.9	1.3	–1.1	–0.7
Selective Sales	1.6	–0.9	–4.7	0.1	–2.8	–1.4
Gross Receipts	–3.4	7.1	35.4	2.2	2.4	0.4
Total Retail Sales	0.8	5.0	–0.3	4.0	–1.9	3.2
Retail Sales						
(Without food)	1.4	5.6	–0.1	4.8	–2.0	3.9
Retail Service Sales[c]	2.3	8.1	8.7	7.0	–0.3	5.4
ACIR Tax Capacity[d]:						
Retail Sales	4.3	10.6	–1.5	10.8	–1.5	6.4
Selective Sales	–2.9	3.3	–1.5	1.9	–4.5	3.1

[a]Tax revenue deflated using the implicit GNP deflator for state and local government purchases. Tax base measures deflated with the implicit GNP deflator for personal consumption expenditures.

TABLE 30 (continued)
Annual Percent Change in Per Capita Sales Tax Revenues and Tax Bases[a]: New York, Neighboring States, and Total United States

[b]Due to data limitations, includes only state government taxes. Selective sales includes taxes on tobacco products, alcoholic beverages, motor fuel, and amusements. Gross receipts taxes include taxes on public utilities and insurance companies.

[c]Includes lodging, recreation, personal, and repair services. Due to coverage changes, this should be viewed as an approximation of trends.

[d]The tax capacity for the general sales tax includes retail sales of goods and selected services. Excludes food and prescription drugs. Selective sales includes estimated sales or quantity sold for various taxable items. See ACIR in source notes for more detail. Annual percent changes from 1979–1982 and 1982–1986.

Source: U.S. Department of Commerce, Bureau of the Census, *Census of Retail Trade, 1977, 1982 and 1987, Census of Service Industries, 1977, 1982 and 1987,* and *Governmental Finances* and *State Government Finances,* various years; and Advisory Commission on Intergovernmental Relations, No. M-134, March 1982, M-142, May 1985, and M-165, March 1989.

states, only New Jersey (1982) and Connecticut (1989) have raised their general sales tax rates during the decade of the 1980s. By contrast, twenty-seven other states raised their general sales tax rate at least once during the 1980s, primarily during the budget crises of 1983.[16] While New York's state sales tax rate is lower than that of any of its neighbors, its combined state and local rate of 7 percent or higher in two-thirds of its counties is among the highest in the region and in the country. New York's per capita general sales tax burden climbed to 33 percent above the national average by 1988 and was higher than that of any of its neighboring states except Connecticut.

Even without rate increases, general sales tax revenues grew faster in New York and its neighbors than total retail sales (measured with and without food [see Table 30]). This implies a heavier taxation of the faster growing components of consumption, namely, services, in the Northeast. New York has a relatively high taxation of services, including telecommunication services, repair charges, installation services, and hotel/motel charges.[17]

The other side of the story is that New York exempts food, prescription drugs, consumer gas and electric utilities, and many services from general sales taxation. This is similar to its neighboring states, except that Connecticut, Massachusetts, and New Jersey also exempt clothing and Massachusetts and Pennsylvania do not exempt utility sales.

Relatively few discretionary tax base actions were taken by New York or its neighbors in the 1980s. Except for a recent (1989) decision to tax mail-order sales, New York held to its sales tax base. Most of New York's neighbors also took little action to adjust their retail sales base to the rising service economy. Connecticut is the one exception. The retail sales tax is the major state government tax in Connecticut, and there were substantial revisions in the base. Exemptions for food less than $1 (1983), clothing less than $75 (1985), and meals less than $2 (1986) were all enacted. In contrast, a major extension of the base took place in 1989 to include numerous services, out-of-state mail-order sales, and meals less than $2.[18]

In summary, the gap between revenue and retail sales growth appears to be due primarily to the exemption of relatively income inelastic commodities, such as food and medicine. While New York taxes some services, many others escape taxation. These include fast-growing sectors, such as health, financial, and legal services. As documented in chapters 2 and 3, the rapid expansion of the service sector implies that New York needs to reexamine its tax system to better capture the growing taxable capacity in the service sector.

SELECTIVE SALES TAXES.   Selective sales taxes accounted for 22 percent of total sales tax revenues in New York in 1987—less than the national average of 29 percent. Selective sales taxes can be divided into those imposed on specific commodities (primarily tobacco, alcoholic beverages, and motor fuels) and those imposed on specific business sectors (primarily public utilities, insurance, transportation, and finance companies).[19] Commodity taxes are typically assessed "per unit" of the commodity (for example, packs of cigarettes) while the selective business taxes are usually a percent of the "gross receipts" of the firm. For New York, selective sales tax revenue was evenly divided between these two sources while nationally two-thirds of revenue come from commodity taxes.

Selective sales tax revenue grew much slower than that from the general sales tax in New York (see Table 30). From 1982 to 1987, real per capita revenues grew at a rate of 1.8 percent per year in New York and the nation, and all of the growth in revenue in New York was due to strong growth in business gross receipts tax revenue. This growth rate was 50 percent above the national average and well above that in all New York's neighboring states except Massachusetts (which has very low gross receipts taxes). By contrast, excise tax revenue per capita actually declined in New York when adjusted for inflation. This compares to declines in Massachusetts and Pennsylvania and slow growth in Connecticut and New Jersey. Selective sales taxes are one revenue source where New York imposes a lower tax burden than the rest of the country and the region.

Why the slow growth in selective sales tax revenues? One reason is the inherently lower income elasticity of taxes levied at a specific rate. Effective rates of excise tax declined for most commodities during the 1980s in New York and for most neighboring states (see Table 29). Particularly, cigarette and gasoline effective tax rates did not keep up with inflation. (New York and Connecticut enacted in 1989 significant increases in nominal cigarette tax rates.)

In summary, revenues from selective sales taxes grew slowly in New York due primarily to a decline in real per capita revenue in excise taxes. This decline was due to both a sharp drop in tax capacity and tax rates that did not keep up with inflation. By contrast, business gross receipt taxes grew strongly in New York due primarily to a rapid growth in tax capacity.

Property Taxes

Property taxes accounted for 23 percent of state and local revenue in New York in 1988 and 22 percent nationally. This is down from 1980 levels in both cases. New York's property tax revenue has grown generally on par with its neighboring states, except for Massachusetts, which has experienced declining per capita revenue (Table 31).

When indexed by the growth in the property tax base, revenue growth has been significantly slower in New York and its neighboring states than in the rest of the country. The property tax base is not easily measured, but census estimates are that assessed value grew by 4.4 percent per year from 1981 to 1986 in New York and full market value grew by 3.5 percent from 1982 to 1987; ACIR's property tax capacity measure grew by more than 9.0 percent per year from 1982 to 1986. While it is difficult to compare these different base measures, they all indicate an increased property tax potential, and all can be

TABLE 31

Annual Percent Change in Per Capita Property Tax Revenues and
Tax Bases[a]: New York, Neighboring States, and Total United States

	New York		Total United States		Connecticut	
	1977–82	1982–86	1977–82	1982–86	1977–82	1982–86
Total Property Taxes	–3.3	2.0	–3.8	2.1	–2.2	2.0
Total Assessed Value[b]	–2.2	4.4	8.9	5.1	3.4	6.1
Full Market Value[c]	–2.3	3.5	NA	NA	NA	NA
ACIR Tax Capacity[d]:	1.7	9.1	–0.1	3.6	5.1	6.4
Residential	7.1	10.7	5.8	5.3	10.1	8.0
Commercial and						
Industrial	–4.3	8.2	–6.4	3.5	–2.8	3.4

	Massachusetts		New Jersey		Pennsylvania	
Total Property Taxes	–7.4	–0.5	–3.6	1.8	–0.7	2.6
Total Assessed Value[b]	9.7	18.4	–1.2	6.2	–4.1	4.9
ACIR Tax Capacity[d]:	4.0	10.7	2.8	6.3	–2.8	3.9
Residential	8.9	13.6	8.0	6.5	0.9	5.9
Commercial and						
Industrial	–3.9	5.7	–4.5	8.6	–8.0	2.5

[a]Tax revenue deflated using the implicit GNP deflator for state and local
government purchases. Tax base measures deflated with the implicit GNP deflator.

[b]Gross assessed value by state and local governments, as estimated in the
Census of Governments. Due to variation in assessment ratios, may not reflect changes
in the full market value.

[c]Full market value (municipal purposes) as reported by the New York State
Comptroller for 1977, 1982, and 1987.

[d]Estimated full market property value from various sources. See ACIR in
source note. Annual percent changes from 1979–1982 and 1982–1986.

Source: U.S. Department of Commerce, Bureau of the Census, *Census of
Governments, 1977, 1982 and 1987*, and *Governmental Finances*, various years;
Advisory Commission on Intergovernmental Relations, No. M-134, March 1982, M-
142, May 1985, and M-165, March 1989; and New York State Comptroller, *Special
Report on Municipal Affairs, 1987*, Table 1–1.

used to show that property tax revenues are declining relative to total property value. The declining effective tax rates on residential property in the region are reported in Table 29. New York's effective rate dropped from 2.8 to 2.1 percent from 1980 to 1987. This was particularly the case in Massachusetts, which experienced an absolute loss in real property tax revenue due to Proposition 2 1/2.

It is important to note here that New York still has some of the highest property tax rates in the country and a per capita property tax burden 60 percent above the national average. With the sharp drop in property taxes in Massachusetts, New York has the highest per capita property tax burden in its region.

Expenditure Growth

Real state and local government expenditures in New York grew by 3 percent per year from 1980 to 1988, significantly faster than in the 1970s. While this growth was on par with the national growth rate and was around the median for the Northeast region, it must be remembered that New York entered the decade with spending levels that were, comparatively, very high. New York continued in the 1980s to spend 50 percent more per capita and 25 percent more relative to personal income than the national average and than most neighboring states.

The questions we will address in this section are: Why did expenditures continue to grow rapidly in New York during the 1980s? Which public services experienced the most growth? Was the growth fueled by rising demand for public services or by the increasing cost of providing a given quality of service? Has the expenditure growth been accompanied by improved service quality? What do these trends imply for public expenditure growth in the 1990s in New York? While data limitations and the complexity surrounding the evaluation of many of these services make a comprehensive analysis impossible, the information presented here sheds light on the reasons for expenditure growth.

Education

Education services received significant public attention in the 1980s. From 1983 to 1986, there were no fewer than nine major national studies on the condition of public schools in this country.[20] Education has consistently come up as one of the leading fiscal issues in surveys of state government officials.[21] Virtually all of these studies share a common concern over the "quality" of students being produced and the efficiency and effectiveness of current school policy. Since strong public schools have been found to be important in business and individual location decisions, educational reform has also been related to state economic development policy.[22]

Despite the high visibility that educational issues have received, this has not been matched by a large growth in public education expenditures. While growth in education expenditures in New York has exceeded growth rates nationally and in neighboring states, it still lags behind total expenditure growth.

ELEMENTARY AND SECONDARY EDUCATION.   Real elementary and secondary education expenditures increased by 2.6 percent per year in New York from 1980 to 1987 (Table 32). This was above the national growth rate and above that of New York's neighbors. New York's per capita expenditures went from 22 percent above the national average in 1980 to 34 percent in 1987. Among New York's neighbors, only New Jersey (17 percent above) and Connecticut (6 percent above) had per capita expenditures above the national average.

New York's growth in expenditures was led by a rapid growth in capital outlays, 5.2 percent a year. This was well above capital growth rates for the nation and New York's neighboring states. Most of this growth was in construction or repair of school buildings versus equipment or land purchases. One cannot say that this expenditure improved New York's competitive advantage in education services. It may have, if these investments improved the quality of the state's education capital stock. On the other hand, it may reflect only a catch-up in maintenance that was too long delayed. One should note that New York's capital expenditures in 1987 were still only 92 percent of the national average.

Current expenditures, which account for 95 percent of total expenditures, also grew strongly in New York. Current expenditures per capita were 37 percent above the national average and were higher than in all of New York's neighboring states. Personnel expenditures accounted for 58 percent of current expenditures in New York (65 percent nationally). Total real payroll grew by 1.7 percent per year in New York during this period, compared to only 0.7 percent nationally and to little or no growth at all in New York's neighboring states.

Employment was a major part of this growth in the 1980s. Payroll increases in New York were driven more by a rapid increase in employment of teachers and staff (2.8 percent per year) than by increased wages (the average payroll per instructional employee declined by 1.1 percent per year in New York and nationally). Using estimates of average teacher salaries from the National Education Association, it would appear that there was, at most, a slight growth in salaries in New York; this despite the fact that, nationally, teacher education and experience have grown steadily over the last several decades.[23]

What has driven the education expenditure growth in New York? One would first look for evidence of an increase in demand for primary and secondary education services. In fact, there was a significant decline in the school-age population in New York of 2 percent or more a year from 1980 to 1987. However, this is entirely a loss in white children, with minority children growing 0.8 percent per year in New York and 1.3 percent nationally. This pattern resulted in a decline in enrollment and average daily attendance, mostly in secondary schools. It is clear, then, that New York's expenditure growth was not being fueled by rising enrollments.

The implication of these data, that there was a significant growth in expenditures per pupil, is borne out by the data: a 4.2 percent increase per year in New York and a 2.6 percent increase nationally. Per pupil expenditures in New York were 60 percent above the national average in 1987. The crucial issue for public policymakers is whether this higher level of per student spending led to improved educational quality. Unfortunately, the lack of good quality measures in education makes this assessment difficult. The most common measure of educational quality is test scores. While the evidence linking high scores to future success (however it might be measured) is weak,[24] they are often used for lack of a better alternative. The results of the Scholastic Aptitude Test (SAT) show that New York went from equal the national average in 1980 to slightly below (98 percent) in 1987 for both verbal and math.[25] While New York has consistently ranked below its neighboring states on SAT scores, it is difficult to make interstate comparisons due to differences in coverage.[26]

TABLE 32

Annual Percent Change (1980 to 1987) in Primary and Secondary Education Expenditures and Measures of Demand for and Cost of Providing Education Services[a]: New York, Neighboring States, and Total United States

	New York	United States	Connecticut	Massachusetts	New Jersey	Pennsylvania
Total Expenditures:	2.6	2.1	1.9	-0.7	2.3	1.3
Capital Outlay	5.2	1.3	-0.3	-5.2	3.6	4.2
Current Expenditures	2.5	2.1	2.0	-0.6	2.3	1.1
Payroll	1.7	0.7	-1.1	-2.9	0.1	-0.8
Employment	2.8	1.8	0.2	-0.8	0.4	0.0
Payroll/Employee	-1.1	-1.1	-1.2	-2.2	-0.4	-0.8
Average Teacher Salary[b]	0.4	0.8	1.8	0.6	0.9	0.8
Demand Factors:						
School Age						
Population (5–17)	-1.9	-0.7	-2.3	-2.8	-2.1	-2.0
White[c]	-2.6	-1.1	-2.7	-3.1	-2.8	-2.2
Black and Other[c]	0.8	1.3	0.7	1.9	0.8	-0.5
Enrollment	-1.4	-0.3	-1.9	-3.0	-1.9	-1.9
Primary	-0.8	0.1	-1.5	-2.5	-1.3	-1.9
Secondary	-2.6	-1.3	-2.6	-4.0	-3.0	-1.9
Average Daily						
Attendance	-1.6	-0.5	-1.9	-3.5	-1.5	-2.1

Cost/Quality Factors:					
Expenditure/Pupil	4.2	2.6	3.9	2.9	3.9	3.5
Payroll/Pupil	3.3	1.2	0.8	0.6	1.6	1.3
Earnings per Employee:					
Consumer Services	1.4	0.5	2.4	2.6	1.8	0.7
Education Services	2.4	1.7	0.8	2.5	1.5	2.4
Health Services	1.1	1.7	3.2	2.7	1.9	2.1
Poverty Population (5–17)[c]:					
Annual % Change	1.0	1.8	-0.9	-1.5	-0.6	0.8
Poverty Rate (1990)	20.3	19.0	11.2	13.1	14.5	17.0
White	15.9	14.1	6.8	10.2	7.9	13.3
Black and Other	45.6	38.7	40.1	42.5	37.1	41.2
Pupil/Teacher Ratio	-2.8	-0.9	-2.1	-1.7	-2.1	-1.0
	(18.5–15.2)	(18.8–17.6)	(15.4–13.3)	(15.7–13.9)	(16.3–14.0)	(17.4–16.2)
High School Graduation Rate[d]	(62.0%–62.5%)	(65.6%–67.1%)	(65.4%–67.8%)	(70.8%–72.8%)	(67.5%–68.5%)	(67.9%–70.1%)

[a] Direct general expenditures deflated using the implicit GNP deflator for state and local government purchases, payroll by deflator for state and local government compensation, and earnings by the implicit GNP deflator. Payroll per employee based on payroll and full-time equivalent employment for instructional employees in October.

[b] Average annual teacher salaries as estimated by the National Education Association.

[c] Detailed estimates available from authors upon request.

[d] Estimate based on high school graduates in a year divided by the average population between fifteen and seventeen.

Source: U.S. Department of Commerce, Bureau of the Census, *1980 Census of Population* and *Current Population Reports,* Series P-26, Nos. 1017 and 1044, and Series P-60, Nos. 163 and 166; *Governmental Finances, Finances of Public School Systems,* and *Public Employment,* various years; Bureau of Economic Analysis, unpublished earnings and employment data; and U.S. Department of Education, *Digest of Education Statistics,* various years.

Another type of quality measure is the number of years of education completed by students or high school graduation rates. Unfortunately, this information is not available at the state level between decennial censuses. There is information by state on the number of high school graduates. When this is compared to the potential graduating population, it is possible to construct a rough measure of high school graduation rates. This rate remained at about 62 percent in New York in the 1980s compared to a national rate of 67 percent (see Table 32).[27] While graduation rates remained stagnant in New York, they grew slightly in New York's neighboring states. Finally, we can look at changes in student-teacher ratios. Although smaller classes have been challenged as an indicator of improved education,[28] they certainly increase the potential for more individualized attention to students. There was a rapid decline, 2.8 percent per year, in student-teacher ratios in New York, from 1980 to 1987. This decline, while occurring nationally, was much stronger in New York, even compared to its neighboring states. While these quality measures are too crude to draw strong conclusions, they provide mixed evidence on whether the strong growth in per pupil expenditures improved educational quality in New York State during the 1980s.

To what extent has this expenditure growth been the result of a rise in the cost of providing a given quality of education to students? Cost increases could be due to either rising resource prices (for example, teacher salaries, material costs, and so forth) or socioeconomic factors that influence educational quality. Since the days of the famous Coleman Report, it has been well established in education research that family background and income can have a crucial impact on a child's success in school.[29] There is also research showing that a child's educational performance can be influenced by the background and performance of other students in the class, the so-called "peer effect."[30] The combination of these factors implies that it will be significantly more expensive to provide comparable education in school districts with a large poverty population.

Examining the evidence would suggest that socioeconomic factors, not rising factor prices, probably had the most important influence on costs in the 1980s. As we discussed previously, real employee salaries appear to have stagnated and possibly declined since 1980. While evidence on material and capital costs is not available, it is unlikely that they grew much faster than the inflation rate in

New York. The number of children below the poverty line is estimated to have grown by 1.0 percent a year in New York and 1.8 percent nationally during the 1980s.[31] Most of this growth was in minority households headed by women (1.8 percent per year in New York). Since poverty rates are much higher in New York than nationally, especially among minority children (46 percent in New York compared to 39 percent nationally), and New York has a larger "at risk" population, the cost of providing the same quality education may be significantly higher in New York.

Two other areas that have been found to strongly affect costs are the number of disabled students and transportation costs.[32] While state level data on disabled students were not available, there was evidence on transportation costs in 1980. New York ranked only twenty-first in the number of students transported; however, it ranked fourth in the cost per student transported and second in cost per bus mile, 76 and 153 percent above the national average, respectively.[33]

In summary, New York increased its real primary and secondary education expenditures faster than the rest of the country or region. This growth appears to have been fueled more by rising per pupil costs than by demand. Whether these expenditures have resulted in improved educational quality is unclear, but it would appear that the cost of providing a given quality of education in New York has increased, primarily due to the rising poverty population.

HIGHER EDUCATION. While not receiving the attention of primary and secondary education, higher education is an important component of a state's public service system. Expenditures on higher education accounted for 20 percent of total education expenditures in New York in 1987 (27 percent nationally). Since the rising service sector increasingly requires mental rather than physical skills, public universities have an important economic development role. It is not by accident that high-tech growth centers, such as Silicon Valley in California and Route 128 in Boston, are located near several major universities. There appears to have been recognition of this link in New York State's economic development program.[34]

Higher education spending in New York grew by almost 3 percent a year from 1980 to 1987 (Table 33). This was slightly above the national average but about the median compared to New York's neighbors. New York's expenditures per capita were only 87 percent of the

TABLE 33

Annual Percent Change (1980 to 1987) in Higher Education Expenditures and Measures of Demand for and Cost of Providing Education Services[a]: New York, Neighboring States, and Total United States

	New York	United States	Connecticut	Massachusetts	New Jersey	Pennsylvania
Total Expenditures:						
Capital Outlay	2.9	2.7	2.4	7.0	5.5	3.3
Current Expenditures	17.6	5.0	9.8	16.3	9.1	9.2
Payroll	1.8	2.5	1.9	6.3	5.2	2.8
Employment	-0.3	0.5	3.6	6.5	1.2	0.0
Payroll/Employee	0.4	1.5	1.6	5.4	1.4	1.4
	-0.7	-1.0	2.0	1.0	-0.2	-1.3
Demand Factors:						
College Age Population (18–24)						
White[b]	-1.2	-1.4	-1.2	-1.9	-0.5	-2.1
Black and Other[c]	-2.1	-1.9	-1.6	-2.3	-1.3	-2.4
	2.5	1.0	3.1	2.7	3.5	0.2
Enrollment	0.1	0.8	0.7	0.3	-0.7	0.9
Residents[c]	-0.4	0.7	0.2	-0.8	-1.2	0.3
Nonresidents[c]	3.3	1.2	3.1	3.1	5.7	3.6
Resident Enrollment/Capita[d]	0.8	2.2	1.3	1.2	-0.8	2.5

Cost Factors:						
Expenditure/Pupil	2.8	1.9	1.7	6.8	6.2	2.4
Payroll/Pupil	-0.4	-0.3	2.9	6.2	1.9	-0.8
Earnings per Employee:						
Education Services	2.4	1.7	0.8	2.5	1.5	2.4
Producer Services	3.8	1.9	2.4	3.3	2.4	1.7
Poverty Population (18–24)[b]:						
Annual % Change	0.0	-1.9	-0.8	-1.8	-0.4	-1.4
Poverty Rate (1990)	19.2	15.3	10.9	12.9	12.1	14.2
White	11.7	12.3	7.5	11.0	8.4	10.9
Black and Other	45.4	28.7	35.0	33.9	26.2	38.0

[a] Direct general expenditures deflated using the implicit GNP deflator for state and local government purchases, payroll by deflator for state and local government compensation, and earnings by the implicit GNP deflator. Payroll per employee based on payroll and full-time equivalent employment for instructional employees in October.

[b] Detailed estimates available from authors upon request.

[c] Residents are students going to school in home state. Based on survey in fall of 1979 and 1986.

[d] Resident students divided by resident population between eighteen and twenty-four years old.

Source: U.S. Department of Commerce, Bureau of the Census, *1980 Census of Population* and *Current Population Reports*, Series P-26, Nos. 1017 and 1044, and Series P-60, Nos. 163 and 166; *Governmental Finances, Finances of Public School Systems,* and *Public Employment*, various years; Bureau of Economic Analysis, unpublished earnings and employment data; and U.S. Department of Education, *Digest of Education Statistics*, various years.

national average in 1987, but they were higher than in neighboring states. As with public schools, the expenditure growth for higher education has been driven primarily by a rapid increase in capital expenditures, almost 18 percent per year. This is three times the national average and well above New York's neighbors, except Massachusetts. However, it should be pointed out that most of this growth was in 1987, and capital expenditures declined by 37 percent in 1988.[35] Even in 1987, New York's per capita spending was just at the national average.

Current higher education expenditures grew by 1.8 percent per year in New York after adjusting for inflation, below the growth rates nationally and in the region. While real personnel expenditures experienced rapid growth in Connecticut and Massachusetts, they actually declined in New York. Decomposing this decline, instructional employment grew slightly while payroll per employee declined in New York and nationally. Higher educational employment per capita was less than 80 percent of the national average while salaries remained at about the national average.

Has higher education expenditure growth in New York been driven by rising demand? The answer would appear to be negative, because enrollment remained stagnant and growth rates were below 1 percent per year in all neighboring states (see Table 33). Resident enrollment actually declined in New York, which is consistent with the drop in college-age population. Despite this drop, there was almost a 1 percent per year growth in New York in resident enrollment per capita. Relative growth in college attendance was even more rapid among New York's neighbors (except New Jersey).

Even with the slow enrollment growth, expenditure per pupil increased by 2.8 percent per year in New York. Has this growth been driven by rising costs? Unfortunately, there are very little data available on higher educational costs at the state level. Clearly, salary growth has not driven higher per student expenditures. College professors in New York appear to have lost ground to comparable private sectors, such as educational services and producer services. Whether New York State can continue to retain good faculty with such a disparity is open to question.

Another possible cost factor is an increase in college enrollment among minority and poor students, who may need special services. While the poverty population among the eighteen to twenty-four age group has remained constant, there has been growth of 2.5 percent per year in minority residents in this age group. Data on enrollment by racial composition and income background are not available. In summary, New York had strong growth in higher educational expenditures in the 1980s, for both current and capital expenditures. Since enrollment has been stagnant, expenditure per student continues to rise. However, given the sparse data on higher education, it is difficult to determine whether cost or quality factors, or some combinations of both, drove this growth.

Health and Welfare

Two of the most rapidly expanding areas of state and local expenditures during the 1980s were the public health and welfare programs. After adjusting for inflation, these categories grew by 3.4 and 4.9 percent, respectively. New York's growth exceeded the national growth rate in both areas and was higher than in most neighboring states. Equally important, the level of per capita expenditures rose to 100 percent above the national average in the case of welfare and 72 percent above the national average in the case of health.

PUBLIC WELFARE. Public welfare spending continued its rapid increase in New York during the 1980s, especially since 1983. Growth in per capita spending in New York was 3.2 percent per year from 1980 to 1988 and 5.3 percent since 1983. Surprisingly, this was higher than the growth rates during the 1970s and well above that for the nation and most of New York's neighboring states. Even controlling for the strong growth in personal income during the 1980s, public welfare expenditures increased by 1 percent per year, twice the national average. Public welfare expenditures per dollar of personal income actually declined in neighbor states.

What led to this strong expenditure growth, especially during the decade of the Reagan administration? Has it applied uniformly to all programs? Has it been driven by new recipients, rising benefits, or higher costs, particularly for medical care? What impact did federal changes in Aid to Families with Dependent Children (AFDC) and Medicaid have on state expenditures? These are some of the questions we will attempt to answer in our brief analysis of growth in welfare expenditures.

As clearly illustrated in Table 34, all of the growth in welfare expenditures in the 1980s in New York was at the state level. While state expenditures grew 14 percent per year, local expenditures

TABLE 34

Annual Average Percent Change (1980 to 1988) in Public Welfare Expenditures and Measures of Demand for and Cost of Providing Public Welfare Services[a]: New York, Neighboring States, and Total United States

	New York	United States	Connecticut	Massachusetts	New Jersey	Pennsylvania
Total Expenditures:	3.4	2.7	3.2	2.2	2.8	0.8
Local	-3.1	0.6	5.3	-4.2	-2.3	2.8
State	14.1	3.4	3.0	2.3	5.8	0.4
Vendor Payroll (Medicaid)	16.1	5.0	5.3	2.5	6.2	4.1
Other Income Support (Primarily AFDC)	-3.4	0.8	0.2	2.1	4.5	2.1
Demand/Eligibility Factors:						
Poverty Population[b]:	1.3	1.8	1.0	0.6	1.4	0.9
18 and under	1.5	2.3	0.0	-0.6	0.2	1.3
Poverty Rate (1990)	24.4	19.9	12.5	14.0	15.4	17.7
65 and over	-1.5	0.2	2.5	1.5	2.5	-0.3
Poverty Rate (1990)	9.2	12.2	9.0	9.8	10.1	9.7
Public Welfare Recipients						
AFDC	-1.1	-0.2	-3.4	-4.6	-5.6	-2.4
SSI	0.5	0.9	2.9	-1.0	1.7	1.0
Food Stamps	-2.3	-1.2	-5.8	-3.7	-6.4	-1.6

Medicaid Recipients	-0.4	0.9	-0.2	-4.1	-2.9	-1.7
AFDC Medicaid Need Standard[c]	0.3	NA	-1.7	-3.9	-2.6	4.7
Cost Factors:						
Expenditure/Poverty						
Population	1.7	0.6	2.1	1.5	1.3	-0.5
Percent of U.S. (1988)	181.0	100.0	184.9	216.8	143.3	127.4
Average AFDC Benefit Per Family:						
Annual Percent Change	-1.1	-1.5	-1.0	0.1	-3.1	-3.1
Percent of U.S. (1988)	136.9	100.0	132.3	138.5	96.9	92.7
Average Medicaid Payment						
Per Recipient:						
Annual Percent Change	4.7	3.9	6.7	8.7	8.9	6.7
Percent of U.S. (1988)	195.8	100.0	184.8	173.1	151.6	97.4

[a]Direct general expenditures deflated using the implicit GNP deflator for state and local government purchases and AFDC and Medicaid payments by the implicit GNP deflator for personal consumption expenditures.

[b]Detailed estimates available from authors upon request.

[c]Standards for AFDC for a four-person family. Percent change from 1979 to 1986.

Source: U.S. Department of Commerce, Bureau of the Census, *1980 Census of Population and Current Population Reports*, Series P-26, Nos. 1017 and 1044, and Series P-60, Nos. 163 and 166; *Governmental Finances and State Government Finances*, various years; *Statistical Abstract of the United States: 1990*; U.S. Department of Health and Human Services, Health Care Financing Administration, *Medicare and Medicaid Data Book*, various years; and Social Security Administration, *Social Security Bulletin*, various years.

declined by 3 percent per year. Even with this change, New York State still has a much more decentralized system of welfare finance, with 44 percent of expenditures at the local level compared to 23 percent nationally. The difference appears to be accounted for by a significant "pass-through" of categorical and other assistance funds to the local level (both city and county).[36] New York State accounted for 30 percent of total national intergovernmental expenditure by state governments for public welfare.

All of the growth in state welfare expenditures in New York came from a rapid increase in vendor payments, more than 16 percent per year (primarily for Medicaid), as opposed to other income support (primarily for AFDC), which actually declined by 3 percent per year (see Table 34). New York was not alone in this regard, with vendor payments growing rapidly while cash assistance declined both nationally and in New York's neighboring states.

Income support programs, such as AFDC and food stamps, were clearly one of the areas that the Reagan administration hoped to reduce in size. The major reduction took place in the 1981 Omnibus Budget Reconciliation Act (OBRA), with eligibility standards tightened considerably and benefits reduced for those with earned incomes.[37] There was an attempt to restrict benefits to only the "truly needy" and to push other recipients off the welfare rolls or into state "Workfare" programs. While the reductions were concentrated in 1981 and were smaller than proposed, it is still estimated that 300,000 to 400,000 families (11 to 14 percent) were removed from the welfare rolls, another 300,000 had their benefits reduced, and 1 million families are estimated to have lost access to food stamps.[38]

These eligibility changes were reflected in the decline in AFDC and food stamp recipients in New York State and nationally (see Table 34). The drop was even more dramatic among New York's neighboring states, with recipient declines of 2 to 6 percent per year. In contrast, there was a slight increase in the number of Supplemental Security Income (SSI) recipients in New York and nationally. The eligibility changes did not generally affect this program, which is directed to the elderly. This is consistent with a long-term trend of improvement of benefits to the elderly as opposed to families with children.[39] In addition, the real benefits to AFDC recipients continued to decline during the 1980s.[40] The average AFDC benefit per family in New York dropped by 1.1 percent per year during the 1980s, which was actually below the national decline. New York's benefit levels were 37 percent above the national average in 1988, on par with those in Connecticut and Massachusetts but well above those in New Jersey and Pennsylvania.

It is not surprising, with a drop in both recipients and benefit levels, that expenditures dropped sharply in New York and elsewhere. Does this imply a reduction in the need for such programs, that is, a decreased level of poverty? The estimates of the poverty population developed for this study show that while AFDC recipients were declining in New York by 1.1 percent per year, the poverty population actually increased by more than 1.0 percent per year. This mirrors trends nationally and in New York's neighbors. The percentage of the poor in New York receiving AFDC dropped from 47 percent in 1980 to 38 percent in 1988. The rise in poverty has been particularly rapid among female-headed households with children (2.8 percent per year).[41]

The second major change in welfare occurring in the Reagan administration was the effort to reform the welfare system beginning in 1986.[42] After two years of debate and compromise, the Family Support Act of 1988 was finally passed by the One-hundredth Congress. While there was a "surprising degree of consensus about the major shortcomings of the existing system," there was strong disagreement over what to do next.[43] Reischauer argues that "the changes made by the legislation were quite modest."[44] The act did little to change benefit levels or the state role in their implementation. There was some extension of benefits to married families with an unemployed spouse in states without coverage. The major change was the replacement of the Work Incentive program with an expanded Job Opportunity and Basic Skills (JOBS) program. This program required AFDC recipients without young children or another exemption to participate in certain educational, job training, and work requirements. In return, benefits were expanded to include child care, transportation, and other work-related costs. States were expected to develop a plan by October 1990 for the implementation of the JOBS program.

In summary, the AFDC program went through several major changes during the 1980s. It is too early to say what the impact of the latest round of welfare reform will be on states, but welfare spending should continue to be a major policy issue in New York and other states. In particular, New York must confront an increasing poverty population that is not being supported by its "safety net." With the rise of female-headed households likely to continue and with poverty rates and welfare expenditures well above the national average, New York State policymakers face some difficult choices related to social welfare policy in the 1990s.

PUBLIC HEALTH.   Health is the most rapidly expanding area of state expenditures. This category of expenditure includes health support for low-income recipients (Medicaid), support for public or private hospitals (hospitals), and outpatient care (health). State Medicaid expenditures in constant dollars increased by 16 percent a year and state and local health and hospital expenditures by 5 percent a year from 1980 to 1988. These growth rates and the level of per capita expenditures were well above national levels.

Vendor payments went from one-third of New York State's welfare budget in 1980 to two-thirds by 1988. What drove this remarkable growth and how does Medicaid coverage in New York compare to its neighbors? There are three possible explanations: an increase in recipients, expanding service levels, and/or increasing medical costs. With respect to the number of Medicaid recipients, there was actually a decline in New York compared to a 1 percent increase nationally (see Table 34). The decline was entirely in AFDC-eligible Medicaid recipients (families with children), while there was substantial growth in the number of elderly recipients (1.7 percent per year) and blind and disabled recipients (3.9 percent per year).[45]

These divergent trends seem to be due primarily to a tightening of the eligibility standards for AFDC Medicaid recipients. The changes to AFDC in the 1981 OBRA also affected Medicaid because AFDC eligibility automatically qualifies a family for Medicaid as well. In addition, states were given more flexibility on targeting their services to certain groups.[46] There was little growth in the AFDC "need standard" in New York, which is the income cutoff needed to qualify for AFDC and Medicaid. Adjusted for inflation, this standard declined sharply in all of New York's neighbors except Pennsylvania (see Table 34).

Despite the recent decline in recipients, New York State still ranks as one of the easiest states to qualify for Medicaid. In 1984, New York ranked fourth in terms of the ratio of Medicaid recipients per capita (12 percent). By comparison, Massachusetts had a ratio of

10 percent, Pennsylvania 9 percent, New Jersey 8 percent, and Connecticut 7 percent.[47] This high proportion of Medicaid patients is due both to a higher poverty rate in New York and Medicaid coverage for both AFDC and SSI, which is one of the broadest in the country.[48]

If growth in numbers of recipients does not explain the rise in Medicaid expenditures, then it must be accounted for by increases in payments per recipients. The average real payment per recipient grew by about 5 percent per year in New York from 1980 to 1988. This was above the national growth rate but below that in neighboring states. The payment level rose from 84 percent above the national average to 96 percent in 1988 and remains above that of surrounding states.[49]

This growth in medical assistance expenditures is partially due to rising health care costs, but there is no strong evidence that the cost is increasing faster in New York. The consumer price index (CPI) for medical services increased at a rate well above that of the CPI for all items (Table 35).[50] Even adjusting for higher medical costs, however, there was a significant rise in payments per recipient. This may be attributed to expanded services or rising benefits provided to hospitals, physicians, or nursing homes. We can provide no evidence that service levels expanded more rapidly than in the rest of the country in the 1980s, but New York, along with Massachusetts, Connecticut, and New Jersey, rank as leading states in terms of the number of "optional services" provided.[51] In addition, New York State ranked third in the country in terms of its reimbursement rates for nursing homes and intermediate care facilities, between 40 and 70 percent above the national average.[52] In a recent comparison of New York with three other states (including California, Michigan, and Georgia), New York's benefit levels were judged to be the most generous in most of the programs affecting children.[53] The one area where New York and its neighbors appear to lag behind is in reimbursements to physicians, which are less than 50 percent of the levels in Medicare.[54] This has led to low availability of physicians who will handle Medicaid patients.

A recent study of state Medicare systems, from the perspective of a low-income family, ranked New York as third in the nation, followed by Massachusetts (4), Connecticut (5), New Jersey (7), and Pennsylvania (19). New York's system was praised not only for its eligibility rules, scope of services, and generous payments but for the use of innovative programs to control costs and target benefits.[55] Cost

TABLE 35

Annual Average Percent Change (1980 to 1988) in Public Health Expenditures and Measures of Demand for and Cost of Providing Public Welfare Services[a]: New York, Neighboring States, and Total United States

	New York	United States	Connecticut	Massachusetts	New Jersey	Pennsylvania
Total Expenditures:						
Local	4.9	2.9	6.6	4.5	2.6	-0.6
State	4.5	3.2	0.4	3.4	0.8	-0.5
Health	5.7	2.5	7.4	4.9	3.5	-0.6
Hospital	7.3	5.4	8.8	3.4	12.6	2.2
	3.5	1.5	6.6	5.7	-0.3	-1.2
Capital Outlay	10.8	-1.1	-2.5	3.5	-6.9	-20.3
Current Expenditures	4.6	3.1	7.0	4.5	3.6	1.1
Payroll	2.7	1.1	7.3	2.8	1.3	-3.1
Employment	0.9	0.3	2.8	0.6	0.2	-2.3
Payroll/Employee	1.8	0.8	4.4	2.3	1.0	-0.9
Demand Factors:						
Total Population:						
18 and under	0.2	1.0	0.5	0.3	0.6	0.1
65 and over	-0.9	0.0	-1.0	-1.4	-1.0	-1.1
	0.9	2.2	2.2	1.3	2.0	2.0
Medicare Recipients	0.5	1.8	1.9	1.1	1.5	1.6
Hospital Usage:						
Inpatient Days	-2.0	-2.5	-2.9	-2.9	-2.2	-3.5
Outpatient Visits	2.4	3.1	2.2	1.0	2.8	0.7

Cost Factors:						
Expenditure/Capita	5.0	1.8	6.4	4.5	2.4	-0.3
Capital/Capita	10.5	-2.1	-3.0	3.1	-7.4	-20.4
Payroll/Capita	2.4	0.1	6.8	2.5	0.7	-3.2
Earnings per Employee:						
Health Services	1.2	1.6	3.5	3.0	2.2	1.9
Hospital Costs[b]:						
Average Cost Per Day	9.5	11.5	12.3	10.9	11.6	12.1
Percent of U.S.	90.3	100.0	116.9	114.4	86.9	99.5
Average Cost Per Stay	9.4	10.8	12.0	9.2	9.3	10.6
Percent of U.S.	120.5	100.0	120.4	124.2	89.7	103.9
CPI-U Medical Care[c]	7.6	8.0	NA	11.7	7.6	9.0
CPI-U All Items[c]	5.3	4.6	NA	5.2	5.3	4.9

[a]Direct general expenditures deflated using the implicit GNP deflator for state and local government purchases, payroll by deflator for state and local government compensation, and earnings by the implicit GNP deflator. Payroll per employee based on payroll and full-time equivalent employment in October.

[b]Total expenses per admission (stay) and per inpatient day for community hospitals from the American Hospital Association Annual Survey. Shown in current dollars to measure the actual price increase.

[c]CPI-U for medial care for New York City area and northeastern New Jersey for New York and New Jersey, Boston area for Massachusetts, and Philadelphia area for Pennsylvania.

Source: U.S. Department of Commerce, Bureau of the Census, *1980 Census of Population and Current Population Reports*, Series P-26, Nos. 1017 and 1044, and Series P-60, Nos. 163 and 166; *Governmental Finances, State Government Finances, and Public Employment*, various years, *Statistical Abstract of the United States: 1990*; U.S. Department of Health and Human Services, Social Security Administration, *Social Security Bulletin*, various years; U.S. Department of Labor, Bureau of Labor Statistics, *CPI Detailed Report*, January 1981 and 1989; and American Hospital Association, *Hospital Statistics*, various years.

containment will become an increasingly important issue in the 1990s as New York may find it difficult to pay for its extensive Medicaid program. This may be particularly true if the projected expansion of Medicaid funds for Acquired Immune Deficiency Syndrome (AIDS) cases comes to pass. A recent study of Medicaid and AIDS cited research showing that AIDS "will probably absorb about 5 percent of the Medicaid budget during the 1990s" and "that many high caseload states will see AIDS-related increases of 10 to 15 percent in Medicaid expenditures."[56] Since New York has the second highest AIDS caseload per capita in the country, it is not surprising that the Hospital Council of New York has estimated that AIDS-related Medicaid expenditures will double from 1988 to 1992.[57]

Besides increasing Medicaid expenditures in New York, there was a rapid growth in expenditures for publicly funded hospital and outpatient (health) care. Expenditures at both the state and local levels grew rapidly during the 1980s, and growth in New York was well above the national average and that of its neighbors except Connecticut (see Table 35). Payrolls grew by 2.7 percent a year (twice the national average), driven primarily by rising compensation (1.8 percent per year). Most of the current expenditure growth was in nonpersonnel expenditures. Although data on these expenditures are not available, it is likely that rising prices of medical supplies and prescription drugs were a large part of this growth. The growth was especially rapid in capital expenditures, 11 percent per year, compared to a decline nationally and among most of New York's neighbors. However, capital expenditures account for only 5 percent of total expenditures.

The most rapid growth in New York and nationally was in outpatient (health category) versus hospital expenditures. State health expenditures in New York grew by 7.3 percent per year compared to 3.5 percent for hospitals from 1980 to 1988 (see Table 35). To a certain extent, this disparity appears driven by trends in medical care usage. Inpatient days in hospitals declined by 2 percent per year in New York (and even more rapidly among New York's neighbors) while outpatient services increased by more than 2 percent per year.

In addition, rising medical care costs appear to be another explanation for this growth. As discussed previously, prices of medical care rose more than 2 percentage points faster than the general inflation rate. Hospital charges grew even more rapidly, with the average cost per day and average cost per stay increasing by more than 9 percent per year in New York and even more rapidly in New York's neighbors during the 1980s. As with Medicaid, the containment of medical costs will become increasingly important for New York, especially if it wants to maintain a generous level of publicly funded medical care.

Highways

Public highways and infrastructure received significant public attention during the early 1980s. Early in the decade, there were gloomy predictions that the nation's public infrastructure was wearing out at an alarming rate and that it would cost upwards of $3 trillion before the end of the century to rectify the problem.[58] While these high infrastructure need estimates have been challenged,[59] there still seems to have been a general consensus in this country in the early 1980s that infrastructure investment should receive high priority.[60] For New York State, the infrastructure "crisis" was symbolized by the collapse of the Schoharie Creek Bridge on Interstate 90 in April of 1987, killing ten people and resulting in millions of dollars of damage.[61]

Have highway investments by state and local governments in New York and other states responded to this crisis? The answer would appear to be that it depends on the state. New York experienced only modest growth, 2.3 percent per year, in real expenditures by its state and local governments on highways (Table 36). This was below the national average of 3.1 percent and New York's neighboring states, particularly Connecticut and New Jersey. The highway expenditure growth rate remained fairly constant during the 1980s, with only slightly faster growth (2.4 percent per year) after 1983. New York's per capita highway expenditures were slightly below the national average in 1988.

Even more telling was the slow growth of only 1.4 percent per year in capital outlays for highways. This was 40 percent of the national average growth rate and pales in comparison with the rates of 12 and 18 percent in Connecticut and New Jersey, respectively. New York's capital outlays per capita were 10 percent below the national average in 1988. The slow growth in capital outlays occurred despite the passage during the 1980s of several major bond issues in New York to fund highway construction. (The "Rebuild New York" Bond Acts of 1983 and 1988 authorized sale of long-term bonds for $1.25

TABLE 36

Annual Percent Change (1981 to 1988) in Highway Expenditures and Measures of Demand for and Cost of Providing Public Highways[a]: New York, Neighboring States, and Total United States

	New York	United States	Connecticut	Massachusetts	New Jersey	Pennsylvania
Total Expenditures:	2.3	3.1	10.5	2.7	11.3	5.0
State	0.8	3.3	12.6	2.0	18.5	7.3
Local	3.6	2.8	6.1	3.5	1.2	-0.3
Capital Outlay	1.4	3.4	12.4	4.6	18.4	7.8
Current Expenditures	3.5	2.8	8.7	0.9	3.3	3.0
Payroll	3.6	1.1	2.2	0.8	2.6	-1.4
Employment	1.0	0.1	-0.1	-1.8	0.0	-1.9
Payroll/Employee	2.5	1.0	2.2	2.6	2.6	0.6
Demand/Service Responsibility Factors:						
Population (over 17)	0.6	1.3	0.9	0.8	1.1	0.5
Automobiles Registered	2.7	1.9	3.5	0.1	3.1	0.7
Annual Vehicle Miles	3.9	3.9	4.3	2.7	1.9	1.8
Principal Arterial	5.1	4.6	4.8	4.2	3.5	2.7
Other	2.9	3.2	3.7	0.3	0.6	1.0
Public Road Mileage	0.1	0.1	0.3	0.0	0.3	-0.1
Federal Aid—Interstate	0.9	0.8	3.5	0.9	2.1	0.2
Federal Aid—Other	0.6	2.8	0.3	0.4	0.0	0.1
Nonfederal Aid	0.0	-0.6	0.2	-0.2	0.4	-0.2

Cost/Quality Factors:						
Expense/Vehicle Mile	-1.5	-0.7	5.9	0.0	9.2	3.1
Capital/Vehicle Mile	-2.5	-0.5	7.7	1.8	16.2	5.9
Payroll/Vehicle Mile	-0.3	-2.6	-2.1	-1.9	0.7	-3.2
Earnings per employee:						
Manufacturing	1.9	1.0	2.5	3.1	2.5	0.5
Distributive Services	1.2	0.7	3.1	2.1	1.8	0.6
Structurally Deficient[b]						
Bridges (% of total)	(50–60)	(15–24)	(5–26)	(13–35)	(12–23)	(13–27)

[a]Direct general expenditures deflated using the implicit GNP deflator for state and local government purchases, payroll by deflator for state and local government compensation, and earnings by the implicit GNP deflator. Payroll per employee based on payroll and full-time equivalent employment in October.

[b]Structurally deficient bridge is defined as one that (1) is restricted to light vehicles only, (2) is closed, or (3) requires immediate rehabilitation to remain open. Range is for 1979 and 1988.

Source: U.S. Department of Commerce, Bureau of the Census, *Current Population Reports*, Series P-26, No. 1044; *Governmental Finances* and *Public Employment*, various years; Bureau of Economic Analysis, unpublished earnings and employment data; and U.S. Department of Transportation, *Highway Statistics*, various years, and *Highway Bridge Replacement and Rehabilitation Program*, various years.

billion and $3 billion for highway and bridge construction and repair, respectively. Part of the explanation for this slow growth appears to lie in declining federal aid for highways. Despite the significant attention that infrastructure received at the federal level, total federal highway aid to state governments actually dropped slightly during the 1980s. The New York state government experienced close to a 3 percent per year drop in real federal highway aid from 1980 to 1988. This compares to growth rates of more than 8 percent per year in Connecticut, New Jersey, and Pennsylvania.

Current expenditures (which account for 48.0 percent of total highway expenditures) grew by 3.5 percent per year in New York from 1981 to 1988. This was above the national average and all of New York's neighboring states except Connecticut. Highway payroll, which represents more than 60 percent of current expenditures, grew by 3.6 percent per year (see Table 36). This was much higher than in New York's neighboring states. Most of this growth was accounted for by rising salaries, 2.5 percent per year, which actually exceeded the growth for comparable private sector activities, such as manufacturing and distributive services. While highway employment appeared to be stagnant in the rest of the country, it grew by 1 percent a year in New York. New York now hires 25 percent more highway employees per capita than the national average.

The growth in highway expenditures in New York was primarily at the local government level, with a growth rate of 3.6 percent. It appears to have been funded in part by a significant increase in state highway aid to local governments, 10.5 percent per year. This compares to no growth in state highway aid nationally and significant decreases by neighboring states. To its credit, the state government appears to have directed its limited funds to that part of the state system most in need. Local highways and bridges have consistently been in poorer condition than state highways, which receive federal aid.[62]

The moderate growth in highway expenditures in New York was not due to a decline in highway usage. While the total number of road miles in the state increased only slightly, there was strong growth (3.9 percent per year) in annual vehicle miles (see Table 36). This growth was at about the national average but exceeded that of New York's neighbors. The strongest growth, more than 5 percent per year, occurred on the major highways. In addition, automobile registrations in the state grew by 2.7 percent per year during this time period.

What does New York's relatively slow growth in highway expenditures imply about changes in the condition of the state's highways? Quality measures for highways, while more readily available, should also be viewed with caution. The U.S. Department of Transportation, as part of the "Highway Bridge Replacement and Rehabilitation Program," has states evaluate the condition of state-controlled bridges on a biannual basis. In 1979, 50 percent of these bridges in New York were deemed "structurally deficient," and this grew to 60 percent by 1988 (see Table 36).[63] By contrast, 24 percent of total U.S. bridges, 26 percent in Connecticut, 35 percent in Massachusetts, 23 percent in New Jersey, and 27 percent in Pennsylvania fell into this category in 1988. In both New York and the nation, there was an increase in the percent of structurally deficient bridges.[64]

State highway condition statistics are also published by the U.S. Department of Transportation; however, due to the small sample size and differences in methodology between states, the accuracy of interstate comparisons is questionable.[65] The New York State Department of Transportation does carry out a "visual inspection" of all miles of state-responsible roads every year. On a scale of one to ten, they rate anything five or below as in "poor" condition. Concerning the overall measure of condition, there was an improvement from 13.0 percent in the poor category in 1981 to 11.8 percent in 1988 (10.9 percent in 1989).[66] Most of this decline occurred by 1985. However, the average rating for state highways (6.82) did not change from 1981 to 1988.

In summary, there is mixed evidence on whether there has been improvement in the condition of New York's highway system. There appears to have been some improvement in state highway condition, while state bridges appear to be in poorer condition. Unfortunately, there are little data on the condition of local highways and bridges, which in the past have been in even worse shape. These results suggest that highway infrastructure funding is likely to remain a major policy issue in the 1990s.

Public Safety

The second most rapidly growing category of expenditures in New York is public safety. Real expenditures in New York grew by more than 5 percent a year since 1980, faster than the national rate and faster than surrounding states. Per capita expenditures for public safety in New York went from 43 percent above the national average in 1980 to 59 percent above in 1988. This compares to an expenditure level 16 percent above the national average in New Jersey, the neighboring state with the highest public safety expenditure burden. Most of New York's growth in this expenditure category occurred at the state level, with an annual rate of close to 8 percent. However, there were significant differences in expenditure trends between the different public safety functions: police, corrections, and fire.

POLICE AND CORRECTIONS.   Police and corrections accounted for roughly 7 percent of total state and local spending in New York in 1988. Corrections expenditures were primarily at the state level (53 percent) and police at the local level (90 percent). The major local governments handling corrections were counties and municipalities and for police were municipalities. As is clear in Table 37, there were significant differences in expenditure trends for these public safety functions.

Police expenditures grew by 3.3 percent per year in constant dollars from 1980 to 1988, which was slightly above the national average and all of New York's neighbors except Connecticut. New York's per capita police expenditures grew to 58 percent above the national average and were higher than those of any of its neighboring states. Two-thirds of these expenditures were for payrolls, which grew by 2.7 percent per year. Payroll growth in New York was driven by both increases in employment (1.6 percent per year) and employee compensation (1.1 percent per year). By comparison, compensation remained constant for the country as a whole. On a per capita basis, New York is now 39 percent above average for employment and 20 percent above average for compensation in the police category.[67]

While police expenditures experienced moderate growth, corrections expenditures skyrocketed in the 1980s, growing by more than 10 percent per year in constant dollars. This compares to a growth rate of 8.4 percent nationally and between 6.0 and 8.0 percent in New York's neighboring states. The growth was equally high for both state and local governments; however, state governments represent most of the spending. Part of the explanation for this rapid growth was due to payrolls, which increased by more than 11 percent in New York (see Table 37). Payroll growth was due almost entirely to a rapid rise in corrections employees, 10.6 percent per year. New York now employs 80 percent more corrections employees per capita than the national average. Employee compensation, on the other hand, grew only slightly faster than inflation; still, salaries are 20 percent above the national average.

What drove the rapid growth in correctional expenditures? Looking at the prison population in state facilities, there was a growth of more than 9 percent per year during this period, a rate slightly above the national average. Since population growth and even the growth of the poverty population below twenty-five years old were well below this rate, there was either a rapid expansion of criminal activity in the state and nation or changes in policy. These policy changes could involve court mandates on prison expansion, enforcement of mandatory sentencing, or expansion of police activity.

Increasing court mandates with regard to state and local correctional facilities have been a major issue for state and local governments.[68] Several recent censuses of state and local jails provide evidence on the magnitude of such mandates.[69] In 1983, 29 percent of local jails and in 1984, 7 percent of state facilities in New York were under court order or consent decrees. This is on par with many of New York's neighboring states. For example, in Massachusetts 42 percent of local jails, in Connecticut 38 percent of state facilities, and in New Jersey 31 percent of local jails were under court order. Unfortunately, data on capital outlay expenditures for corrections are available at the state level only, so it is difficult to track how these mandates have affected local jail construction. New York, Massachusetts, and Pennsylvania had increases in real capital outlays for corrections of 20 percent per year or more since 1980. The national average was close to 10 percent. On the other hand, state capital outlays actually declined in Connecticut and New Jersey once adjusted for inflation.

With regard to police activity, the most general activity measure is the number of arrests by type of crime. Arrest statistics, though, are not available in published form back to 1980. What is available are measures of crime rates by type of crime. Ideally, this would provide some indication of the quality of police services, that is, the level of "safety" in a community. However, these represent only reported crimes and there is evidence of significant underreporting of criminal activity. The gap between actual and reported crime rates appears to vary by the type of crime, age and sex of the victim, and region of the country (Box 11). Crime rate information may indicate only an increased demand on police services.

TABLE 37

Annual Percent Change (1980 to 1988) in Public Safety Expenditures and Measures of Demand for and Cost of Providing Public Safety Services[a]: New York, Neighboring States, and Total United States

	New York	United States	Connecticut	Massachusetts	New Jersey	Pennsylvania
Total Expenditures:	5.2	4.6	4.8	2.6	4.1	1.2
Local	4.4	4.0	3.7	1.1	2.7	0.4
State	7.9	6.0	6.9	7.6	7.3	2.8
Police	3.3	3.0	4.5	2.3	3.2	-0.3
Payroll	2.7	1.5	3.5	0.6	1.2	-1.6
Employment	1.6	1.5	1.7	0.1	0.6	-0.4
Payroll/Employee	1.1	0.0	1.7	0.5	0.6	-1.1
Corrections	10.6	8.4	7.1	7.7	7.2	5.5
Payroll	11.2	7.1	6.0	7.2	7.4	3.6
Employment	10.6	6.9	3.1	6.1	6.2	5.1
Payroll/Employee	0.6	0.1	2.8	1.1	1.1	-1.4
Fire	2.4	3.7	3.0	0.4	1.2	-0.4
Payroll	2.3	1.7	1.1	-0.3	0.3	-1.6
Employment	0.5	0.5	0.0	-1.0	-0.7	-0.9
Payroll/Employee	1.8	1.2	1.0	0.7	1.1	-0.6
Demand Factors:						
Poverty Population[b]:						
Under 25	1.1	1.1	-0.2	-1.0	0.1	0.5
White	0.9	1.5	-1.2	-1.7	-1.2	0.6
Black	1.4	0.4	1.1	1.5	1.3	0.4

Prison Population:	9.3	8.4	8.1	9.8	14.1	10.3
Percent White (1987)	49.9	48.6	32.8	59.4	34.0	43.3
Percent Black (1987)	50.1	51.4	67.2	40.6	66.0	56.7
% of Capacity (1984)	105.0	117.0	108.0	173.0	119.0	138.0
Cost/Activity Factors:						
Earnings per Employee:						
Manufacturing	1.5	0.9	2.2	2.8	2.2	0.4
Distributive Services	0.8	0.3	2.3	1.5	1.2	0.1
Crime Rate[c]	-1.1	-0.5	-1.8	-2.4	-2.3	-2.0
Violent Crimes	0.8	1.2	1.2	0.4	-0.5	-0.1
Percent of U.S.	172.2	100.0	71.5	97.2	91.5	56.8
Property Crimes	-1.5	-0.7	-2.0	-2.8	-2.6	-2.2
Percent of U.S.	103.7	100.0	92.3	87.0	93.7	56.0

[a]Direct general expenditures deflated using the implicit GNP deflator for state and local government purchases, payroll by deflator for state and local government compensation, and earnings by the implicit GNP deflator. Payroll per employee based on payroll and full-time equivalent employment in October.

[b]Detailed estimates available from authors upon request.

[c]Reported crimes per capita. Due to variation between reported and actual crimes in different areas, this may not accurately reflect the relative level of criminal activity in different areas.

Source: U.S. Department of Commerce, Bureau of the Census, *1980 Census of Population* and *Current Population Reports,* Series P-26, Nos. 1017 and 1044, and Series P-60, Nos. 163 and 166; *Governmental Finances, State Government Finances and Public Employment,* various years, *Statistical Abstract of the United States: 1990;* U.S. Department of Justice, Federal Bureau of Investigation, *Crime in the United States;* and Office of Justice Programs, *Sourcebook of Criminal Justice Statistics,* various years.

Box 11. Crime Rate Statistics

The major source of crime rate statistics is the Uniform Crime Report (UCR) developed by the Federal Bureau of Investigation (FBI) in conjunction with state and local police departments. Information is collected on the number of arrests, clearances (crimes solved usually by the arrest of a suspect), and reported crimes by type of crime.[a] Essentially, the UCR is based on an incident reporting system where police officers fill out an incident report. This report is then checked by a UCR coding clerk before being sent to the FBI.

While the UCR system of state and local police departments has gone through periodic audits, there is still a lot of room for discretion. This discretion occurs first in whether an incident is reported as a crime. This can depend on whether the officer expects the complainant to press charges and the credibility that the officer places in his or her complaint.[b] Since both of these may be influenced by the socioeconomic status of the victim, it is likely that the misreporting that does take place is not random.

Finally, the UCR records only reported crimes. There is strong evidence that significant underreporting of criminal activity exists. The Bureau of Justice Statistics in conjunction with the Bureau of the Census carries out the National Crime Survey (NCS) of approximately fifty thousand households. The results of this survey show that in 1985, only 36 percent of all crimes were reported to police. This underreporting varies by the type of crime (for example, rape, 39 percent; theft, 70 percent), age (for example, less than nineteen, 22 percent; more than fifty, 40 percent), and region of the country.[c] There is a tendency for the reporting of a crime to go up the higher the probability of an arrest. This implies that it is possible to get the perverse result that an increase in expenditures on police actually increases the crime rate because victims are now more willing to report crimes. In other words, caution must be taken in using the crime rates reported in the UCR as a measure of actual criminal activity.

---

[a] UCR information is reported annually in the national publication, *Crime in the United States*, from the FBI. For New York, this information is reported in the *Crime and Justice Annual Report* published by the New York State Division of Criminal Justice Services.

[b] James Lynch, "Changes in Police Organization and Their Effects on the Divergence of the UCR and NCS Trends." Unpublished paper presented at the 35th Annual Meeting of the American Society of Criminology, Denver, Colorado, November 9–13, 1983.

[c] For results from the NCS, see U.S. Department of Justice, *Criminal Victimization in the United States, 1985* (Washington, D.C.: U.S. Government Printing Office, May 1987).

In the case of New York, there was a 0.8 percent increase in violent crimes per capita and a 1.5 percent decrease in property crimes during the 1980s, for an overall decrease in reported crimes per capita of 1.1 percent per year. This decrease exceeded that for the nation but was below neighboring states. In the area of violent crime, New York continued to experience rates 70 percent above the national average, while property crime rates are comparable to those for the country as a whole.

In summary, New York state and local governments increased their expenditures significantly in the areas of police and especially corrections. The expenditure growth in corrections appears to be driven by court mandates on state and local prisons and a rise in the prison population. With New York State's prisons still above capacity in 1984 (see Table 37), it is likely that prison overcrowding will continue to drive expenditure growth in corrections in the 1990s. It is also likely that the increasing number of poor children and young adults in New York will adversely affect the crime rate because most crimes are committed by persons under thirty.[70] Finally, recent evidence shows that 80 percent or more of males and females arrested in New York City in December 1988 were using drugs, as were close to 90 percent of young adults (twenty-one to thirty years old).[71] It is likely, then, that the demand on police services, particularly in the central cities, will continue to be high in the 1990s.

FIRE PROTECTION.   While expenditures on police and corrections experienced strong growth in the 1980s, expenditures by local fire departments grew modestly in New York, 2.4 percent per year (see Table 37). This growth rate was well below the national average but above all New York's neighbors except Connecticut. New York continues to spend 35 percent more per capita on fire than the national average. Since personnel costs are the majority of fire expenditures (60 to 70 percent), most of this growth was in payrolls, with a growth rate of 2.3 percent. Fire employment grew slowly in New York as well as nationally (see Table 37). Most of the payroll growth was in employee compensation, which grew by close to 2 percent per year in constant dollars. New York local governments in 1988 had per capita employment and compensation 20 percent above the national average.

Why have fire expenditures grown only modestly compared to other public safety functions? The explanation seems to lie in the declining numbers of fires. With the success of fire prevention programs, the total number of fires declined by 5.4 percent per year from 1981 to 1986.[72] Instead, the role of local fire departments has begun to change into one of emergency response to fire, medical, or hazardous waste emergencies. The number of emergency responses by fire departments grew by 10 percent per year from 1981 to 1985.[73] In particular, the growth of costly emergency medical service responsibility among local fire departments may have a significant expenditure impact.

Besides the changing responsibilities of fire departments, another issue that may affect costs in the 1990s is increasing use of paid personnel. As of 1988, 80 percent of local fire departments were volunteer in New York.[74] The remainder were split between fully paid and mixed paid and volunteer departments. Still, volunteer departments, especially in suburban areas, are finding it increasingly difficult to recruit and retain volunteers.[75] In their recent review of fire services in New York State, the Legislative Commission on State-Local Relations cited this as the principal problem facing volunteer departments today.[76] Since it is likely that expenditures in paid departments are higher,[77] this may become an important cost issue in the 1990s. Finally, recent evidence has shown for New York that factors such as building age and condition (and, implicitly, economic status) can have a significant impact on fire protection costs.[78] This implies that the older central cities in New York may face rising expenditures for fire protection in the 1990s.

Conclusions

Underlying New York's government sector growth in the 1980s is a complicated set of factors. Despite the complexity, some consistent trends stand out.

First, New York's revenue growth was driven by growth in its underlying tax base, not by discretionary increases in tax rates. In fact, the top marginal rate of the state personal income tax had been cut in half in the 1980s. In addition, New York State has not increased its sales tax rate, and a combination of inflation and increasing property values has led to declines in the effective rate for both selective sales and property taxes.

Second, the tax burden is very high by comparison with the rest of the country. It is important to remember that New York has a very decentralized tax system, with local income, sales, and property taxes accounting for a large share of the overall tax burden. While state government tax rates are not out of line with neighboring states, the combined state and local tax rates are relatively high, especially in New York City. New York's high tax burden relative to the nation and to its neighbors did not decrease in the 1980s. While New York has begun to move in the right direction to make its tax system more "competitive," it still has a long way to go.

Third, the growth in state and local government education, health, and welfare expenditures was not driven by an increase in recipients. In all three areas, there has been a reduction in the number of beneficiaries. There was, however, an increase in per recipient expenditures. While it is difficult to assess whether service quality has improved in these areas, it is clear that there have been rising costs. For education, the cost increase was most likely due to the increasing number of poorer, disadvantaged students in the central cities. For health, the increase was driven by rapid growth in medical and hospital costs. Finally, New York continues to offer a much more generous package of services (including education) to its low-income residents than the average state.

Fourth, for highways and public safety, there was growth in "demand" for the services. There was a significant increase in traffic volume on the state's highways and a large rise in the prison population in New York. The expenditure increases for both services were influenced by assessments at the beginning of the 1980s of inadequacies in capacity or in the condition of the existing public facilities, such as highway infrastructure and prisons. There was also significant growth in compensation for highway, police, and fire employees. It is likely that replacement of infrastructure and prison overcrowding will remain significant budgetary pressures in the 1990s.

The story, then, is that New York's expenditure growth in the 1980s was driven less by its capacity to finance than by its rising costs and its desire to renew the public infrastructure, to improve the real salary position of state and local government employees, and to respond to demands for better health, education, and welfare services.

The story for the 1980–88 period was pretty much the same as for 1970 to 1975—expenditure growth rather than revenue constraints dominated budgetary planning.

It is quite clear that New York will face some tough fiscal choices in the 1990s. On the one hand, New York has made a concerted effort to provide better than average health, welfare, and education services and likely will try to maintain this level of service. The socioeconomic changes of the 1980s, particularly the large increase in poor households with children, will almost certainly increase the future cost of providing these social services. On the other hand, New York's high expenditure levels do not come without the price of high tax burdens, which may adversely affect state economic growth in the 1990s.

Notes

1. For a good review of state tax actions in the 1980s, see Steven Gold, "Developments in State Finances, 1983 to 1986," *Public Budgeting & Finance* 7 (Spring 1987): 5–23.

2. ACIR's tax capacity is based on federal income tax liability adjusted for deductibility of state and local taxes.

3. Real capital income grew by 4 percent per year in New York, 5 percent in Connecticut, and 6 percent in Massachusetts. This compares to growth rates for wage and salary income of 3.7, 4.7, and 4.9 percent, respectively, from 1980 to 1988.

4. Gold, "Developments in State Finances, 1983 to 1986."

5. Pennsylvania raised its personal income tax rate from 2.2 to 2.45 percent. Connecticut instituted a tax on interest income for incomes more than $50,000 and raised the rate for dividend income. The discretionary tax analysis is based on the annual publication, developed by the National Conference of State Legislatures, *State Budget Actions* (Denver: NCSL, various years). See Table E-11 in Appendix E for a review of major tax actions in New York and its neighbors.

6. Pennsylvania allowed its income tax to return to its original 2.2 percent rate by 1985.

7. Revenue was estimated to decrease by 11 percent due to federal tax reform in both Rhode Island and Vermont. See Advisory Commission on Intergovernmental Relations, "Preliminary Estimates of the Effect of the 1986 Federal Tax Reform Act on State Personal Income Tax Liabilities," Staff Information Report (Washington, D.C.: ACIR, December 8, 1986), Table 3.

8. Ibid.

9. New York passed the Tax Reform and Reduction Act of 1987 in January of 1987, and Maine was to follow a year later with income tax reform. The number of tax brackets in Maine was reduced from 8 to 4, and the top rate decreased from 10 to 8 percent in 1988.

10. For a brief summary of New York's reform, see New York State Department of Taxation and Finance, "New York State's Tax Reform and Reduction Act of 1987," No. 900 (Albany: New York State Department of Taxation and Finance, May 1987).

11. Other exceptions include Connecticut's expansion of its capital income tax in 1983 and Massachusetts's rate increase in 1989 from 5 to 5.75 percent for earned income.

12. New York State passed the Business Tax Reform and Rate Reduction Act in August of 1987, reducing the net income tax rate from 10 to 9 percent (8 percent for small businesses) and eliminating or reducing some credits and deductions. In July of 1988, the state passed a bill to bring New York City's General Corporation Tax into compliance with the state tax and to reduce rates from 9.0 to 8.85 percent.

13. Since Massachusetts has corporations pay an excise tax equal to the greater of several tax calculations, it is difficult to identify a particular tax rate. According to the publication *State Budget Actions* put out annually by the National Conference of State Legislatures, Massachusetts did not make a major discretionary change in its corporate income tax base from 1983 to 1989.

14. Grouped under New York City corporate income taxes by the Bureau of the Census are the General Corporation Tax, the Unincorporated Business Tax, and the Financial Corporation Tax.

15. New York State Department of Taxation and Finance, Office of Tax Policy Analysis, *Statistical Report* (Albany: New York State Department of Taxation and Finance, various years), Table 7.

16. Advisory Commission on Intergovernmental Relations, *Significant Features of Fiscal Federalism, 1990*, Vol. 1 (Washington, D.C.: ACIR, 1990), Table 25. See Gold, "Developments in State Finances, 1983 to 1986," for an excellent review of state government responses to budget problems in 1983.

17. For a brief summary of sales taxation of consumer services in New York State, see New York State Department of Taxation and Finance, "Sales and Use Tax Information for Consumers," No. 760 (Albany: New York State Department of Taxation and Finance, 1986). New York City actually taxes a broader range of services, including parking vehicles, credit rating, protective services, and miscellaneous personal services. See New York State Department of Taxation and Finance, "Sales Tax Information on Selected Services in New York City," No. 846 (Albany: New York State Department of Taxation and Finance, 1989).

18.   The review of discretionary actions in this section is based on the publication *State Budget Actions,* developed by the National Conferences of State Legislatures. See Table E-11 for a review of major tax actions in New York and its neighbors.

19.   Gross receipts taxes in New York include a tax on sales of public utilities and transportation companies and insurance company premiums.

20.   These studies are cited in the excellent literature review by Eric Hanushek, "The Economics of Schooling: Production and Efficiency in Public Schools," *Journal of Economic Literature* 3 (September 1986): 1141–1177. Probably the most well known of these was from the National Commission on Excellence in Education, *A Nation at Risk: The Imperative for Educational Reform* (Washington, D.C.: U.S. Government Printing Office, April 1983).

21.   The National Conference of State Legislatures (NCSL) annually asks state fiscal officers what are the top fiscal issues in that state during the year. From 1983 to 1988, education was cited as a leading fiscal issue for at least four years by twenty-seven states on average, including New York and most of its neighboring states. The results are summarized in the publication *State Budget Actions,* published annually by the NCSL.

22.   This section borrows heavily from the work of Michael Wasylenko. See, in particular, "Employment Growth and the Business Climate in New York and Neighboring States," Metropolitan Studies Program Occasional Paper, No. 140 (Syracuse: Syracuse University, 1990); and "Business Climate, Industry and Employment Growth: A Review of the Evidence," Metropolitan Studies Program Occasional Paper, No. 98 (Syracuse: Syracuse University, 1985).

23.   Hanushek, "The Economics of Schooling: Production and Efficiency in Public Schools," Table 7.

24.   Ibid.

25.   These results are published by the U.S. Department of Education, National Center for Education Statistics, *Digest of Education Statistics, 1989* (Washington, D.C.: U.S. Government Printing Office, 1989), Table 113.

26.   For example, in New York, 72 percent of graduates take the SAT while in Connecticut 81 percent take it, Massachusetts 73 percent, New Jersey 69 percent, and in Pennsylvania 63 percent. Ibid.

27.   The New York State Department of Education estimates high school dropout rates. There was little change in the rate, approximately 6.5 percent during the 1980s. See the Nelson A. Rockefeller Institute of Government, *1985–86 New York State Statistical Yearbook* (Albany: Nelson A. Rockefeller Institute of Government, 1986), Table D-13.

28.   See Hanushek, "The Economics of Schooling: Production and Efficiency in Public Schools," for a discussion of this issue.

29.   James Coleman, Ernest Campbell, and Carol Hobson, *Equality of Educational Opportunity* (Washington, D.C.: U.S. Government Printing

Office, 1966). While Coleman's methodology has been challenged, there are numerous studies showing the influence of family background on performance. See Hanushek, "The Economics of Schooling: Production and Efficiency in Public Schools."

30. See, for example, Vernon Henderson, Peter Mieszkowski, and Yvon Sauvageau, "Peer Group Effects and Education Production Functions," *Journal of Public Economics* 10 (1978): 97–106; and Anita Summers and Barbara Wolfe, "Do Schools Make a Difference?" *American Economic Review* 67 (September 1977): 639–652.

31. Since poverty statistics are not available at the state level between decennial censuses, they had to be estimated from available data. These estimates were made by the authors using several publications from the U.S. Bureau of the Census: *1980 Census of Population* (Washington, D.C.: U.S. Government Printing Office, 1983); "Projections of the Population of States, by Age, Sex and Race: 1988 to 2010," *Current Population Reports*, Series P-25, No. 1017 (Washington, D.C.: U.S. Government Printing Office, October 1988); and "Poverty in the United States, 1987," *Current Population Reports*, Series P-60, No. 163 (Washington, D.C.: U.S. Government Printing Office, February 1989). State data in 1980 were extrapolated to 1988 by race, age, and family type (female-headed and other) using projections by state of age and racial composition and national poverty statistics for 1987. These results were then compared to the poverty estimates by state from 1985 to 1987 by Robert Plotnick, "How Much Poverty Is Reduced by State Income Transfers?" *Monthly Labor Review* 112 (July 1989): 21–26, Table 1.

32. See Kerri Ratcliffe, Bruce Riddle, and John Yinger, "The Fiscal Condition of School Districts in Nebraska: Is Small Beautiful?" *Economics of Education Review* 9 (January 1990): 81–99.

33. See U.S. Department of Education, National Center for Education Statistics, *Digest of Education Statistics, 1983-84* (Washington, D.C.: U.S. Government Printing Office, 1985), Table 28.

34. Specifically, the New York State Science and Technology Foundation administers the Centers for Advanced Technology, which are a cooperative venture between ten universities in the state and private companies. Their objectives are to produce "industrially relevant" research and development, train technical personnel, and create a link between business and higher education.

35. By comparison, real capital expenditures grew by 11 percent per year from 1980 to 1986 and 9 percent per year from 1980 to 1988.

36. Of the $5.6 million (current dollars) in local public welfare expenditures in 1988, $5.2 million (92 percent) appears to have been funded by intergovernmental aid from the state. U.S. Bureau of the Census, *Governmental Finances 1987-88* (Washington, D.C.: U.S. Government Printing Office, 1990), Table 29, and *State Government Finances in 1988* (Washington, D.C.: U.S. Government Printing Office, 1989), Table 12.

37. For an excellent review of the proposals and record of the Reagan administration in changing the welfare system in the early 1980s, see D. Lee Bawden and John Palmer, "Social Policy: Challenging the Welfare State," in *The Reagan Record,* eds. John Palmer and Isabel Sawhill (Cambridge: Ballinger Publishing Co., 1984).

38. Ibid.

39. One estimate shows that the percentage of elderly removed from poverty by government transfers increased from less than 60 percent in 1970 to close to 80 percent by 1985, with slight growth occurring during the Reagan years. In contrast, the number of female-headed families removed from poverty decreased from a peak of 20 percent in 1971 to less than 10 percent by 1985. The decline was particularly steep after 1979. See Sheldon Danziger, "Fighting Poverty and Reducing Welfare Dependency," in *Welfare Policy for the 1990s,* eds. Phoebe Cottingham and David Ellwood (Cambridge: Harvard University Press, 1989), Figure 2.2.

40. See Robert Moffitt, *Has State Redistribution Policy Grown More Conservative? AFDC, Food Stamps and Medicaid, 1960-84,* Institute for Research on Poverty Discussion Paper, DP No. 851–88 (Madison: University of Wisconsin, January 1988). Moffitt argues that the decline in the AFDC benefit levels, which are set by the states, is not an indication of increasing conservatism at the state level. Instead, it is an attempt to shift welfare financing onto the federal government through the substitution of federally funded food stamps for state-financed AFDC benefits.

41. For a discussion of the issue of child poverty and government policy, see Danziger, "Fighting Poverty and Reducing Welfare Dependency"; Congressional Budget Office, *Reducing Poverty Among Children* (Washington, D.C.: U.S. Government Printing Office, May 1985); and U.S. Congress, Joint Economic Committee, *Poverty, Income Distribution, the Family and Public Policy* (Washington, D.C.: U.S. Government Printing Office, December 1986).

42. One of the early reform proposals was provided by the Governor's Task Force on Poverty and Welfare, *A New Social Contract: Rethinking the Nature and Purposes of Public Assistance* (Albany: Governor's Task Force on Poverty and Welfare, December 1986).

43. For an excellent discussion of the passage and content of the Family Support Act of 1988, see Robert Reischauer, "The Welfare Reform Legislation: Directions for the Future," in *Welfare Policy for the 1990s,* pp. 10–40. See also Karen Britto, "The Family Support Act of 1988: Welfare Reform," *State Federal Issue Brief,* National Conference of State Legislatures, Vol. 2 (February 1989).

44. Reischauer, ibid., p. 11.

45. These rates are based on changes among Medicaid recipients from 1980 to 1985. See U.S. Department of Health and Human Services, Health

Care Financing Administration, *Medicare and Medicaid Data Book* (Washington, D.C.: U.S. Government Printing Office, 1988 and 1983). These results are consistent with those found nationally by John Holahan and Joel Cohen, *Medicaid: The Trade-Off Between Cost Containment and Access to Care* (Washington, D.C.: Urban Institute Press, 1986).

46.   For a discussion of Medicaid changes due to the 1981 OBRA, see Holahan and Cohen, ibid.; and Embry Howell, David Baugh, and Penelope Pine, "Patterns of Medicaid Utilization and Expenditures in Selected States: 1980–84," *Health Care Financing Review* 10 (Winter 1988): 1–15.

47.   Holahan and Cohen, ibid., Table 11.

48.   Of the nine coverage categories listed for AFDC and eight for SSI, New York covers all but two. Among New York's neighbors, only Pennsylvania approached this level of coverage. See U.S. Department of Health and Human Services, Health Care Financing Administration, *Medicare and Medicaid Data Book 1988*, Tables 4.1 and 4.3. This result is consistent with a recent study done on state Medicaid programs. From the standpoint of a low-income household, they ranked Pennsylvania first or second in eligibility, New York fourth, Massachusetts sixth, New Jersey ninth, and Connecticut tenth. See Public Citizen Health Research Group, *Poor Health Care for Poor Americans: A Ranking of State Medicaid Programs* (Washington, D.C.: Public Citizen Health Research Group, 1987).

49.   While Pennsylvania is quite liberal in its eligibility standards, its level of benefits is actually below the national average. This appears to be due to both a narrow set of covered services and low levels of reimbursements to participating physicians and hospitals. See Public Citizen Health Research Group, ibid., pp. 142–144.

50.   Since the general inflation rate is estimated from a sample of urban consumers, it is not available on a state level. The inflation rates shown in Table 35 are for New York City/northeastern New Jersey (New York and New Jersey), Boston (Massachusetts), and Philadelphia (Pennsylvania).

51.   U.S. Department of Health and Human Services, Health Care Financing Administration, *Medicare and Medicaid Data Book, 1988*, Table 4.7.

52.   James Swan, Charlene Harrington, and Leslie Grant, "State Medicaid Reimbursement for Nursing Homes, 1978–86," *Health Care Financing Review* 9 (Spring 1988): 33–50.

53.   Marilyn Rymer and Gerald Adler, "Children and Medicaid: The Experience in Four States," *Health Care Financing Review* 9 (Fall 1987): 1–20.

54.   Holahan and Cohen, *Medicaid: The Trade-Off Between Cost Containment and Access to Care*, Table 21; and Public Citizen Health Research Group, *Poor Health Care for Poor Americans: A Ranking of State Medicaid Programs*.

55.   Public Citizen Health Research Group, ibid. These programs include areas of enhanced service (maternal and child health and home-based personal care) and cost containment (prospective, case-mix reimbursement

system). See Holahan and Cohen, *Medicaid: The Trade-Off Between Cost Containment and Access to Care*, for a further discussion of cost containment.

56.   Anthony Pascal, Marilyn Cvitanic, and Charles Bennett, "State Policies and the Financing of Acquired Immunodeficiency Syndrome Care," *Health Care Financing Review* 11 (Fall 1989): 91–104.

57.   Cited in ibid., pp. 91–104.

58.   This estimate was made by Associated General Contractors of America, *America's Infrastructure: A Plan to Rebuild* (Washington, D.C.: Associated General Contractors, 1983); and Pat Choate, "House Wednesday Group Special Report on U.S. Economic Infrastructure," unpublished manuscript. Both are cited in Charles Hulten and George Peterson, "The Public Capital Stock: Needs, Trends and Performance," *American Economic Review* 74 (May 1984): 166–173. One of the most cited studies on infrastructure is Pat Choate and Susan Walter, *America in Ruins: Beyond the Public Works Pork Barrel* (Washington, D.C.: Council of State Planning Agencies, 1981).

59.   See Hulten and Peterson, ibid.; and John Kamensky, "Budgeting for State and Local Infrastructure: Developing a Strategy," *Public Budgeting & Finance* 4 (Autumn 1984): 3–17.

60.   For a good review of this issue related to highways in New York State, see New York State Legislative Commission on State-Local Relations, *New York's Highway System, a Vital Economic Asset* (Albany: New York State Legislative Commission on State-Local Relations, February 1986).

61.   The total losses from bridge replacement, traffic restoration, and lost revenues for businesses on I-90 are estimated to be $44 million. According to a spokesman for the New York State Thruway Authority, most of this is covered by insurance. In addition, there are liability cases for the ten casualties that are still pending as of July 1990.

62.   In 1980, it was estimated that 11.6 percent of minor roads and 75.0 percent of nonfederal aid bridges (mainly local) were in need of repair. This compares to 5 percent of major roads and 42 percent for federal aid bridges. U.S. Department of Transportation, Federal Highway Administration, *Highway Statistics 1981* (Washington, D.C.: Government Printing Office, 1981); and *Highway Bridge Replacement and Rehabilitation Program* (Washington, D.C.: Government Printing Office, 1980). For a good discussion of this problem, see New York State Legislative Commission on State-Local Relations, *New York's Highway System.*

63.   U.S. Department of Transportation, Federal Highway Administration, *Highway Bridge Replacement and Rehabilitation Program*, various years. As defined in these reports, "A structurally deficient bridge . . . is one that (1) has been restricted to light vehicles only, (2) is closed, or (3) requires immediate rehabilitation to remain open" (p. 6, Eighth Annual Report).

64.   The New York State Department of Transportation develops its own ratings of bridge condition. While the ratings show fewer deficient

bridges, they also indicate worsening conditions in the 1980s. The number of deficient bridges has increased from 38 percent of total bridges in 1979 to 48 percent in 1990. Based on information provided by the New York Department of Transportation. In 1990, 37 percent of state-controlled bridges were deficient compared to 55 percent of nonstate (local) bridges.

65. Out of the 110,000 miles of roads in New York State, only sixteen thousand are sampled as part of the Highway Performance Monitoring System (HPMS) used by the U.S. Department of Transportation (DOT). The sample is then "blown up" to the total sample by the type of road and volume of traffic on the road. These results are published by the U.S. Department of Transportation, Federal Highway Administration, *Highway Statistics* (Washington, D.C.: U.S. Government Printing Office, various years). In reviewing the highway condition data in the HPMS system for New York, we noticed some significant disparities between these results and those published by New York State as part of its pavement condition survey. Since New York's survey was of all miles of state-responsible roads, it was deemed to be more reliable and was used for this analysis. These results are published by the Planning Division of the New York Department of Transportation, *Pavement Condition of New York's Highways*.

66. These results are for the "Touring Route Survey," which consists of state-owned highways and certain non state-owned highways. New York State Department of Transportation, *Pavement Condition of New York's Highways* (Albany: New York Department of Transportation, various years).

67. Only New Jersey exceeds New York's per capita levels for employment (44 percent above the national average), and no state has higher per capita compensation.

68. For an analysis of the effect of court mandates on state and local correctional expenditures, see Linda Harriman and Jeffrey Straussman, "Do Judges Determine Budget Decisions? Federal Court Decisions in Prison Reform and State Spending for Corrections," *Public Administration Review* 43 (July/August 1983): 343–351; and Jeffrey Straussman and Kurt Thurmaier, "Budgeting Rights: The Case of Jail Litigation," *Public Budgeting & Finance* 9 (Summer 1989): 30–42.

69. U.S. Department of Justice, Bureau of Justice Statistics, *1984 Census of State Adult Correctional Facilities* (Washington, D.C.: U.S. Government Printing Office, 1987); and *Census of Local Jails, 1983* (Washington, D.C.: U.S. Government Printing Office, 1988).

70. New York State Legislative Commission on State-Local Relations, *New York's Police Service, Perspectives on the Issues* (Albany: New York State Legislative Commission on State-Local Relations, November 1985), Table 23.

71. U.S. Department of Justice, Office of Justice Programs, *1988 Drug Use Forecasting Annual Report* (Washington, D.C.: U.S. Department of Justice, March 1990).

72.   For a discussion of the changing nature of fire protection, see New York Department of State, Office of Fire Prevention and Control, *Fire in New York, 1986* (Albany: New York Department of State, 1987); and New York State Legislative Commission on State-Local Relations, *New York's Fire Protection System, Services in Transition* (Albany: New York State Legislative Commission on State-Local Relations, February 1988). These trends are occurring nationally as well. See Federal Emergency Management Agency, *Fire in the United States, 1984* (Washington, D.C.: U.S. Government Printing Office, 1987).

73.   For an excellent review of these changing roles, see New York State Legislative Commission on State-Local Relations, ibid.

74.   For a breakdown of local fire departments by government type and type of personnel hired, see William Duncombe, *Evaluation of Factors Affecting the Cost of Public Services with an Application for Fire Protection*, doctoral dissertation (Syracuse: Syracuse University, 1989).

75.   For example, Onondaga County in 1989 had an advertising campaign (which borrowed heavily from Albany County) to recruit volunteers.

76.   They attribute this problem to the changing demographic and economic structure in this country. Volunteer fire departments rely heavily on traditional social institutions to recruit and retain members, the job often being passed down between generations of the same family. Recruitment, particularly during the day, came mainly from blue-collar workers. With the decline of many rural villages and the growth of suburban communities with service-based economies, the social stability and economic structure that facilitated recruitment of volunteers has declined. See New York State Legislative Commission on State-Local Relations, *New York's Fire Protection System, Services in Transition*.

77.   One study finding this result was John Hilke, "The Impact of Volunteer Firefighters on Local Government Spending and Taxation," *Municipal Finance Journal* 7 (Winter 1986): 33–44.

78.   See Duncombe, *Evaluation of Factors Affecting the Cost of Public Services with an Application for Fire Protection*.

6

Fiscal Health and Responsiveness

The 1980s were a time when both the economy and tax base expanded in New York State. Instead of using this strong growth in tax capacity to reduce tax burdens, New York chose to use it to maintain its relatively large public sector in the 1980s. This is not an inherently bad public policy, but it does carry two important implications. One is the possibility of a decrease in the rate of economic growth as firms and individuals select locations with a more favorable tax climate. The other is the possibility of poor fiscal health, the subject of this chapter.

The first question to be examined here is: What did an expanding public sector imply for the fiscal health of state and local governments in New York? While the measurement of fiscal health or condition is admittedly a controversial subject, the examination of a variety of fiscal health indicators suggests that the underlying fiscal health of New York is around the national average and at the median for the Northeast region. It has enough fiscal capacity that it should be able to support average public services without undue strain. The decision by policymakers to provide better than average service levels has placed the actual fiscal position of the state in jeopardy. In addition, many central cities in New York continued in the 1980s to be "on the edge" of financial security.

The second question taken up in this chapter is: How has expenditure growth in the 1980s affected the ability of New York's public sector to respond to the prospective changes of the 1990s? A number of external factors may threaten the fiscal health of the state in this decade. By already expanding its public sector to what appears to be the limit, New York has reduced its ability to respond to external shocks, such as major cutbacks in federal aid, changes in federal tax and policy, and national economic fluctuations.

Fiscal Health

One of the most heavily investigated and controversial areas in public finance is state and local government fiscal health. What does it mean and how do we measure it? Numerous studies of fiscal health or condition have been motivated by a concern that particularly state governments and the older central cities have been adversely affected by changes in the macroeconomy, socioeconomic changes, and reductions in federal aid. The conclusions from this work, about who is distressed and who is not, vary depending on the question asked and on who is doing the asking. For example, the federal government may carry out a fiscal distress analysis to determine whether New York should receive a greater share of federal aid, but state officials may think of measuring distress in terms of budget balance or in terms of whether a proposed capital improvements program will be carried out. With this qualifier in mind, we can turn to the literature on fiscal health to ask how New York compares with the region and with the rest of the nation. Three types of fiscal health measures are considered: (1) surplus/deficit measures, which are of most direct concern to state and local officials; (2) bond ratings and debt ratios, which are of interest to lenders and investors; and (3) measures of underlying fiscal capacity and expenditure need, which attempt to abstract from the actual decisions of the governments.

Surplus/Deficit Measures

The question of most interest to state and local officials, and probably to the general public, is: "How are we going to balance the budget?" The place to begin an analysis of New York's position with regard to budgetary balance is with an analysis of national trends, that is, with an analysis of the surplus situation for the entire state and local government sector. The surplus or deficit position of the sector is estimated by the U.S. Bureau of Economic Analysis (BEA) and regularly reported in the National Income Accounts (NIA). Excluding revenues and expenditures of pension funds, the NIA surplus indicates, as summarized by Bahl, "the excess of current revenues and grants over all current and capital expenditures. A positive surplus indicates a net year-end savings and an amount available for debt retirement or for adding to cash balances. A negative surplus, or deficit, indicates that net borrowing must be undertaken to cover capital expenditures."[1]

The NIA surplus, not surprisingly, is sensitive to the business cycle, with deficits in recessions and surpluses in expansions. Using this measure of surplus, state and local governments during the first half of the 1980s appeared to be in relatively good shape.[2] Deficits were fairly small during the recessions of the early 1980s, and sizable surpluses were built up from 1984 to 1986 (averaging $12 billion a year in 1982 dollars). However, by the end of 1986, the state and local sector was in deficit. These deficits have continued to increase and reached $25 billion by 1989 (in 1982 dollars).[3] Most of the deficit was at the state government level (77 percent of the total in 1988).[4] The fiscal shortfalls facing New York at the end of the 1980s, then, were not out of step with what was happening in the entire state and local government sector.

STATE GOVERNMENTS. Unfortunately, the BEA does not disaggregate its surplus estimates for specific states or even regions of the country.[5] Individual states, of course, report their budgetary balances—to the general public and the legislature—but these are neither comparable across states nor with the NIA measure. For New York, though, it can be reported that there was a deficit in the General Fund for three consecutive years through fiscal year 1990.

Another approach is to consider changes in the stock of reserves, the fund balances, which a state holds. Several organizations do publish estimates of state General Fund balances on an annual basis.[6] While this is an incomplete picture of state finances (because it does not include other funds), the General Fund is usually the main focus of budget deliberations. As Gold notes in analyzing balances in the General Fund compared to all major funds from 1979 to 1983:

> . . . that it is best to focus primary attention on the General Fund if one is concerned about changes in state fiscal conditions. General Fund balances fluctuate much more than balances in most other funds. While the aggregate of other funds may have larger total balances than the General Fund, if the balances are relatively stable, they do not have to be considered.[7]

Using data from the National Conference of State Legislatures (NCSL) on General Fund balances, it is possible to analyze the posi-

tion of individual state governments in the 1980s. Table 38 presents
the end-of-year balances of the General Fund (and any "rainy day"
funds) as a percent of General Fund expenditures for northeastern
states. Though rules of thumb about the "right" balance to carry are
easily challenged, many analysts think of a benchmark of 5 percent as
a sufficient cushion to respond to fiscal emergencies. The General
Fund balances appeared to be cyclically sensitive in the 1980s. Only
one state nationally had a negative balance in 1980, but there were
eight states in this position in 1982. Close to thirty states were above
the 5 percent threshold in 1980; however, this dropped to ten states
by 1982. Especially hard hit were the energy states, which had
enjoyed sizable balances in the late 1970s.[8]

General Fund balances grew after 1982 and averaged 5.7 percent
of expenditures in 1989; this despite the relatively poor performance
of the energy states. Many Northeast and Midwest states, in particular, have enjoyed significant surpluses since 1984. The projections for

TABLE 38

State Year-end General Fund Balances[a]
As a Percent of General Fund Expenditure

	1978	1980	1982	1985	1988	1989 (Estimated)	1990 (Projected)
New York	0.1	0.1	0.0	0.5	0.2	0.0	0.0
Connecticut	4.9	0.0	–1.7	16.2	6.4	1.7	2.6
Maine	8.4	3.6	2.8	2.4	7.7	9.3	2.4
Massachusetts	5.5	1.1	1.6	2.0	0.0	0.1	0.0
New Hampshire	11.3	3.9	–2.4	11.5	7.2	4.9	5.3
New Jersey	7.0	5.9	2.0	10.6	7.8	6.8	1.1
Pennsylvania	–0.1	1.1	0.0	3.6	1.7	4.5	1.1
Rhode Island	3.7	5.2	0.0	5.6	10.1	3.6	2.5
Vermont	2.5	–3.1	0.0	–5.7	10.9	4.9	2.5
U.S. Average	NA	NA	NA	4.5	2.6	5.7	3.0

[a]Balances of General Fund and the rainy day fund, if one exists. Also includes
transfers to or from other funds.

Source: National Conference of State Legislatures, *State Budget Actions*,
various years. Information for years prior to 1982 was based on surveys by the
National Association of State Budget Officers.

1990, though, indicate a downturn in fund balances, especially among northeastern states. Only one state (New Hampshire) is projected to have a balance above 5 percent in 1990.

New York had little or no end-of-year balance during the 1980s. At least in the General Fund, little fiscal cushion has been accumulated for the 1990s. Certainly there has been no recent growth in the General Fund balance. New York State has incurred a cash-basis operating deficit in the General Fund for each of fiscal years 1988, 1989, and 1990.[9]

One might offer several explanations for this. The most obvious explanation, and the one that turns out to be correct, is that the deteriorating General Fund position reflects a generally deteriorating fiscal situation. Another possibility is that the General Fund position is a misleading barometer because it does not take into account transfers between funds, and New York may be holding large, unrestricted balances elsewhere. NCSL has recently begun reporting transfers to and from the General Fund. There have consistently been sizable transfers from the General Fund in New York to other funds. These transfers were between 5 and 7 percent of General Fund expenditures in 1987 and 1988 but dropped to 2 percent in 1989. New York does make transfers to several funds and holds significant balances in both the debt repayment and capital funds. Most of these transfers are for debt service purposes, and these monies are not sources of current revenue financing. Moreover, the combined balance sheet of all governmental funds showed an accumulated deficit of $1.6 billion in March 1989.[10]

What one can say from this analysis is that New York had pushed its fiscal condition to the edge by the end of the decade: tax rates were high, reserve balances were low, and there was a chronic budget deficit.

LOCAL GOVERNMENTS. During the 1970s and 1980s there has been concern that many central cities are fiscally distressed, that is, they are unable to finance an adequate level of public services. The causes of this situation have to do with the flight of high-income taxpayers to the suburbs, an old and deteriorating infrastructure, the loss of direct federal aid, and changes in demographic composition and economic structure. Because of the difficulty of defining an absolute measure of fiscal distress, most studies developed crude rankings of

cities based on a range of economic and fiscal indicators. These studies seem to be saying, "We cannot tell you how bad the situation is by
looking at the distress index for Buffalo, but we can tell you it is a
better or worse situation than in Newark."

Despite some variation in results,[11] most studies found that cities
in the Northeast or Midwest generally were among the most "distressed." For example, northeastern cities commonly included were
Boston, Buffalo, Hartford, Newark, New York City, Pittsburgh, and
Rochester.[12]

Some very interesting information on the financial condition of
large city governments in the 1980s is available in Dearborn's continuing studies of audited financial statements.[13] His estimates, summarized in Table 39, indicate that many large cities built a reasonably
comfortable financial position by the mid-1980s and that city financial
surpluses/deficits are cyclical, with the trough reached in the year after
a recession. He found that General Fund balances as a percent of
revenue more than doubled between 1976 and 1984. These results
led Dearborn to conclude that large cities in 1984 were "in perhaps
the best financial condition they have been in since 1971."[14]
Northeastern cities, on the other hand, did not fare nearly as well.
Those cities in his sample from the Northeast generally performed
poorly, with Boston and Buffalo in deficit and New York City and
Pittsburgh with very low surpluses during the 1980s.

The National League of Cities (NLC) did not reach as positive a
conclusion as Dearborn, but their survey of the actual and prospective
fiscal condition of 660 cities in 1984 to 1986 indicated surprising fiscal
strength.[15] More than one-half of all cities began 1986 with a General
Fund surplus in excess of 6 percent of total expenditures. Nearly 60
percent of the cities expected to use part of their existing balance to
finance 1986 operations. However, the results of their 1987 survey
indicated generally slower revenue growth and declining cash balances. Unfortunately, the NLC does not provide data on individual
cities so it is not possible to examine how New York cities have fared.

Bond Ratings and Debt Ratios

Another valuable perspective on the fiscal health of state and
local governments is that of the private sector.[16] This approach to
analyzing fiscal health focuses on whether a government is a good
place to invest money or to start or expand a business. Such an assess-

TABLE 39

Selected Major Cities' General Fiscal Condition
Balance (or Deficit) As a Percent of Total Revenues[a]

	1971	*1976*	*1981*	*1984*
Northeast:				
Boston	13.4	–10.7	–7.5	–6.0
Buffalo	2.1	–15.0	–0.3	0.0
New York City	–9.2	–31.1	0.5	0.1
Philadelphia	–6.1	–10.2	4.4	1.8
Pittsburgh	7.9	5.6	1.1	0.7
Unweighted Average	1.6	–12.3	–0.4	–0.7
Midwest: Unweighted Average (10 Cities)	–3.6	1.3	2.3	3.2
South: Unweighted Average (9 Cities)	8.7	8.8	9.3	6.4
West: Unweighted Average (6 Cities)	11.7	5.7	7.8	10.2
Unweighted Average (All Cities)	3.8	2.0	5.0	4.7

[a]Estimate of surplus (deficit) for all government funds. See source for description of limitations with these data and adjustments made to assure consistency.

Source: Philip Dearborn, "Fiscal Condition in Large American Cities, 1971–84," in Michael McGeary and Laurence Lynn, *Urban Change and Poverty* (Washington, D.C.: National Academy Press, 1988), Table 7.

ment encompasses not only an evaluation of economic health of the jurisdiction but whether the financial management practices of the government are sound. Are government officials willing to make the hard decisions to balance the budget and, most importantly, to avoid future financial emergencies? In theory, it is a forward-looking approach: it asks about the potential of a government to repay its debt over the life of the bond issue.

The most comprehensive private sector measures of government financial health are the credit ratings developed by Standard & Poor's and Moody's Investors Service. These ratings are an attempt to assess the overall creditworthiness of the government and involve the assessment of several factors: debt level and structure, financial condition and structure, administrative efficiency, and the strength of the economy.[17] While rating agencies collect and analyze significant amounts of financial and economic data, there is inevitably a large amount of subjective judgment involved. Rating agencies came under heavy criticism in the mid-1970s for the "black box" nature of this process, especially given the influence of these ratings on the interest rates paid by governments.[18] The weaknesses in such ratings were highlighted by the upgrading of New York City ratings right before the fiscal crisis of 1975.[19]

Since that time, rating agencies have been more open about rating decisions, and it is fair to say that there have been significant improvements in the quality of the rating process. The changing focus of rating agencies is reflected in the results of the numerous studies on the "determinants" of bond ratings. While early research found debt ratios to be the primary factor influencing bond ratings,[20] studies in the 1980s found economic factors to have the primary influence on bond ratings, followed by financial and debt variables.[21]

Whether or not bond ratings are an accurate assessment of fiscal health, these ratings are very influential in determining the marketability of government bonds and ultimately the interest rates jurisdictions must pay on their debt. Bond ratings from Moody's Investors Service for state governments in New York and its neighboring states, and for large cities in each state, are reported in Table 40. The highest ranking provided by Moody's is Aaa and the lowest C. Ratings in the A categories are generally considered favorable investments; B categories, medium grade; and C categories, poor credit risks.

New York State maintained a relatively low Moody's A rating for most of the 1980s. This rating was upgraded to A1 by 1988 but has recently been downgraded by both Standard & Poor's and Moody's. Standard & Poor's, in their notification of the downgrading, cited the fact that the "accumulated deficit will likely exceed $5 billion" and that there is a "lack of governmental consensus on the magnitude of the problem and the absence of a credible plan to address it in a fiscally responsible manner."[22] This downgrading does not appear to have rippled through to most local governments in New York, at least not yet.[23]

TABLE 40

Moody's Municipal Bond Ratings

For General Obligation Debt[a]

	1976	*1980*	*1982*	*1984*	*1988*	*1990*
New York:	A1	A	A	A	A1	A
Albany	A	Baa1	Baa1	Baa1	Baa1	A
Buffalo	Baa	Baa	Baa	Baa	Baa	Baa1
New York City	Caa	B	Ba1	Baa	Baa1	A
Rochester	Aaa	Aa	Aa	A1	A1	A1
Syracuse	Aa	Aa	Aa	Aa	Aa	Aa
Connecticut:	Aa	Aa	Aa	Aa	Aa1	Aa
Hartford	Aaa	Aa	Aa	A1	Aa	Aa
Massachusetts:	A1	A1	A1	A1	Aa	Baa
Boston	Aa	Baa	Ba	Ba1	Baa1	A
Springfield	Aa	A1	A1	A1	A	Baa
New Jersey:	Aa	Aaa	Aaa	Aaa	Aaa	Aaa
Newark	Baa	Baa	Baa	Baa	Baa	Baa1
Pennsylvania:	A1	A	A	A	A1	A1
Philadelphia	A	Baa	Baa	Baa	Baa	Ba
Pittsburgh	A1	Baa1	Baa1	Baa	Baa1	Baa1

[a]Credit rating by Moody's Investors Service for general obligation bond without bond insurance.

Source: Moody's Investors Service, *Municipal & Government Manual,* various years; and *Moody's Bond Record,* July 1990.

New York is not the only northeastern state to face dropping bond ratings. Massachusetts has had its bonds downgraded several times since 1988 and Connecticut's bonds were also downgraded in 1990. New Jersey was put on "creditwatch" by Standard & Poor's in early 1990, although as of mid-1990, its ratings had not decreased.[24] Some cities, including Springfield and Philadelphia, had their ratings reduced recently as well.

What do rating declines suggest about the fiscal health of a state or local government? This is difficult to determine without an insider's view of the rating process. For certain, the agencies are advising investors that there are relatively safer places to invest. However, because of the limited number of categories, bond ratings are fairly "blunt instruments" for assessing state and local government fiscal health. How much deterioration has occurred when a bond rating is lowered? It is fair to say that there is a preponderance of evidence that there are "fiscal problems" that either have not been resolved or not been addressed. It would appear that the recent downgrading of bonds in New York State is based on the assessment that New York has not been addressing mounting deficits over the last several years. It is somewhat ironic that New York's bond rating has been lowered at a time when its fiscal capacity has been increasing. The problem in the rating agencies' eyes would seem to be with New York's fiscal management.

A key factor in evaluating the creditworthiness of a government is the debt burden. This reflects a long-term commitment that can affect a community for decades. While there is justification for using long-term debt to spread payments for a project among future beneficiaries, if these debt burdens are too high, they imperil the future fiscal health of the government. Another important issue is the use of short-term debt. Since revenue collections may be "lumpy," it is part of sound financial management for a community to use short-term borrowing to even out its cash flow. If this debt grows as it rolls over into future years, though, it may indicate an improper use of short-term debt—the financing of operating expenditures. New York City's abuse of short-term borrowing is the classic case in point.[25]

It is no easy matter, theoretically or empirically, to determine whether a state or local government has borrowed too much. The most common approach to evaluating debt burdens is to develop a series of debt ratios and to check these against national benchmarks.[26] Using census data on debt for all state and local governments, we have developed a set of simple debt ratios for New York and neighboring states and compared these to the national average (Table 41). If long-term debt outstanding is adjusted for differences in personal income and tax capacity, New York is shown to have a higher debt burden than the national average and its neighboring states. However, the gap closed considerably during the 1980s, with New York only 20 to 30 percent above the national average in 1988.

Cash and investments (outside of insurance trust funds) were expressed as a share of total debt outstanding to provide a rough indicator of how much of long-term debt is covered by liquid assets. The lower the number, the poorer the coverage. New York is below the national average, as are most states in the Northeast. Short-term debt burden is defined here as the ratio of the amount outstanding to total own-source revenue. New York's use of short-term debt is double the national average but is in the median in comparison with neighboring states. Finally, to get at the debt drain on revenues, the following indicator was developed: the percent of own-source revenue claimed by debt service payments. By this measure, New York is at the national average, and relative debt service payments decreased considerably in the 1980s.[27] In summary, these results suggest that New York has long-term and short-term debt burdens well above the national average, but the gap decreased considerably in the 1980s. Tax-supported debt outstanding fell from 4.8 percent of personal income in 1980 to 4.2 percent in 1989. Short-term debt, however, has increased with the need to finance a recurring general fund deficit.

Fiscal Capacity and Expenditure Need

The surplus or balance measures provide valuable indicators of the actual fiscal health of a government, but they can disguise its underlying fiscal health. The finding of an operating surplus:

> ...could mean a buoyant revenue system and truly indicate fiscal health. On the other hand, the excess could reflect no more than a temporary embarrassment of riches resulting from service cutbacks, reductions in capital expenditures and employment, deferred compensation, and so on.[28]

In other words, information on budgetary surpluses or deficits does not necessarily tell us whether a jurisdiction has the financial capacity to provide an adequate level of public services in the future.[29]

For this reason, a significant body of research has addressed the "underlying" or "structural" fiscal health of a government. This research generally has broken fiscal health into two parts: the fiscal capacity of the community and its expenditure needs.[30] Fiscal capacity measures the potential revenue that a community could raise using

TABLE 41

Debt Ratio Indexes for Long-term and Short-term Debt[a]:
New York and Neighboring States

	New York	Connecticut	Massachusetts	New Jersey	Pennsylvania
Long-term Debt Outstanding/Personal Income:					
1970	136.0	106.9	89.4	79.3	113.2
1980	162.2	100.3	105.1	94.7	116.3
1988	121.8	80.1	88.6	93.6	108.6
Long-term Debt Outstanding/ACIR Tax Capacity[b]:					
1975	194.2	134.2	122.0	110.4	132.5
1980	203.1	113.9	121.6	109.2	131.4
1988	133.1	79.7	87.4	102.1	100.1
Cash + Investments/Long-term Debt Outstanding[c]:					
1970	81.6	71.9	58.5	113.3	65.0
1980	75.7	69.3	78.8	89.6	68.1
1988	78.6	87.7	78.7	99.6	82.3
Short-term Debt Outstanding/Own-source Revenue					
1970	291.2	422.8	137.0	157.6	72.5
1980	194.4	239.9	300.6	247.9	117.1
1988	216.2	122.7	271.6	225.3	114.6

Debt Service/Own-source
Revenue[d]:

1970	126.3	157.0	141.3	88.9	135.5
1980	182.0	143.3	125.4	103.1	128.0
1988	104.1	102.8	90.7	118.3	112.0

[a]Debt deflated using the implicit GNP deflator for state and local government purchases. National average equals 100.

[b]ACIR tax capacity estimates were not available for 1970; therefore, 1975 estimates were used as an alternative.

[c]All cash and security holdings except those for insurance trust funds.

[d]Since data on principal payments are not available, this is approximated with total long-term debt retired.

Source: U.S. Department of Commerce, Bureau of the Census, *Governmental Finances*, various years; and Advisory Commission on Intergovernmental Relations, *1986 State Fiscal Capacity and Effort*, Report M-165, March 1989, and unpublished data for 1988 provided by ACIR.

average tax rates or burdens on its citizens. Expenditure needs or cost indexes indicate the level of expenditures required to provide a standard package of public services of average quality. Both measures abstract from actual fiscal performance. As defined by Ladd and Yinger, "standardized fiscal health" is the difference between the revenue-raising or fiscal capacity of a community and "standardized expenditure need."[31]

In this section, we will present the available evidence on fiscal capacity, expenditure needs, and standardized fiscal health for the total state and local sector in New York and for specific local governments. In addition, we will examine the evidence on actual tax and expenditure burdens.

FISCAL CAPACITY.   The concentration of research on the measure of fiscal capacity is due to the general concern with equalization and to the use of such measures in federal and state grant distribution. We review three measures of fiscal capacity here, discuss their strengths and weaknesses, and use them to evaluate changes in fiscal capacity in New York.

The most obvious measure of the underlying fiscal capacity of a community is the income of its residents. All taxes and charges that fall on households must be paid either from their income or from their accumulated wealth. "Personal income" as estimated by the BEA includes income from wages and salaries, dividends, rents, interest, transfer payments, other labor income, and income of small proprietors (see chapter 3). Per capita personal income in New York as a percent of the U.S. average is presented in Table 42. These data suggest that New York has a tax capacity per capita that is 17 percent above the national average and that it rose significantly in the 1980s. The tax capacities are even higher in many neighboring states.

The use of personal income as a measure of fiscal capacity has been criticized. Part of the criticism is directed toward the fact that this is an incomplete measure of income.[32] Personal income does not measure some forms of imputed income or undistributed corporate income (that is, unrealized capital gains). Moreover, the personal income measure does not take into account the ability of communities to "export" taxes onto nonresidents. The best example of this is the energy states that can tax the use of their oil or gas reserves (often in the form of severance taxes). Most of this oil and gas is being con-

TABLE 42

State and Local Government Tax Capacity Indexes[a]
for the Northeastern States

	Per Capita Income		ACIR Tax Capacity		Per Capita Gross State Product	
	1980	*1988*	*1980*	*1988*	*1980*	*1986*
New York	108	117	90	109	102	117
Connecticut	122	140	112	143	109	127
Maine	83	92	80	98	77	85
Massachusetts	107	126	96	129	96	114
New Hampshire	99	118	97	126	86	104
New Jersey	117	133	105	124	102	117
Pennsylvania	100	98	93	94	90	89
Rhode Island	96	102	84	99	82	90
Vermont	86	93	85	105	81	92

[a]National average equals 100.

Source: U.S. Department of Commerce, Bureau of Economic Analysis, *Survey of Current Business*, August 1987 and 1989 and May 1990; and Advisory Commission on Intergovernmental Relations, *1986 State Fiscal Capacity and Effort*, Report M-165, March 1989, and unpublished data for 1988 provided by the ACIR.

sumed outside the state, so it is likely that the bulk of the taxes are paid either by out-of-state consumers or owners of the firm. Personal income of state residents is a measure that would miss this tax advantage. The ability to export taxes can significantly increase the tax capacity of certain energy or tourist states.

One measure that partially corrects for exporting is "gross state product" (GSP), developed by the BEA. It is defined as "the gross market value of the goods and services attributable to labor and property located in a state. It is the state counterpart of the nation's gross domestic product."[33] By taking into account the output generated by firms in a state, whether owned by state residents or not, GSP partially controls for tax exporting.[34] The GSP is not without its weaknesses, however. It excludes some forms of income (transfer payments) and wealth (real property), which are in the tax bases of state and local governments. Using per capita GSP, New York would appear to have had an even stronger growth in fiscal capacity, rising from 2 percent above the national average in 1980 to 17 percent above in 1986 (see Table 42). This increase may be partially accounted for by significant growth in international and domestic financial services in New York City, which is counted as part of the state's "output."

The Advisory Commission on Intergovernmental Relations (ACIR) has developed a measure of tax capacity that more directly attempts to estimate the capacity to raise revenue from each of the most common state and local taxes. As discussed in chapter 4, the ACIR estimates the amount of revenue that a "representative tax system" (RTS) would yield if average tax rates were used in every state. The advantage of this measure is that it allows for estimates of tax capacity for individual taxes and it takes account of the ability of states to "export" taxes through the use of special severance or tourist taxes. By the RTS measure, New York's tax capacity grew from 10 percent below the national average in 1980 to 9 percent above by 1988.[35] Using any of these measures, New York's per capita fiscal capacity grew significantly during the 1980s and is now 10 to 20 percent above the national average.

New York's ability to finance taxes has clearly gone up. What has happened to actual tax burdens, that is, to what extent has this increase in taxable capacity been used? Total state and local taxes per dollar of each of the measures of tax capacity, as a percent of the U.S. average, can be used as measures of tax effort. New York's *relative* tax burden went up slightly with respect to personal income but had fallen in the 1980s for the other two measures. Tax effort dropped from between 40 and 60 percent above the national average in 1980 to between 30 and 50 percent above in 1988. One cannot get too euphoric about this finding because New York's tax effort, by all of these measures, remained one of the highest in the nation and quite far out of line with the average practice.

EXPENDITURE NEED AND FISCAL HEALTH.   It is not just the capacity to raise taxes that determines fiscal health. This needs to be set against the expenditure claims on this revenue. Ideally, the second part of a fiscal health measure would be an estimate of the cost of providing some average bundle of public services. This measure should capture the fact that it can be more expensive to provide a given quality of service in some communities than others.

These higher costs can be partially due to higher prices for the resources that a government uses in producing its services (for example, public employee salaries). In addition, some communities have a more harsh environment for producing services, and this can also affect costs.[36] For instance, it is clearly less expensive (per capita) to provide a given level of "public safety" in a wealthy suburb than in a large central city. Expenditure need or cost indexes must reflect both of these sets of factors. There have been several attempts to estimate expenditure need indexes and measures of standardized fiscal health. Evidence from these studies for New York State is presented below.

As discussed in chapter 4, Robert Rafuse of the ACIR has developed estimates of expenditure needs using work load measures.[37] His measures of "representative expenditures" closely parallel the representative tax system developed by the ACIR. Essentially, he has collected information on the recipients of different public services and used this to construct work load indexes by service and state. He then divides the total national expenditures for each public service (for example, on highways) by the total work load (for instance, miles of road) to develop a national average "unit cost" measure. The final step is to multiply this average unit cost by the actual work loads in each state. The result is an estimate of the expenditures required to provide public services of average quality in each state.

The estimates of total expenditure needs by state for 1984 are presented in index form in column 2 of Table 43. Surprisingly, New York has an expenditure need or cost index (96) slightly below the national average (100). This is a composite number: New York is estimated to have public service costs for welfare and public safety close to 10 percent above the national average; costs for education and health around the average; and highway expenditure needs only 60 percent of the national average. The low highway needs estimate was due undoubtedly to the relatively low level of highway mileage per capita in the state.[38]

Using this index of expenditure need and the RTS index of tax capacity, it is possible to construct a measure of relative "potential" fiscal health for state and local governments in New York. This is found by subtracting expenditure needs from tax capacity and dividing by tax capacity. After normalizing the result around a mean of 100, the resulting index indicates whether a state imposing national average tax burdens can provide public services of national average quality. A value above 100 indicates strong fiscal health and below 100 relatively

TABLE 43

State and Local Government Expenditure Need, Effort, and Fiscal Health Indexes[a]: For the Northeastern States

	Fiscal Health Index (1984)[b]			Representative Expenditure (1984)[c]	Expenditure Effort Indexes Per Dollar of Income[d]		
	ACIR Tax Capacity	Expenditure Need	Fiscal Health		1980	1984	1988
New York	98	96	100	148	126	125	126
Connecticut	124	88	129	115	80	78	82
Maine	88	102	87	89	105	107	103
Massachusetts	111	91	115	115	103	90	91
New Hampshire	110	93	113	87	84	77	72
New Jersey	114	91	119	118	89	87	87
Pennsylvania	88	92	97	94	91	89	90
Rhode Island	86	91	95	122	113	112	104
Vermont	95	100	93	104	114	119	110

[a]National average equals 100.
[b]Fiscal health index is calculated by subtracting the ACIR tax capacity from representative expenditure needs per capita, that is, the per capita gap in capacity. This gap is then divided by per capita tax capacity.
[c]Direct general expenditures per capita divided by per capita representative expenditures.
[d]Direct general expenditures per capita divided by personal income per capita.

Source: U.S. Department of Commerce, Bureau of Economic Analysis, Survey of Current Business, August 1987 and 1989; Bureau of the Census, Governmental Finances, various years; Robert Rafuse, "A Representative-Expenditure Approach to the Measurement of the Cost of the Service Responsibilities of States," in Federal-State-Local Fiscal Relations, Technical Papers, Vol. 1 (Washington, D.C.: U.S. Department of Treasury, 1986); and the Advisory Commission on Intergovernmental Relations, 1986 State Fiscal Capacity and Effort, Report M-165, March 1989.

poor fiscal health. The result, for 1984, suggests that New York is in average fiscal health (an index of 100 in Table 43). Again, it is important to emphasize what this finding does and does not mean. It does mean that New York should be able to provide an average level of public services and tax at a rate no higher than the national average. By contrast, all neighboring states, except Pennsylvania, enjoy above-average fiscal health, that is, at an average level of tax effort they could provide an above-average level of public services. There is tremendous variation in fiscal health, ranging from Colorado (120) to Alabama (49).

Actual expenditures in New York were of course higher than those expected by almost any standard. Dividing actual expenditures by either representative expenditures (column 4 in Table 43) or personal income (columns 5 to 7) shows that New York continued in the 1980s to have expenditure levels well above the national average and above those of most other states. The ratio of actual expenditures to expected expenditures, according to the Rafuse index, suggests that New York actually spent 48 percent more than would have been expected if the goal were to provide an average level of public services. The crucial issue is whether these higher expenditures indicate higher quality services or just the higher costs of providing the same quality service in New York. While we are not able to come to any definitive conclusion, it appears that both factors account for New York's higher expenditures. Rafuse's measures correct for higher factor prices in New York; however, they do not appear to take into account the effects of a harsher environment on costs. With a large poverty population generally located in older central cities, and an older infrastructure, New York State (and its cities) would appear to have a much harsher environment for the provision of services, such as public education, public safety, welfare, and highways.

Ladd and Yinger have attempted to control for the impact of the environment on costs in developing indexes of fiscal health for large American cities.[39] They developed a cost index that controlled both for factor prices and important "environmental factors" and subtracted this from an estimate of fiscal capacity[40] to produce a measure of "standardized fiscal health." The results for major cities in the Northeast for 1972 and 1982 are presented in columns 1 and 2 of Table 44.[41] These indexes are standardized around the national average in 1972 so that it is possible to examine both the relative health of the city in one year and how fiscal health has changed over time.[42]

TABLE 44

Fiscal Health Indexes for Major Northeastern Cities[a]

	Standardized[b]		Actual[c]	
	1972	1982	1972	1982
Albany	16.2	8.8	9.9	30.2
Boston	−5.1	−11.9	−28.8	2.3
Buffalo	−25.7	−52.6	−19.0	−26.2
Hartford	7.0	−15.0	3.5	1.3
New York City	−81.5	−104.6	−71.1	−63.2
Newark	−31.9	−109.7	7.6	−21.5
Philadelphia	−34.9	−59.9	−3.6	−23.1
Pittsburgh	−10.6	−7.8	−5.3	−34.7
Providence	−1.1	−11.2	2.0	11.3
Rochester	−5.4	−0.4	−35.8	−21.1
National Average	0.0	−10.9	0.0	−4.9

[a]The index is standardized around the average for all cities in 1972. Indexes for a city indicate how the fiscal health of that city compares to the average for 1972.

[b]Standardized fiscal health is the difference between the underlying revenue-raising capacity and expenditure needs of a city, not the actual fiscal behavior of city officials.

[c]Actual fiscal health is the difference between the "restricted" revenue-raising capacity (which takes into account actual taxes available and grants) and actual expenditure needs (which adjusts for differences in service responsibilities).

Source: Helen Ladd and John Yinger, *America's Ailing Cities: Fiscal Health and the Design of Urban Policy* (Baltimore: The Johns Hopkins University Press, 1989), Tables A5.1 and A9.1.

The results indicate that, on average, the standardized fiscal condition of all cities was about 11 percent worse in 1982 than in 1972. This declining fiscal health was primarily due to the deteriorating economic base in some major cities. The decline in standardized fiscal health was especially dramatic for Buffalo, New York City, Newark, and Philadelphia. Using this measure, New York City had the second worst underlying fiscal health in 1982 and Buffalo ranked seventh worst. Of the other New York cities in the sample, Albany's fiscal health between 1972 and 1982 was above the national average, while Rochester's fiscal health improved slightly but remained below average. These results indicate how important a harsh socioeconomic environment is on both fiscal capacity and costs.

Ladd and Yinger also estimated what they called "actual fiscal health."[43] This measure attempts to control for the actual fiscal institutions that exist in a state. For example, fiscal capacity is adjusted for the actual taxes available to a local government and the impact of state aid, and expenditure needs are adjusted for the actual service responsibilities of a city. A comparison of standardized and actual fiscal health estimates (the latter are reported in columns 3 and 4) indicates whether state fiscal institutions improve or decrease the fiscal health of a city. It is clear from Table 44 that states have lessened the fiscal distress of many central cities through their use of state aid and assignment of tax bases and service responsibilities. With this adjustment, the actual fiscal health of Albany, Boston, Hartford, and Providence was above the national average in 1972 and 1982. In contrast, the actual fiscal health of Buffalo, New York City, Newark, Philadelphia, Pittsburgh, and Rochester was significantly worse than average in 1982.

Fiscal Health Conclusions

The results of this review of fiscal health measures of New York and the Northeast are mixed. Rafuse's estimates of fiscal health for all state and local governments suggest that New York has an average underlying fiscal health. Ladd and Yinger's estimates, on the other hand, indicate that central cities in the Northeast are in worse fiscal health than Rafuse's estimates would suggest. Having particular problems were New York City and Buffalo. Unfortunately, both estimates stop in the mid-1980s, so it is difficult to tell how New York State and its local governments have fared in the economic expansion during most of the past decade.

Fiscal Responsiveness

While the high tax burdens in New York do not necessarily imply poor fiscal health or a poor business climate, they do indicate that New York has chosen to live on the financial edge of its resources. By choosing not to adopt a more conservative fiscal philosophy, New York has left itself little maneuvering room to adjust to future financial emergencies. This strategy inevitably intensifies the debate surrounding every fiscal decision: It would be fair to say that it will be difficult for New York to further increase taxes without potential political and economic consequences.

The fiscal position of New York, like that in most states, will be as significantly affected in the 1990s by uncontrollable, external events as by its own policy initiatives. Those states least able to accommodate these shocks will face the tightest fiscal constraints. New York may be among the more vulnerable. This would suggest that New York needs to build a fiscal cushion in order to withstand these shocks and to accommodate the fiscal implications of structural changes that are under way. Those states with least pressure to build a fiscal margin are those where economic growth will be rapid enough to cover both external shocks and internal policy mistakes.

In examining this hypothesis, we take up several issues that will at least partly shape the fiscal health of New York in the 1990s. The state will not be able to significantly bend these trends, at least in the short run, and the issue will be the way in which the fiscal behavior in New York is adjusted to deal with these external influences. The external events we consider here are federal aid reduction; federal macroeconomic policy; the longer run effects of the 1986 federal tax reform; state industrial policy; and poverty and the underclass.

Federal Aid Reduction

As discussed in chapter 4, real or inflation-adjusted federal grants to state and local governments (in 1982 dollars) fell from $109.7 billion in 1978 to an estimated $93.4 billion in 1989.[44] While most of the reductions took place in fiscal years 1982 and 1983, there has been little growth in real federal aid since 1985. Most of the growth that did take place was in entitlement programs for welfare and health—more than 3 percent per year from 1980 to 1989. In contrast, federal capital grants declined by more than 2 percent per year during the 1980s.

The narrative in the 1991 federal budget projects that there will be slow growth in real federal aid from 1989 to 1995.[45] Given the present federal budget crisis, even these projections may be optimistic. Based on a continuation of past trends, real grants to individuals are projected to grow by close to 5 percent per year while capital grants are projected to decrease by 6 percent per year. However, growth in entitlement grants is projected to be concentrated in Medicaid, with a growth rate of 6.6 percent per year. Medicaid is expected to grow from 28 percent of federal aid in 1989 to 38 percent in 1995. Grants for family support—AFDC—are expected to show almost no growth once adjusted for inflation during the next five years. This compares to a growth of 3 percent per year from 1985 to 1989. Finally, highway grants are expected to continue decreasing in real terms, more than 4 percent per year.

How will New Yorkers fare in the competition for what is likely to be little growth (in real terms) in federal aid? Historically, at least, New York's governments have been affected less severely than governments in the rest of the nation (as discussed in chapter 4) because of their concentration in welfare grants. While Medicaid grants are projected to continue their strong growth, this is not the case for AFDC. New York, with a rapidly growing population of poor households with children, is likely to be adversely affected by the slow growth in AFDC payments.

A second reason New Yorkers have avoided some of the consequences of federal aid retrenchment is their strong representation in Congress. New York's real per capita federal aid was $556 in 1988, 46 percent above the national average (third highest state in the country), notwithstanding the fact that its per capita income was 17 percent above the national average. Excluding public welfare, New York's per capita federal aid was actually below the national average in 1988. The number of New York's representatives, their congressional seniority, and their membership on the House Ways and Means and Senate Finance committees are factors contributing to the city's (and state's) competitive advantage in securing federal aid.[46] With relatively slow population growth in the 1980s, New York will lose a significant amount of its political influence in Congress after the next round of reapportionment.

Federal Macroeconomic Policy

Deficit reduction is almost certainly on the federal agenda, and the fiscal position of New York state and local governments will be significantly impacted by the way in which the federal government chooses to deal with the budget deficits in the coming years. The choices would seem to be further reduction in federal grants, expenditure reduction in both defense and domestic programs, elimination of certain tax expenditures (preferential tax treatments that impose a revenue loss), and tax increase.

As noted above, the next round of reductions in federal aid to state and local governments will almost certainly cut New York more deeply than has been the case in the past. Reductions in direct federal expenditures will have a similar effect. New York receives approximately the national average per capita amount in direct federal expenditures, and New York firms have benefited significantly from primary and secondary defense contracts.

Another federal deficit reduction strategy is to reduce tax expenditures. If this is a direction in which the administration chooses to move, the deductibility of state and local government income and property taxes could be likely targets. The 1986 tax reform has already eroded much of the value of these deductions by reducing the marginal rate and by reducing the number of itemizers. Because of this, the political opposition to eliminating these tax expenditures may not be as great this time around. Removing the remainder of the deductibility subsidy would increase the overall tax burden on state taxpayers who itemize. This would probably have the net effect of making taxpayers much more resistant to discretionary rate increases by state and local governments and, hence, would probably dampen the growth in state and local government budgets. Such action would disproportionately hurt higher taxing states and those that rely more heavily on individual income taxes, such as New York. New York's tax burden is 30 to 50 percent out of line, and the gap would increase with reduction in the subsidy, making New York's competitive position even weaker.

The least talked about (by the White House) deficit reduction measure is a tax increase. This may not harm the New York fisc as much as the other possibilities. Often discussed is a federal energy tax on consumption of oil products. This will affect New York's fiscal position in two ways: first, it is in competition for the gasoline tax base with the state government and it is a drain on personal income; second, it will increase the price of energy, which is already quite high in New York. An increased personal income tax rate, the standard remedy for a deficit, will increase the value of deductibility to New York State itemizers and increase the extent to which the federal government subsidizes New York's higher level of state and local government taxes. However, it also would reduce the amount of disposable income, the base that state and local governments ultimately tax. A national value-added tax would contain no such subsidy but would be a net drain on the total amount of income that would be available for state and local government taxation.

The 1986 Tax Reform

The centerpiece of the 1986 federal tax reform (TRA86) was reduction of the top marginal tax rate and introduction of a "three-rate" system of 15, 28, and 33 percent. An analysis of the implications of TRA86 for state and local government finances suggests the need to consider a "price effect" and an "income effect." With respect to the former, reductions in federal tax rates decrease the value to taxpayers of federal deductions for state and local government taxes and municipal bond interest. Considering that the top marginal tax rate was 70 percent as recently as 1980, it is clear that the "price" of state and local government services has increased dramatically for itemizers who previously could shift a much larger share of their state and local taxes to the federal government (Box 12). This price effect is reinforced by the elimination of deductibility of state and local government sales taxes.[47]

The other potential effect is an increase in the disposable income of taxpayers, that is, with lower federal tax rates, the taxpayer will now have more money with which to buy other goods, including state and local government services.[48] In fact, there was a revenue windfall in the first year (for states that used the federal base) because the base for state income taxes was automatically broadened. This was a one-time gain, though, and the overall effect of the reform was revenue-neutral (if business taxes are taken into account) or there actually may have been a reduction in after-federal-tax income if payroll taxes are considered.

The bigger questions, then, have to do with the price effects of TRA86 and its implications. Fiscal planners in New York would do well to consider two important implications: the prospects for less revenue growth and for more competition between central city and suburbs for state aid.

REVENUE GROWTH. Whether the revenue-enhancing "income effects" of expected economic growth or the revenue-dampening "price effects" of lower federal tax deductions and rates will dominate

---

**Box 12. The Federal Tax Reform and the
Reduction of the Tax Price in New York**

How much does payment of a tax dollar cost an individual? A simple answer might be had from the formula:

$$P = (1 - dr)$$

where P = the price of a state and local tax dollar
    d = the percentage of the tax that is deductible
    r = the federal marginal income tax rate

If an individual does not itemize, or if we are considering sales taxes or user charges (which are not deductible), then d = 0 and P = 1. That is, the price a person must pay for \$1 in state and local government expenditures is \$1 in taxes. If the tax is fully deductible and the marginal tax rate is 28 percent, P = .72.

For a more detailed exposition of the potential price effects, see Paul N. Courant and Daniel Rubinfeld, "Tax Reform: Implications for the State-Local Public Sector," *Journal of Economic Perspectives* 1 (Summer 1987): 87–100.

---

is still an open question. The strength of the price effect depends on two things: the change in the tax price and the price elasticity of demand for state and local government services. By how much has the government expenditure price (P) risen in New York? We can roughly estimate this from the formula:

$$P = \frac{(E - F) \times (1 - dr)}{E}$$

where E = expenditures
    F = federal aid
    r = marginal tax rate
    d = percent of state revenues that are deductible

The marginal federal tax rate faced by the average New York taxpayer is 15 percent,[49] 40 percent of state and local government taxes are deductible, and federal aid accounts for 12 percent of total state and local government expenditures. By this computation, the price of \$1 of government expenditure in 1988 was eighty-three cents. The same computation in 1980 would show a tax price of seventy-three cents. The price of a dollar of state and local government expenditures rose by 13 percent because of a combination of federal aid reductions, elimination of sales tax deductibility, and reduction in the federal tax rate. Is this tax price higher in New York than in the rest of the country, and has it risen by more? The comparable tax price for all state and local governments rose from seventy-four cents in 1980 to eighty-two cents in 1988, a 10 percent increase.

A reasonable hypothesis is that the increased cost of local government will lead to more resistance to tax increases in New York because New Yorkers pay higher taxes and itemize more than taxpayers generally.[50] In fact, the same computation as above shows that the higher price of state and local taxes for those who itemize will, all else being equal, reduce the demand for public services. The question is, by how much? There is considerable disagreement around this subject, and no clear answer has yet emerged.[51] A reasonable proposition, based on historical behavior, is that the demand for state and local government services is more price inelastic in New York than in the rest of the country, that is, that the increased tax price will have less of a dampening effect. Still, there will be some increased resistance to state tax increases; coupled with federal aid cuts, this suggests that the amount of state revenues available for local government assistance also will be reduced.

A longer run revenue-dampening effect will come from the 1987 New York State and New York City income tax reforms. These changes will reduce the revenue responsiveness to economic growth or the elasticity of their tax systems: they reduce rate progressivity (and, hence, revenue increases due to "bracket creep") and eliminate the higher rate on unearned income. Since income from property sources, notably dividends, interest, and rents, is the fastest growing component of personal income, lower tax elasticity is the likely result.

The growth of local property tax revenues may also be dampened. Lower marginal income tax rates and the disallowance of "passive" real estate losses as offsets against regular income reduce subsidies both to housing consumption and investment. On the consumption side, this may reduce the demand for homes among itemizers, which, in turn, would reduce growth in real estate values and the property tax base.[52] On the investment side, removal of tax preferences for new plant and equipment may discourage new construction. Thus, both components of growth in the property tax base, new construction and reassessment, would be dampened.

Federal tax reform should result in a shift of investment from manufacturing to the service sector. This results because the 1986 reform removed investment subsidies that benefited manufacturers disproportionately because they invest relatively more in plant and equipment. The negative effects of this change will be felt most deeply in the manufacturing belt in upstate New York. The New York City economy, with 86 percent of its employment outside the goods-producing sector, should benefit from this shift in investment.

INCREASED CITY-SUBURBAN COMPETITION. Another consequence of federal tax reform could be increased competition between cities and suburbs for a smaller pot of state aid money. This could result if (1) there is slowed growth in state government revenues as discussed above and/or (2) the "price" of local government services rises more in suburbs than in central cities. The growth in state revenues will almost certainly slow, as a result of federal aid reductions, the rising tax price, other federal reform issues described above, and state policies that have lowered the income elasticity of the income tax. Whatever the revenue effect turns out to be, history suggests that state aid to localities will grow even more slowly.[53] State aid to local governments as a percentage of total state government spending decreased from 45 percent in 1980 to 36 percent in 1988.[54]

The second half of the competition story is that it will be more difficult for local officials to use property taxes to pick up the slack from slow growth in federal aid and state assistance. This will be especially true for elected suburban government officials. Because capital-intensive firms, which increasingly locate in the suburbs, already will have experienced a significant tax increase by removal of investment tax preferences under TRA86, they will strongly resist further local tax hikes. Tax increases also will be opposed staunchly by homeowners whose benefits from property tax and home interest deductibility were reduced by the federal reforms. The net cost of their state and local taxes has been estimated to increase by as much as 10 to 20 percent, which contrasts with the effect on (largely nonitemizing) renters who will benefit disproportionately from income tax relief.[55] Since more than 70 percent of suburban housing is in owner-occupied dwellings (compared to less than 30 percent in New York City), suburban residents will experience disproportionately high property tax increases.[56]

This skewing against suburban property owners—individuals and firms alike—may cause them to increase their pressure on state officials for relief in the form of increased aid, especially school aid. Such proposals are not likely to fall on deaf ears in the suburban-dominated state legislature. Since the residents of cities do not suffer as much as suburbanites from the federal reforms related to property taxes, suburbanites may have a strong case for compensatory changes in state allocations. If the increased state aid is "funded" from cuts in social programs, city residents will be doubly damned.

State Industrial Policy

President George Bush's administration has made it clear that there will not be a national industrial policy, that is, the government will not attempt to pick winners. This leaves it to state and local governments to decide on whether and how they will compete with one another for industry. If the competition takes the form of pre-ferential tax treatment and industrial subsidies, which it usually does, then there is the question of how it is to be paid for.

New York's participation in tax incentive programs is somewhat of a paradox. The taxes levied in New York are at the highest rates in the nation. Some of this is then given back in the form of tax forgive-ness or tax expenditures, which narrows the tax base and forces up the tax rate. The cost of the incentive programs, then, is borne by some combination of a higher general rate of tax and a diversion of expendi-tures toward economic development purposes. This is one more explanation of why New York's tax burdens are so out of line with the rest of the country.

The other way to compete is with generally lower tax rates. While there is no consensus that lower taxes promote economic development, many would argue that New York is a special case because its taxes are so high and because there is uncertainty about what the fiscal future may hold. Moreover, the adverse consequences of New York's high tax burdens may be exacerbated by federal tax reform. The general competitive position (relative to New York) of states with lower taxes, fewer itemizers, and no income taxes will be improved. Before the New York State and New York City income tax reforms were announced, estimates were that the 1986 federal tax reform would cause high-income residents to experience a 5 percent tax increase if they lived in New York City, whereas they would enjoy a 4 percent reduction if they lived in New Jersey or Connecticut.[57] The ACIR estimated that New York State residents would experience a 9 percent increase in personal income tax liabilities due to the federal reform if the state made no windfall adjustments; it classified New York as one of fourteen states whose residents would have a large increase.[58]

What would be the outline of an industrial policy for New York State and New York City that is designed to recapture losses in competitive position resulting from its own fiscal policies and perhaps from the federal tax reform? With respect to taxes, the top priority would be to lower marginal tax rates in the top brackets to ameliorate against what many believe is the chief deterrent to New York locations.[59] Another option would be to reimburse some of the losers from the federal reform, particularly manufacturers. With respect to expenditures, priorities would be shifted toward infrastructure investments, which help industry generally, and to industry-specific uses, such as investments in the scientific capacity of universities, in order to stimulate and attract high-tech activities.

It would be difficult to provide hard evidence that would support such a package of reforms. The benefits are unsure and the costs are high. The marginal income tax reductions under way in New York probably do move the state toward a healthier business climate. Moreover, the reduced progressivity in the income tax will reduce its automatic growth and indirectly limit the growth in state government. Most would agree that these are needed changes and that they benefit all taxpayers, but to target industrial sectors, such as manufacturers, for tax preferences, to subsidize inefficient firms to stay in the state, and to chase high-tech activities with incentive packages are strategies where the net returns may be very small.

The costs, on the other hand, can be great. Taxes on all other activities will be higher to make up for revenues given away on the incentive program or competing social programs will not be financed because of these economic development initiatives. From the perspective of the New York state budget, the implication is that cities would suffer because economic development policies are neither pro-urban nor pro-poor.[60]

Effects on Poor People

Despite the income growth in New York in the 1980s, and despite the fact that per capita income in the state is 17 percent above the national average, New York State appears to have a disproportionately heavy concentration of the poor. Unfortunately, there are no current data on income distribution, so we developed our own estimate of poverty rates (see Table 20, chapter 4). New York's poverty rate in 1990 is estimated to have been 15 percent, compared to 13.5 percent nationally. Assuming trends in the 1980s continue, we project that the rate will reach 15.6 percent in New York by the turn of the century. This growth will be driven by rapid growth in female-headed and minority households that historically have had higher incidences of poverty.

The concentration of the poor in New York State is partially uncontrollable in that its origins may be traced to a national economy that has not produced enough jobs for unskilled workers, the growth in female-headed households, access to jobs, drug abuse, and (some would say) a low minimum wage.[61] Some of these causal factors are beyond the control of state and local governments, which is why the ultimate solution to the poverty problem requires a national policy. This does not say, though, that New York state and local governments cannot do a great deal to alleviate the problem and improve the quality of life of low-income families. Indeed, some aspects of the poverty problem **require** adjustments in local policies. Consider three issues. First, some see the root cause of joblessness among the urban poor as having to do with a skills mismatch—an education system that has not properly trained one segment of the population for the jobs of the 1980s.[62] Others see the problem as access, in that low-skill jobs are increasingly locating in the suburbs and some combination of fiscal zoning, housing discrimination, inadequate public transportation, and the social alienation of a white suburban workplace all conspire to perpetuate joblessness among inner city blacks.[63] Both of these underlying causes call state and local government responsibilities into question: education, transportation, zoning, and interlocal cooperation. A third issue is public assistance policy. It is unclear whether New York's generous programs of maintenance have helped the problem as much as was intended. There are arguments that the security of high welfare benefits in New York held poor families there at a time when they should have been encouraged to migrate to other parts of the country where long-run economic opportunities might have been better.

The story, then, is that the obligation to provide services to the poor constitutes an important claim on New York state and local budgetary resources. An interesting question is whether the federal tax reform helped or hurt New York's ability to provide services to its poor. One answer is that the urban poor are affected only indirectly by federal tax reform because they typically do not pay income taxes. Another is that it is the potential indirect effects that are most important. The long-run income elasticity of the reformed federal income tax will be lower, which suggests that its revenue yield will be lower (unless offset by higher rates of national economic growth). This implies, in general, less federal revenue to allocate, which in turn probably implies more federal aid cuts and reductions in income-maintenance programs. The New York State income tax will be less income elastic, with similar implications for state aid and for direct urban social spending. These fiscal prospects do not bode well for solutions to the already grim poverty problem, particularly in New York City. Recent proposals to alleviate poverty call for major new spending initiatives to improve the basic living conditions for poor New Yorkers,[64] but the state and city may not be able to raise the new funds without adding to the already high level of taxation or diverting funds for some other purpose. Likewise, what may be the more fundamental education skills and transportation dimensions of the problem will be less well addressed.

There are more optimistic notes about poverty alleviation. Federal, state, and city changes in the income tax removed many low-income New Yorkers from the tax rolls and had a direct effect on the take-home pay of low-skill workers. The most hopeful of scenarios about tax reform and poverty is that the stress on fiscal restraint and other economic development measures may stimulate growth in the national and local economies—raising the lot of the poor like boats on a rising tide. However, New York City's record in the 1980s, as well as that of other cities, suggests that the rising-tide argument is wishful thinking.[65] Economic expansion is most likely to occur in the service sector, where the skills mismatch between resident laborers and local jobs appears to be growing even more substantial.[66] If tax reform accelerates the relocation of manufacturers, the attendant upgrading of the local economy may cause the city's poor to face even greater employment problems.

Conclusions

The detailed review of fiscal health measures in this chapter has provided mixed evidence on the fiscal condition of New York's state and local governments at the end of the 1980s. Measures of the underlying health of the state and local government sector place New York at about the national average, that is, its underlying fiscal capacity is just large enough to allow it to support an average level of public services at an average tax rate. This represents some improvement in underlying fiscal health, largely due to the rapid income and fiscal capacity growth in the state in the 1980s. The actual performance of the New York fiscal condition is much less favorable. Expenditures were well above normal levels, the tax rates were among the highest in the nation, and the 1980s ended with three successive general fund deficits. It would not be farfetched to say that New York State has chosen to live near the financial edge.

What is less clear is how the changing demographics and economic structure in the state will affect the cost of providing public services. Ladd and Yinger's estimate for central cities in New York would suggest that a rising poverty population is likely to significantly increase the cost of providing high-quality social and educational services in the 1990s.

One thing that is clear about New York's financial decisions in the 1980s is that they have not been fiscally conservative. New York did not use its rapid income growth in the 1980s to substantially decrease its relatively high tax burdens and provide itself with a fiscal cushion for the 1990s—nor did it save. New York faces many economic and fiscal uncertainties in the 1990s that could significantly affect its fiscal health. The federal government, confronted with a mounting deficit, may take substantial action to reduce expenditures and raise revenues. Two of the more likely outcomes, which will hurt New York, are reduced federal aid and elimination of state and local income and property tax deductibility on the federal income tax. Downturns in the national and international economy are also likely to hit New York hard this time around because so much of the growth of the 1980s was built on international financial services in New York City.

The recent slowdown in the regional economy, with its severe effects on state tax collections and deficits, is an indication of the effect of poor fiscal planning. As will be outlined in chapter 7, policymakers in New York need to learn from the lessons of the 1980s if the state is to avoid a repeat of financial emergencies in the 1990s.

Notes

1. Roy Bahl, *Financing State and Local Government in the 1980s* (New York: Oxford University Press, 1984), p. 37.

2. For a detailed review of state and local finances up until 1987, see Roy Bahl and William Duncombe, "State and Local Government Finances: Was There a Structural Break in the Reagan Years?" *Growth and Change* 19 (Fall 1988): 30–48.

3. For the latest information on state and local fiscal position, see David Sullivan, "State and Local Fiscal Position in 1989," *Survey of Current Business* 70 (February 1990): 26–28.

4. For recent estimates for state and local sectors, see Donald Peters, "Receipts and Expenditures of State Governments and of Local Governments: Revised and Update Estimates, 1985–88," *Survey of Current Business* 69 (October 1989): 24–25.

5. There have been attempts to use the finance data provided by the U.S. Bureau of the Census to estimate surpluses and deficits, but the problems associated with their use were deemed too severe to justify developing such estimates for New York. For a discussion of these problems, see Philip Dearborn, "Fiscal Conditions in Large American Cities, 1971–1984," in *Urban Change and Poverty*, eds. Michael McGeary and Laurence Lynn (Washington, D.C.: National Academy Press, 1988).

6. These include the National Conference of State Legislatures (NCSL) in the publication *State Budget Actions;* and the National Association of State Budget Officers and National Governors Association in the publication *Fiscal Survey of the States*. In this chapter, we use the general fund balances published by the NCSL.

7. Steven Gold, "State Government Fund Balances, Financial Assets, and Measures of Budget Surplus," in *Federal-State-Local Fiscal Relations, Technical Papers*, Vol. 2 (Washington, D.C.: U.S. Department of the Treasury, 1986), p. 596.

8. Between fiscal years 1979 to 1983, Texas and Alaska accounted (on average) for 45 percent of total general fund balances. By fiscal year 1986, both states were in deficit. See Gold, ibid., p. 625; and NCSL, *State Budget Actions, 1987* (Denver: NCSL, 1987), p. 72.

9. A thorough discussion of the state's budgetary position may be found in New York State, "Official Statement: 1990 Tax and Revenue Anticipation Notes" (Albany: New York State, June 8, 1990).

10. New York State, "Offering Statement: 1989–1990 Tax and Revenue Anticipation Notes" (Albany: New York State, March 27, 1990), pp. 26–27.

11. Bahl has pointed out concerning the results of these studies, "The answer one gets . . . depends on the sample of cities chosen for the comparison, the variables included in the analysis, the method used to estimate an index, and the cutoff index selected for distress." See Bahl, *Financing State and Local Government in the 1980s*, p. 55.

12. See Bahl, ibid., Table 3–4, for a good review of these studies. Examples include Katherine Bradbury, "Urban Decline and Distress: An Update," *New England Economic Review* (July/August 1984): 39–55; and Richard Nathan and Charles Adams, "Understanding Central City Hardship," *Political Science Quarterly* 91 (Spring 1976): 47–62.

13. Philip Dearborn has for many years followed the budgetary position of large cities. His earlier work was for the Advisory Commission on Intergovernmental Relations (ACIR) and provided a good comparative view of the changing financial condition of cities. His most recent analysis is published in "Fiscal Conditions in Large American Cities, 1971–84," Table 7.

14. Dearborn, ibid., p. 281.

15. National League of Cities, *City Fiscal Conditions* (Washington, D.C.: National League of Cities, 1986 and 1987).

16. For one analysis from this perspective, see Cathy Daicoff Macsherry, "Assessing Revenue-Raising Ability: A Private-Sector View of Changes," in *Measuring Fiscal Capacity*, ed. H. Clyde Reeves (Boston: Oelgeschlager, Gunn & Hain, 1986).

17. See Standard & Poor's Corporation, *Credit Overview* (New York: Standard & Poor's Corp., 1983); and Moody's Investors Service, *Moody's on Municipals* (New York: Moody's Investors Service, 1989).

18. See Twentieth Century Fund, *The Rating Game* (New York: Twentieth Century Fund, 1974).

19. Edward Gramlich, "The New York City Fiscal Crisis: What Happened and What Is to Be Done?" *American Economic Review* 2 (May 1976): 415–429.

20. See Roy Bahl, "Measuring the Creditworthiness of State and Local Governments: Municipal Bond Ratings," in *1971 Proceedings of the Sixty-Fourth Annual Conference on Taxation of the National Tax Association* (Columbus: National Tax Association, 1971); and Daniel Rubinfeld, "Credit Ratings and the Market for General Obligation Municipal Bonds," *National Tax Journal* 26 (March 1973): 17–27.

21. See, in particular, George Cluff and Paul Farnham, "A Problem of Discrete Choice: Moody's Municipal Bond Ratings," *Journal of Economics and Business* 37 (December 1985): 277–302; and "Standard & Poor's versus Moody's: Which City Characteristics Influence Municipal Bond Ratings?" *Quarterly Review of Economics and Business* 24 (Autumn 1984): 72–94.

22. Standard & Poor's Corporation, "New York State Lowered to 'A'," *Creditweek* (April 2, 1990), p. 15.

23. However, budgetary problems in late 1990 in New York City indicate that downgrading of its bond rating may be imminent. See "Bond Market Woe for New York City," *New York Times* (October 9, 1990), p. A16.

24. See Standard & Poor's Corporation, "New Jersey on

CreditWatch," *Creditweek* (March 19, 1990), p. 10.

25.   See Gramlich, "The New York City Fiscal Crisis: What Happened and What is to Be Done?"

26.   For a good summary of the use of debt ratios, see Robert Berne and Richard Schramm, *The Financial Analysis of Governments* (Englewood Cliffs, NJ: Prentice Hall, 1986), chapter 6.

27.   This result may be partially due to inaccuracies in the measure we used. Since information on principal payments is not available, we used long-term debt retired as a proxy.

28.   See Bahl, *Financing State and Local Government in the 1980s*, p. 49.

29.   For a good discussion of the difference between "budgetary" fiscal distress and "structural" fiscal distress, see Bradbury, "Urban Decline and Distress: An Update."

30.   For several good discussions of the theoretical basis of such measures, see Helen Ladd and John Yinger, *America's Ailing Cities: Fiscal Health and the Design of Urban Policy* (Baltimore: Johns Hopkins University Press, 1989); and Richard Musgrave and Peggy Musgrave, *Public Finance in Theory and Practice*, 5th ed. (New York: McGraw-Hill Book Co., 1989), pp. 479–480.

31.   Ladd and Yinger, ibid., p. 8.

32.   For a good discussion of the problems with both personal income and ACIR's representative tax capacity estimates, see Stephen Barro, "Improved Measures of State Fiscal Capacity: Short-Term Changes in the PCI and RTS Indexes," in *Federal-State-Local Fiscal Relations: Technical Papers*, Vol. 1 (Washington, D.C.: U.S. Department of the Treasury, 1986).

33.   For a discussion of the gross state product (GSP) and estimates by state and sector from 1963 to 1986, see Vernon Renshaw, Edward Trott, Jr., and Howard Freidenberg, "Gross State Product by Industry, 1963–86," *Survey of Current Business* 68 (May 1988): 30–46.

34.   For a good discussion of the strengths and weaknesses of the GSP as a fiscal capacity measure, see Robert Aten, "Gross State Product: A Measure of Fiscal Capacity," in *Measuring Fiscal Capacity*.

35.   Barro has recently criticized the representative tax system (RTS) on a number of grounds. In his estimation, most of these problems tend to dampen RTS tax capacity estimates for high-income states, especially in the Northeast. His corrections to the RTS index for New York in 1980 increase New York's index value from 90 to 106. See Barro, "Improved Measures of State Fiscal Capacity: Short-Term Changes in the PCI and RTS Indexes."

36.   This point was first raised by David Bradford, Robert Malt, and Wallace Oates, "The Rising Cost of Local Public Services: Some Evidence and Reflections," *National Tax Journal* 22 (June 1969): 185–202.

37.   Robert Rafuse's results and methodology are summarized in "A

Representative-Expenditure Approach to the Measurement of the Cost of the Service Responsibilities of the States," in *Federal-State-Local Fiscal Relations: Technical Papers*, Vol. 1.

38. Ibid.

39. Ladd and Yinger, *America's Ailing Cities: Fiscal Health and the Design of Urban Policy*.

40. Their measure of fiscal capacity is a much more direct attempt to control for the problems with the other measures. Their measure of fiscal capacity involves simply the total income in a community multiplied by (1 + e), where e is the tax burden on nonresidents as a percent of the tax burden on residents, that is, the ratio of tax exporting. If e equals 0, there is no exporting; if e equals 1, then half of the taxes are exported. For a discussion of their methodology and results, see Ladd and Yinger, ibid., chapter 3.

41. Their total sample was seventy-one cities.

42. To find the fiscal health of cities in 1982 normalized around a national average of zero, simply add 10.9 to all 1982 estimates presented in Table 44.

43. Ladd and Yinger, *America's Ailing Cities*, chapters 6 to 9.

44. Based on estimates by the U.S. Office of Management and Budget in the *Budget of the United States Government*, Fiscal Year 1991 (Washington, D.C.: U.S. Government Printing Office, 1990), pp. 321–327.

45. Real federal aid is projected to grow by 1.4 percent per year. See U.S. Office of Management and Budget, ibid.

46. An analysis of the effects of congressional representation on the distribution of federal grants, consistent with this explanation of New York's larger share, is Randall G. Holcombe and Asghar Zardkoohi, "The Determinants of Federal Grants," *Southern Economic Journal* 48 (October 1981): 393–399.

47. One estimate for the entire United States is that the "price" of state services will increase 8 percent because of the total elimination of deductibility of the sales tax. See Dennis Zimmerman, "Federal Tax Reform and State Use of the Sales Tax," in *Proceedings of the 79th Annual Meeting of the National Tax Association–Tax Institute of America* (Columbus: National Tax Association, November 1986), pp. 325–331.

48. There is, in addition, the possibility that the tax reforms may stimulate national and local economic growth and could expand the local tax base.

49. The marginal tax rate was calculated by dividing taxable income by returns to get average taxable income. This was then compared to the tax table (for married couple filing jointly) to determine the marginal rate. Since taxable income is skewed to the left, this is likely to overstate the taxable income of the median taxpayer. Since taxable income was not available for

New York in 1988, the average for the total United States was used. The average taxable income for New York was very close to that for the whole country in 1980. More information on this calculation is available from the authors upon request.

50.   The New York State budget director reported that "some 44.7 percent of New York returns claim itemized deductions on their federal returns, compared with 35.1 percent nationally—percentages that have been increasing over time for the state and the nation." R. Wayne Diesel, "Federal Tax Reform: The Impact on New York State," *Citizens Budget Commission Quarterly* 5 (Summer-Fall 1985): 2.

51.   Edward Gramlich, "The Deductibility of State and Local Taxes," *National Tax Journal* 38 (December 1985): 447–464; Daphne Kenyon, "Direct Estimates of the Effects of Tax Deductibility on State Tax Mix and the Level of State Taxing and Spending," unpublished paper, 1985; Robert Inman, "Does Deductibility Influence Local Taxation?" NBER Working Paper, No. 1714 (Cambridge: National Bureau of Economic Research, October 1985); Martin Feldstein and Gilbert Metcalf, "The Effect of Federal Tax Deductibility on State and Local Taxes and Spending," *Journal of Political Economy* 95 (August 1987): 710–736; and Paul N. Courant and Daniel Rubinfeld, "Tax Reform: Implications for the State-Local Public Sector," *Journal of Economic Perspectives* 1 (Summer 1987): 87–100.

52.   These effects are discussed in James R. Follain and Patric H. Hendershott, *Tax Reform and Real Estate: The Impact of the Senate Finance Committee Plan* (Washington, D.C.: Urban Institute, 1986).

53.   This theme is developed in Cynthia Green, "State Aid," in *Setting Municipal Priorities 1986*; eds. Charles Brecher and Raymond Horton (New York: New York University Press, 1985).

54.   U.S. Bureau of the Census, *Governmental Finances* (Washington, D.C.: U.S. Government Printing Office, various years).

55.   These estimates are based on a simulation of federal, state, and local taxes paid by middle- and upper-income New York City renters and suburban homeowners before and after the full implementation of federal, state, and local tax reform. The simulation results are available from the authors.

56.   U.S. Bureau of the Census, *Annual Housing Survey: 1983, New York, NY* (Washington, D.C.: U.S. Government Printing Office, May 1985), Tables B-1 and C-1, pp. C-46, C-88.

57.   Office of the State Comptroller, "The Potential Impact of Federal Tax Law Changes on New York City and New York State" (Albany: New York State Comptroller, 1987).

58.   Advisory Commission on Intergovernmental Relations, "Preliminary Estimates of the Effect of the 1986 Federal Tax Reform Act on State

Personal Income Tax Liabilities," Staff Information Report (Washington, D.C.: ACIR, December 8, 1986).

59. Perhaps the best review of the literature on the effects of taxation on industry location is Michael Wasylenko, "The Effect of Business Climate on Employment Growth," Report to the Minnesota Tax Study Commission (St. Paul: Butterworths, June 28, 1984). For a good review of the implications of this issue for New York, see Dick Netzer, "What Should Governors Do When Economists Tell Them That Nothing Works?" *New York Affairs* 9 (1986): 19–36.

60. Roy Bahl, "Industrial Policy and the States: How Will They Pay?" *Journal of the American Planning Association* 52 (Summer 1986): 310–318.

61. A good review is Isabel V. Sawhill, "Poverty in the U.S.: Why Is It So Persistent?" *Journal of Economic Literature* 26 (September 1988): 1073–1119.

62. John D. Kasarda, "Jobs, Migration, and Emerging Urban Mismatches," in *Urban Change and Poverty*, eds. Michael McGeary and Laurence Lynn (Washington, D.C.: National Academy Press, 1988), pp. 148–188.

63. Keith Ihlanfeldt and David Sjoquist, "The Impact of Job Decentralization on the Economic Welfare of Central City Blacks," *Journal of Urban Economics* 26 (July 1989): 110–130.

64. An ambitious program of investment in human capital is outlined in the Governor's Task Force on Poverty and Welfare, *A New Social Contract: Rethinking the Nature and Purposes of Public Assistance* (Albany: Governor's Task Force on Poverty and Welfare, December 1986).

65. For an assessment of the general approach, see Sheldon Danziger and Peter Gottschalk, "A Framework for Evaluating the Effects of Economic Growth and Transfers on Poverty," *American Economic Review* 75 (March 1985): 153–161; and for a review of the New York City experience, see Emanuel Tobier with Walter Stafford, "People and Incomes," in *Setting Municipal Priorities 1986*, pp. 54–83.

66. William Julius Wilson, "The Urban Underclass in Advanced Industrial Society," in *The New Urban Reality*, ed. Paul E. Peterson (Washington, D.C.: Brookings Institution, 1985), pp. 129–160.

PART III

New York's Finances in the 1990s

7

Lessons from the 1980s

New York State needs to establish a fiscal target: a distribution and level of state and local government expenditures that can be supported by the growth in the state economy, a realistic expectation about federal aid receipts, and an acceptable tax burden for state residents. New York's fiscal problems in the late 1980s, those that occurred in the 1970s, and, if history is any predictor, those that will occur in the 1990s, all stem from the same root cause: a virtual absence of fiscal planning. With the first (Hugh L.) Carey administration a notable exception, the New York state governments since 1970 have not been willing to ask themselves where the fiscal situation was headed or, more important, what level of public expenditures could be afforded.

If Governor Mario M. Cuomo's administration is now ready to question itself on this issue, it would do well to remember four important lessons from the 1980s: (1) long-term fiscal planning, and not the annual management of budget crises, is the route to fiscal stability; (2) the revenue *and* expenditure side of the budget must be considered in planning the state fisc; (3) the state *and* the local government sectors must be taken into account in planning state fiscal policy; and (4) fiscal windfalls ought not to be squandered because they come along much too infrequently.

Long-term Fiscal Planning

Most of New York's annual budget crises have been long in the making. Although most of the problems—usually depicted as revenue shortfalls—could easily be predicted, each has been treated as a holi-

235

day surprise, with resolution sought by a mad scramble for eleventh-hour solutions. This is the antithesis of sound fiscal planning.

The fact is that the seeds for New York's current fiscal problems, including its 1989 and 1990 deficits, were sown several years ago. Expenditure decisions, such as commitments to improved social services, salary increases and enhanced fringe benefits, the addition of new employees, and heavy borrowing, all carried implications for the future size of the state's budget. On a per capita basis, the expenditure gap between New York and the rest of the United States widened. Virtually every category of expenditure exceeded the national average rate. Between 1980 and 1988, state and local government employment in New York (per ten thousand population) increased at a rate of 1.7 percent per year while the rest of the states, on average, were reducing their per capita employment levels; the rate of increase of real payroll per employee in New York was two-thirds above the national average.

What constitutes a "reasonable" growth in public expenditures? Many in New York and other states have argued that the growth in personal income forms some feasible limit to what can be spent. If the goal is to hold the public sector at a constant share of personal income, then the personal income rule should be amended. In periods when federal aid is declining, a constant expenditure-income share would imply that taxes would have to be increased to compensate for the reduced federal subsidy. The slow growth in expenditures relative to personal income for New York in the 1980s actually led to a substantial increase in tax burden—it required some tax increase to compensate for the reduced federal assistance.

Another approach to defining a reasonable limit would be to relate New York's fiscal performance to that of the rest of the country. The argument here would be that New York is so far out of line with tax and expenditure patterns in other states that its primary objective should be to narrow the disparity.

It is a fact that New York was expanding the size of its public sector both relative to its own private sector and to that in other states in the 1980s. If governments in New York had consciously chosen this high road, they should also have been planning a revenue strategy to increase the rate at which personal income would be taxed. On the one hand, they did. Taxes grew at 3.4 percent per year during this period, and the average tax burden rose from 14.7 to 15.8 percent of personal income. On the other hand, discretionary reductions in the top marginal rate of the individual income tax reduced the elasticity of the revenue system, that is, its automatic responsiveness to real income growth and inflation. This comes at a time when federal aid growth is likely to be slow and when national economic growth is slowing. It should come as no surprise that New York State came face-to-face with a revenue shortfall in the late 1980s. The budget deficits of fiscal 1988 to 1990 have been ripening for some time.

It is surprising that there is still not some active movement by the state to engage in long-term fiscal planning; nor does the state even seem ready to acknowledge the longer term consequences of the shortfall in fiscal years 1989 and 1990. The kinds of solutions proposed to deal with these budget deficits indicate the belief that this is a short-run problem that can be dealt with by temporary measures, for example:

- Increased short-term borrowing in the market;
- Borrowing from surpluses in state funds; or
- Deferring certain expenditures and tax rebates to the next fiscal year.

Certainly, a part of the problem is that the state government is unwilling to make the hard choices required but, more importantly, the state has not institutionalized its capability to do economic and fiscal planning.[1] That is, it has not set up a mechanism to tell it what the hard choices are.

There is no shortage of fiscal modeling work in New York, but it is neither long term in outlook nor is it coordinated. There are at least three places within the state government where fiscal analysis and planning may take place: the governor's division of the budget, the senate, and the assembly. In no case does the state use a forecasting model that is tailored to its own economic structure and can be used to make five-year projections. The budget division drives its five-year revenue projections with assumptions about the growth in a few key indicators (primarily population and personal income), but these appear to be based on ad hoc guesses or perhaps "consensus" from national models and some "top down" assumptions. The assembly does make its own forecast, but this is based on a consensus of the estimates provided by several leading forecasting services rather than its own econometric model. The senate makes use of the forecasts from Wharton Econometrics for New York. The point is that longer term economic projections based on a New York analysis are not regularly issued and do not appear to be part of the system.

There is wide variation in the sophistication of the fiscal projection models. The revenue forecasts developed by the budget division appear to be ad hoc, that is, it is not at all clear from the published results how the projections are derived and whether or not they imply any changes in policy. The State Assembly Ways and Means staff has developed an impressive modeling capability, but the projections are primarily short run (one- and two-year) and are not driven by a correspondingly detailed economic model. The senate apparently uses an outside contractor for its forecast.

On the expenditure side, there is virtually no long-term planning. One cannot find a systematic analysis of the long-run implications of annual discretionary expenditure decisions: for example, the true maintenance cost of a capital outlay program, the "uncontrollables" built into future budgets by present compensation agreements, or the revenue and program implications of losses in categorical federal assistance. Expenditure forecasting in New York, like revenue projections, is essentially a one-year exercise.

The first lesson that New York can learn from the late 1980s is this: If the budget deficit is due to a combination of external events and discretionary policy that have slowed revenue growth, and increased uncontrollable expenditures, then the problem will not be solved with quick annual fixes and it will not be solved in one year. The experience with the fiscal year 1989 budget deficit is a case in point. The "solution" to what appeared to be a total shortfall of $2 billion (by comparison with original budgeted amounts) in fiscal year 1989 was to look for temporary measures, but small and piecemeal expenditure reductions, temporary hiring freezes, raiding other state funds, and short-term borrowing will not solve the basic underlying problem of an imbalance between the ability of the economy to generate revenues and the propensity of the legislature to spend.

Even if the problem is recognized as a chronic imbalance and the state legislature takes upon itself the task of dealing with the underlying problem, it will take several years and a detailed plan. For instance, if the inclination is to hike the tax share of personal income to cover the gap, the increment has to be phased in because of the political resistance to higher taxes and because of what are perceived as unfavorable effects on the competitiveness of New York locations. Adjustments on the expenditure side of the budget also require a multiyear planning effort.

The Budget Has Two Accounts

The second lesson is that the New York budget has both a revenue and an expenditure account, and fiscal planning and discretionary fiscal actions cannot approach these as though they are independent. This seems so obvious, but it is a violation of this principle that got the state in fiscal trouble in the 1970s and that caused it new problems in the 1980s. The reason this lesson is not easily learned—in New York or in any state—is that it forces politicians to make hard and therefore unpopular choices between higher taxes or lower public expenditures. Now with federal aid and the deductibility subsidy down and the price of state and local government taxes up, state and local governments in New York are under more pressure than before to match their expenditure desires with the revenues they can raise.

Consider first the tax side. Per capita state and local government taxes in New York in 1988 were 65 percent above the U.S. average. This compromises the competitive position of the New York economy and may dampen its economic growth potential. Largely for the interstate competition reason, and because voters (and politicians) find tax rate increases so painful, few policymakers in New York would argue that the long-run solution to fiscal balance lies in higher taxes. In fact, New York politicians have shown a decided preference for lower taxes by their discretionary actions in recent years: (1) the income tax reductions to return the "windfall" due to the 1986 federal tax reform, and (2) the state income tax reductions that occurred throughout the 1980s.

If higher taxes are not to be the fiscal choice in New York, then a lower rate of growth in government expenditures must be considered. The state must bring its budget into line with its financial capacity. The fact is that per capita expenditures of state and local governments in New York, and probably public service levels, are well above those in the rest of the nation.

What are the implications of an expenditure-reduction strategy? Most are unwanted because some painful cuts will surely be part of the package. First, the competitive position of the state may actually be harmed by expenditure reductions if public service levels are compromised. Many surveys of the determinants of locational preferences of businesses point to public services—notably transportation and education—as important factors. Second, there is a backlog of needs with respect to the New York State infrastructure that must be covered. It will be difficult to carry out such a program in the face of overall expenditure retrenchment. Third, there are great pressures on state resources to provide better services, particularly for those with low income. The underclass, homeless, working poor, and immigrants all can make important claims on available state resources. Fourth, problems such as the cost of medical insurance are on the horizon as big ticket items that the state must face up to. Finally, there are uncontrollables in the state budget that cannot be backed away from: entitlement programs, a certain level of state aid for local government programs, pension commitments, and debt servicing and repayment obligations.

With these kinds of claims on New York's public revenues, it is clear that expenditure austerity cannot occur overnight. Where this leads us is in the direction of a program of long-term and gradual expenditure retrenchment. The approach will have to be gradual, for example, reduce payroll expenditures by attrition rather than by massive layoffs, undertake no new initiatives, retire debt, slow or eliminate real payroll increases, eliminate frills where they can be identified, and most important of all, look for opportunities to retrench without compromising the quality of life in the state.

Such opportunities may exist. The following observations are suggestive:

- A state that relies less heavily on manufacturing may require less capacity in the energy sector and less expenditure on certain other infrastructure services.
- The changing population composition may imply less demand for educational services.
- A slower population growth suggests less need for public employees.
- There may be opportunities to privatize some services that are "priceable" or are simply no longer within the reach of the state's financial resources.

Are there ways to avoid these hard choices? The answer is that there are, but state planners need to be careful in distinguishing what are realistic possible outcomes from what are wishful thoughts. If the state's economy were to grow significantly faster than that in the rest of the country, then the level of taxes in New York could be brought into line without as great an expenditure and public service sacrifice. The same result would occur if federal aid were increased significantly to New York or if the public sector were to become more productive. However, it would be a risky business for the state to base its long-run fiscal plan on any of these possibilities.

More likely, the state is in for a painful period of expenditure retrenchment that can be made less painful by a faster rate of state economic growth or some softening by Washington on federal aid reduction. The numerical example in Box 13 gives some idea of how painful the process might be.

The State and Local Government Sector

The third lesson is that long-term fiscal planning in New York has to take into account not just the state government but the entire state and local government sector. Too often there is the temptation to resolve one level's fiscal problems at the expense of another. The federal government did this to the state and local government sector during the Reagan years, New York State proposed to do it to the local governments during the fiscal crisis of 1989 to 1990, and the New York City bailout in the mid-1970s was dumped in the lap of the state. Off-loading is convenient, but it is not a good route to fiscal soundness.

When New York sets its long-term goals for defining a stable public sector, it should be done as a partnership between the state and local government sectors. This implies that the state government should have a thorough knowledge of the financial operations of New York local governments[2] and should be in the process of continuously evaluating the appropriateness of the structure of intergovernmental fiscal relations. The state government should make regular estimates of the fiscal impacts of its actions on the local government sector as a way of second-guessing its policy program.

The first step to integrating state and local government fiscal planning is to identify the nature of the linkages. The state and local

Box 13. Expenditure Retrenchment

Suppose New York State set as its goal a reduction in the per capita tax burden of state and local governments to 15 percent above the national average by 1995. Fifteen percent would be approximately equal to its expected per capita personal income advantage if New York's income grew at the national rate. What would this imply about the necessary expenditure retrenchment? In order to make this comparison, we will make the following assumptions about (real) annual growth rates for[a]:

	New York	United States
Population	0.2	1.0
Real Federal Aid	0.5	0.5
Own-source Revenue	—	4.1

The results of this analysis show that real per capita expenditures in New York would have to decline by 3.4 percent per year over this period to reach the target.

If the goal were set instead at a level of per capita taxation 30 percent above the national average, the implication would be a decline in real per capita expenditures of more than 1 percent per year. These declines compare to a growth rate in per capita expenditures of 2.7 percent per year in the 1980s.

---

[a] The growth rate for population and own-source revenue (for the total United States) is assumed to continue at the annual growth rate from 1980 to 1988. Federal aid is assumed to experience only slow growth over this period as the federal government attempts to reduce its budget deficit.

government sectors in New York are tied together inextricably in at least the following ways:

- When New York's competitive taxing position is considered, the issue is the aggregate amount of taxes levied and the overall structure of taxes. It makes little difference to a corporation considering a New York location that its state government company income taxes are low if in fact its local government property taxes are correspondingly high, and so on. If a tax incentive package for industry at the state level is given at the expense of higher local government property taxes, then how much has been gained?

- Federal aid received in New York is meant for the support of both state and local government services. It must be shared, just as the New York tax base must be shared. Indeed, some federal aid is even shared by mandate.
- State and local governments provide public services to the same population, and the right way to think about state fiscal policy is to think of the total amounts spent on behalf of residents of the state. The relationships are complicated, however. Some autonomy of local government budgets is compromised by state mandates, some local government services are supported by state aid programs with various conditions and formulas, and irresponsible spending programs at the local government level may come back to haunt the state budget in later years.
- The economic base that guarantees repayment of state and local government debt must also be shared. Since there is a limit to the amount of debt that can properly be issued, some method must be found to allocate that amount between the two levels of government.

The basic theme is that the state government could take an attitude of either sharing its financing base and expenditure responsibilities and finding the right role for the state versus the local government sector or it can compete with its local governments. The position here is that sharing and a carefully thought-out division of fiscal powers and responsibilities is the better way to go.

New York has not traditionally approached the issue of state-local fiscal relations in this way. The debate that swirled around the fiscal year 1990 budget proposals was a good case in point. The governor's initial position was to reduce state aids and to give local governments more taxing authority. One might summarize his views in two statements. "Speaking in a year-end news conference today, Mr. Cuomo said the state had lost control over too much of its money by giving it to local governments. . . . 'I would prefer systems where we gave the local governments less and gave them the capacity to raise their own revenue so that their people can make judgments as to what you want to pay taxes for and what you want to spend on,' he said. 'The government closest to the people is the best. Let them make more of the decisions.' "[3]

The first of these statements is clearly in the spirit of competition; the second is more reasoned and suggests a desire for greater fiscal decentralization in New York. However, the decentralization approach requires that the state (1) define a set of local taxing powers that is commensurate with expenditure responsibility, (2) set up an equalizing state aid program to accompany this taxing program, and (3) remove some mandates and restrictions on taxing powers so that "their people can make judgments as to what you want to pay taxes for and what you want to spend on."[4] In contrast, the governor took a position against local income taxation and suggested only a local property transfer tax. The spirit of the governor's statement about fiscal decentralization is defensible, even admirable, and clearly in the direction of a shared state-local responsibility, but there is no policy program to accompany this rhetoric, and what there is suggests a continuation of the competitive approach.

Now consider the local government position. On the one hand, state off-loading of its deficit by grant reduction or increased expenditure mandates increases the local government's deficit. New York City officials estimated that the proposed fiscal changes in the governor's January 1989 budget message—a reduction in state assistance and a mandated increase in Medicaid spending—would cost New York City $368 million and raise the estimated fiscal year 1990 budget gap to $863 million.[5] One might legitimately raise the question of the extent to which this shifting of budget deficits solves the state's basic problem.[6]

On the other hand, the story is not simply one of the state's budget deficit *causing* a local government budget deficit. New York City, for example, increased its rate of pay for public employees in the 1980s by an amount that far outstrips the growth in personal income and has increased its public employment rolls by a substantial amount. The governor's position is quite correct in this regard—if the local government opts to spend at a higher rate, then it should be responsible for financing this level of expenditure.

Don't Waste Windfalls

The fourth lesson is: Don't squander windfalls. They come along too infrequently. New York entered the 1980s as an overdeveloped public sector with per capita expenditures 39 percent above the national average, per capita taxes 58 percent above, and per capita income only 7 percent above. Looking ahead in 1980, the prospects were for an income growth at or below the national average rate and for substantial reductions in federal aid, with no New York favors from the Reagan administration.

In fact, the 1980s brought New York a windfall. Per capita personal income grew at a rate of 40 percent above the national average and federal aid to New York State did not decline as much as in the rest of the country. The state was presented a golden opportunity to begin to bring its public sector into line with that of the rest of the country while minimizing the hardships imposed on public service recipients and on state and local government workers.

In fact, the state chose to spend this windfall, and instead of reducing its fiscal position relative to other states, it widened the disparity. By 1988, per capita expenditures in New York had grown to 47 percent above the national average and per capita taxes to 65 percent above. Consider what could have been the case. If New York state and local governments had held own-source revenues in line with personal income growth after 1980, expenditures could have increased by 2.5 percent per year in real terms over that seven-year period, even given the slow growth in federal aid that did take place. Under this scenario, per capita own-source revenue would have been reduced to 44 percent above the rest of the nation by 1988 (54 percent was the actual).

The problem to be faced now is that these windfalls probably will not continue. The consequence is that an important part of New York's fiscal "cushion" will be removed and the annual budget crises of the next few years will be even worse than those of the recent past. One cannot say whether personal income will continue to grow above the national rate in New York, but some would argue that it will not. In 1989, New York's personal income grew only 70 percent as fast as the national average.

The reductions in federal aid are almost certain to spread to New York in the coming years, especially with new cuts in social service assistance in the offing. Will New York continue to do as well in the federal aid competition? Probably not. First, both total federal grants and welfare—AFDC—assistance are projected to experience little growth in real terms. Second, the 1980s saw a shift toward the use of formulas for allocating federal aid, a structural change that was designed to reduce the advantage of states, like New York, whose officials are skilled at "grantsmanship." It is doubtful that a state with per capita income 17 percent above the national average and a national population share of 8 percent will continue to receive 11 percent of total federal aid. Sooner or later, New York's share of federal aid is likely to be brought into greater conformity with its financial capacity and population share. In this connection, it should be noted that New York's congressional strength, which has helped shield the state and city from federal aid retrenchment, will be weakened by the next reapportionment of the U.S. House of Representatives.

Nevertheless, New York State and New York City officials continue to be cautiously optimistic (and a bit ambiguous) in their assumptions about federal aid. In 1989, the state's division of the budget anticipated real growth of more than 2 percent yearly to 1991, with most of the increase to be passed on to local governments.[7] The city's Office of Management and Budget forecasts that projected financial gaps will be covered partially by incremental state aid increases of $200 million per year.[8] City officials were also optimistic in assuming that the 1988 federal budget would more closely resemble Congress's budgetary priorities than the president's. However, they now anticipate a sharp drop in direct federal aid. New York City officials also assume that cuts in federal assistance will not result in increased city spending—that is, that the city will not substitute its funds.

Notes

1. Both the state assembly and the private sector have called attention to the inadequacy of dealing with a long-term structural problem with temporary solutions. See New York State Assembly Ways and Means Committee, "Fiscal Change and Financial Sense: Budgetary and Financial Reform in New York State" (Albany: New York State Legislature, February 1989); and Citizens Budget Commission, *New York State's Road to Fiscal Soundness: The Detours and Guidelines for a Return* (New York: Citizens Budget Commission, January 1989).

2. To some extent, this is done by the state comptroller's office. See, for example, Office of the State Comptroller, *Special Report on Municipal Affairs* (Albany: New York State Comptroller, 1988).

3. "Cuomo to Urge Shifting Burden of Budget Gap," *New York Times* (December 28, 1989), p. 1.

4. Ibid.

5. As reported in Citizens Budget Commission, "Review of New York's 1990 Preliminary Budget" (New York: Citizens Budget Commission, 1989), p. 9.

6. Governor Mario M. Cuomo, "Message to the Legislature" (Albany: State of New York, January 4, 1989), pp. 139–144.

7. New York State, Division of the Budget, "Five-Year Projections, Fiscal Years 1986–87 through 1990–91" (Albany: New York State Division of the Budget, 1986), pp. 20–24.

8. New York State Financial Control Board, *New York City Financial Plan, Fiscal Years 1988-91* (New York: New York State Financial Control Board, July 14, 1987), Table 4, p. 16.

8

Conclusions

The 1980s were good years for the New York economy, perhaps better than even the most Pollyanna futurists would have hoped for. Population and employment increased, reversing the declines of the 1970s, although neither grew as fast in New York as in the rest of the country. Personal income did increase at a higher rate than in other states, and per capita income grew to 17 percent above the national average, about the same advantage the state held in 1972.

The public sector in New York also grew in the 1980s. Per capita expenditures rose to 47 percent above that in the average state in 1988 versus 36 percent in 1980. Taxes as a percent of personal income increased from 14.6 to 15.7 percent over this same period, and tax effort in New York was 65 percent above the national average in 1988. The average government worker in New York made 16 percent more than the average U.S. state and local government worker, and for every ten thousand residents, New York had 112 more state and local government employees than did the average state. Clearly, the public sector in New York had become overdeveloped relative to its economic base and relative to that in other states. Reductions in federal aid and the erosion of the value of federal income tax deductibility brought about by the 1986 tax reform have accentuated the disparity with the rest of the country by forcing New York to finance a greater share of its expenditures from locally raised revenues.

What does the future hold for the New York economy? Do the trends of the 1980s signal a healthy New York economy with a comparative advantage that can sustain its growth into the 1990s? Perhaps the primary reason for the New York turnaround was the strong growth in the New York City area economy, mainly in the areas of finance and international business. The "opening" of the U.S. economy, the strong dollar and the federal deficit, prolonged GNP growth, and a booming securities market all conspired to help New York rediscover what may be its uniqueness and comparative advantage.

Aside from this important growth sector, however, there is no strong evidence that New York has gained an economic advantage over other states or that it has removed some important bottlenecks to growth. The performance of the manufacturing sector in New York was an extension of what went on in the 1970s. Employment in the goods-producing sector continued to decline during the 1980s, and this accounted for only 4 percent of earnings growth. There is no reason to expect a general flow of jobs back to New York in the 1990s. The relative cost of doing business has not declined, the cost of living has increased relative to much of the United States, and the share of national income earned in New York has increased only slightly (from 8.4 percent in 1980 to 8.5 percent in 1989). Almost everyone who has predicted the future of the New York economy in the past twenty-five years has been wrong because major turning points have not been foreseen. At the risk of making the same error here, we suggest that New York State will continue to grow, although below the national rate. The road, though, is not likely to be smooth.

While the New York economy seems much stronger and is performing much better now than when it entered the 1980s, there are a great many uncertainties and weaknesses that must be accounted for in state fiscal planning:

- The state is vulnerable to external forces, perhaps more than ever before. Because it has gained so much from the strong U.S. dollar in the 1980s, the state economy will be strongly influenced by changes in the international economy. The state also could be affected adversely by changes in federal macroeconomic policy. Among these are elimination of the remaining amount of deductibility of state and local government taxes, continued cutbacks in federal aid, and the changing national trade policy that might reduce the opportunities for U.S. business to compete effectively in the international economy.
- The New York state government sector has grown perhaps to a point where it is too big, and it would appear that it is not

under control. The state does not seem to have any target for
the overall size of the budget. This creates some uncertainty
on the part of business investors about what the future business climate will be and on the part of those who would invest
in the state infrastructure because it is not clear how the state
will be able to sustain such a large public sector in the long run.

- The price of state and local taxes in New York has been
  increased by the combination of federal aid reductions and the
  1986 federal tax reform. This increase can potentially reduce
  the flow of revenues to the state and force a cutback in the size
  of the expenditure budget.

- New York continues to lose population to other states and to
  have an employment base that grows more slowly than that in
  other states. The source of the population gain in New York in
  the 1980s was natural increase and foreign immigration.

- There is a heavy concentration of the poor in New York, and
  these families and individuals require a heavy social service
  investment and have a high priority claim on state resources.

Given this list of uncertainties and weaknesses, what policy
actions should the state consider or bring under study? The first order
of business is that New York needs to stabilize its public sector in the
1990s. It is important that the state undertake a program of long-term
planning and that it establish some objectives to guide its tax and
expenditure decisions. Perhaps at the top of the list is the determina-
tion of a target level of taxation and public expenditures that are
affordable, that is, that can be sustained by expected growth in the
state economy and federal aid and that can withstand any shocks that
might result from federal macropolicy or the possible adverse performance of the U.S. economy.

A reform of the state tax structure might be high on the list of
policy actions. New York is a more complicated economy now than it
was at the time the tax system was designed. Instead of continuing to
force a 1960 tax system through a 1990 economy and income distribution, it may be time to consider a comprehensive overhaul of the
tax structure. The important changes in the economy to be addressed
by such a reform are that the share of income earned in wages and
salaries has declined from three-fourths to less than two-thirds, the
consumption and production of services have increased as a share of

total state product, and the determinants of the performance (and stability) of the state economy have changed dramatically. A broadening of the state's tax base to more effectively capture the service sector and nonwage income,[1] and a lowering of the average effective rate of taxation, might be high agenda items for reform in the 1990s.

The state might consider the option of dropping its preferential tax treatment and industrial subsidy incentive programs in favor of generally lower rates. The argument goes that states, in general, do not have a particularly good track record of picking winners, that preferential tax treatment may turn out to be little more than giveaways, and that the best tax incentive may well be a generally lower rate anyway.

More consideration should be given to privatizing some services and to financing others with user or benefit charges. New York lags behind the nation in the extent to which it has been willing to charge beneficiaries for services provided. A review of the long-term implications of the fixed commitments, including debt, pensions and "entitlements," should be undertaken. This estimate will play an important role in helping the state define the kind of expenditure discretion it has in planning its longer term retrenchment.

At the top of the reform agenda, however, is public expenditure policy. In the last analysis, if New York state and local governments tax too much, it is because they spend too much. A commitment to reduce government expenditures in New York, though, implies undertaking long-run planning, establishing priorities, and making some hard choices. For example:

- Are 610 state and local government employees per ten thousand population too many, and is an average payroll per worker 16 percent above the national average too great a disparity?
- Is the quality of some public services simply better than the state can afford?
- Is too much or too little being spent on income distribution services?
- Has the proper division of expenditure responsibility between the state and local government sectors been reached? Are local governments sufficiently accountable for their expenditure decisions, and do they have the resources and fiscal discretion necessary to be accountable?

- Has the state overextended itself in terms of the long-run debt and pension commitments it has made? Has the time come to reexamine current expenditure policies in anticipation of meeting these long-run claims?
- Does the changing structure of the state economy offer an opportunity to reduce the size of the government budget? In particular, does the shift from a goods-producing to a service economy lead to lesser demand for infrastructure?
- Are state expenditures on economic development-related services yielding a return that warrants continuing these outlays? At issue here are not only tax incentives but industrial development subsidies, subsidies to private institutions of higher education in the state, and so forth.

New York is a state with a long tradition of engaging in careful study of its fiscal activities. Despite the good work of these various commissions, there still is not a fiscal planning process in New York nor is there an objective forum whereby the hard choices are discussed.[2] The state appointed a commission to rethink the state's tax structure, and the effort continued throughout much of the 1980s. The fact is, however, that the commission's studies and recommendations did not lead to a major comprehensive reform, and although (quite independent of this commission) New York has been engaged in an income tax reduction effort, the overall tax share of personal income has actually risen. Why have such efforts not led to a new era of fiscal planning in New York? The problem, it might be argued, is that the right questions have still not been asked. For example, the need is not for tax reform, it is for fiscal reform; the question is less the legal structure of tax than whether the tax system fits the new economy; the issue is much more how the whole state and local government tax system fits together than it is how each tax impacts the state; and the major policy issues have to do with forecasts of future events and uncertainties. Until the right questions are put on the table, it is unlikely that New York State will make great progress in putting its fiscal house in order.

New York can learn much from its experience in the 1980s, lessons that can help the state and its local governments reach a more sustainable fiscal position in the 1990s. The state needs to establish a fiscal target for the level of state and local government expenditures that can be supported by the growth in the state economy, a realistic expectation about federal aid receipts, and an acceptable tax burden for state residents. New York's fiscal problems in the late 1980s were partially the result of the virtual absence of long-range fiscal planning. The New York state governments in the 1970s and 1980s have not been willing to ask themselves where the fiscal situation was headed or, more important, what level of public expenditures could be afforded.

If the Cuomo administration is now ready to question itself on this issue, it would do well to remember four important lessons from the 1980s: (1) long-term fiscal planning, and not the annual management of budget crises, is the route to fiscal stability; (2) the revenue *and* expenditure side of the budget must be considered in planning the state fisc; (3) the state *and* the local government sectors must be taken into account in planning state fiscal policy; and (4) fiscal windfalls ought not be squandered because they come along much too infrequently.

Notes

1. Fox and Murray estimated that the inclusion of services that can be reached would have increased sales taxes by 61 percent in 1982 in New York. See William F. Fox and Matthew Murray, "Economic Aspects of Taxing Services," *National Tax Journal* 41 (March 1988): 19–36.

2. An *objective* forum would be one in which the business, academic, and government communities could come together to openly air the problems and argue the merits of alternative policy strategies. One such forum is that organized by Raymond Horton and Charles Brecher concerning priorities for New York City.

APPENDIX A

Geographic Definitions

FIGURE A–1
Regions Within New York State

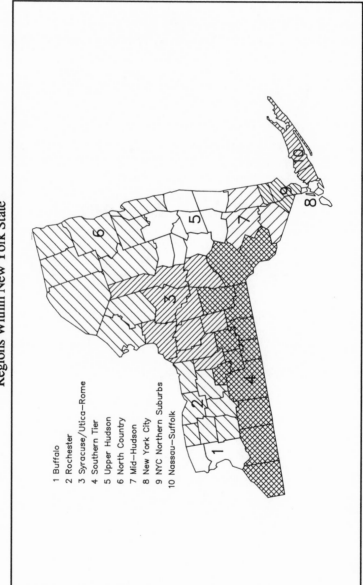

1 Buffalo
2 Rochester
3 Syracuse/Utica–Rome
4 Southern Tier
5 Upper Hudson
6 North Country
7 Mid–Hudson
8 New York City
9 NYC Northern Suburbs
10 Nassau–Suffolk

Source: Regions defined in *Project 2000* reports

Introduction

The levels of geographic disaggregation used in this study are the metropolitan statistical area (MSA) and "region" as defined by the state. All regions of New York State contain at least one metropolitan area. This provides a sufficient disaggregation to capture the diversity of economic change in New York State without getting lost in details. The following are the definitions of regions and MSAs used:

1. Region: The regional definitions used in the *Project 2000* reports were used in this study (Figure A-1; Table A-1). It is recognized that diversity exists within these regions and that other regional definitions have been used by state agencies; however, this division appears to us to capture the most important regional differences in the state.

2. Metropolitan Statistical Area (MSA): The definitions of MSAs developed by the U.S. Bureau of the Census (MSA, PMSA, and CMSA) were used for this study (see Table A-1). The MSA concept is used by other U.S. government agencies, including the Bureau of Labor Statistics and the Bureau of Economic Analysis from whose sources we draw our employment and income data. (See Office of Management and Budget Report 83-20, June 1983, for the revised metropolitan area definitions.)

TABLE A-1

Geographic Divisions Within New York State
Used in This Report

Region	MSAs
Buffalo Region:	Buffalo CMSA:
Erie County	Erie County
Niagara County	Niagara County
Rochester Region:	Rochester MSA:
Livingston County	Livingston County
Monroe County	Monroe County
Ontario County	Ontario County
Orleans County	Orleans County
Wayne County	Wayne County
Genesee County	
Wyoming County	
Syracuse/Utica-Rome Region:	Syracuse MSA:
Madison County	Madison County
Onondaga County	Onondaga County
Oswego County	Oswego County
	Utica-Rome MSA:
Herkimer County	Herkimer County
Oneida County	Oneida County
Cayuga County	
Cortland County	
Otsego County	
Seneca County	
Upper Hudson Region:	Albany–Schenectady–Troy MSA:
Albany County	Albany County
Greene County	Greene County
Montgomery County	Montgomery County
Rensselaer County	Rensselaer County
Saratoga County	Saratoga County
Schenectady County	Schenectady County
Columbia County	
Fulton County	
Schoharie County	

TABLE A-1 (continued)

Geographic Divisions Within New York State
Used in This Report

Region	*MSAs*
North County Region:	Glen Falls MSA:
Warren County	Warren County
Washington County	Washington County
Clinton County	
Essex County	
Franklin County	
Hamilton County	
Jefferson County	
Lewis County	
St. Lawrence County	
Southern Tier Region:	Binghamton MSA:
Broome County	Broome County
Tioga County	Tioga County
	Elmira MSA:
Chemung County	Chemung County
Allegany County	
Cattaraugus County	
Chautauqua County	
Chenango County	
Delaware County	
Schuyler County	
Steuben County	
Sullivan County	
Tompkins County	
Yates County	
Mid-Hudson Region:	Poughkeepsie MSA:
Dutchess County	Dutchess County
	Orange MSA:
Orange County	Orange County
Ulster County	

TABLE A-1 (continued)

Geographic Divisions Within New York State
Used in This Report

Region	MSAs
New York City Suburbs Region:	This is equal to the New York
Putnam County	City PMSA minus New York City:
Rockland County	Putnam County
Westchester County	Rockland County
	Westchester County
Long Island Region:	Nassau-Suffolk PMSA:
Nassau County	Nassau County
Suffolk County	Suffolk County
New York City	New York City

APPENDIX B

Population Data

TABLE B-1

Population Trends and Projections by Regions and Metropolitan Areas
in New York State

Region/ Metropolitan Area (MSA)[a]	Average Annual Percent Change				Percent of Total State Population			
	1960–70	1970–80	1980–88	1990–2000	1970	1980	1988	2000
Buffalo MSA	0.3	–0.8	–0.7	0.1	7.4	7.1	6.6	6.5
Rochester Region	1.7	0.1	0.1	0.4	5.8	6.1	6.0	6.3
–Rochester MSA	1.8	0.1	0.1	0.4	5.3	5.5	5.5	5.7
Syracuse/Utica Region	0.9	–0.1	0.0	0.4	6.5	6.7	6.6	6.8
–Syracuse MSA	1.2	0.1	0.1	0.4	3.5	3.7	3.6	3.7
–Utica/Rome MSA	0.3	–0.6	–0.3	0.3	1.9	1.8	1.7	1.8
Southern Tier Region	0.6	0.3	–0.1	0.3	5.5	5.9	5.7	5.8
–Binghamton MSA	0.7	–0.2	–0.2	0.0	1.5	1.5	1.5	1.4
–Elmira MSA	0.3	–0.4	–0.8	0.1	0.6	0.6	0.5	0.5
North Country Region	0.2	0.4	0.4	0.8	2.6	2.9	2.9	3.2
–Glen Falls MSA	1.0	0.7	0.7	0.7	0.6	0.6	0.6	0.7
Upper Hudson Region	0.8	0.4	0.2	0.4	5.2	5.6	5.6	5.7
–Albany MSA	0.8	0.3	0.2	0.3	4.4	4.8	4.8	4.8
Mid-Hudson Region	2.0	1.3	1.1	0.9	3.2	3.8	4.0	4.3
–Poughkeepsie MSA	2.4	1.0	0.8	0.8	1.2	1.4	1.5	1.6
–Orange MSA	1.9	1.6	1.5	1.2	1.2	1.5	1.6	1.8
New York City	0.1	–1.1	0.5	0.1	43.3	40.3	41.1	39.1
North NYC Suburbs	1.9	0.2	0.1	0.3	6.5	6.9	6.8	6.9
Long Island	2.7	0.2	0.2	0.4	14.0	14.8	14.7	15.4
Total New York State	0.8	–0.4	0.2	0.3	100.0	100.0	100.0	100.0
–Metropolitan Areas	0.9	–0.5	0.3	0.3	91.3	90.4	90.5	89.9
–Central Counties[b]	0.3	–0.9	0.3	0.1	58.7	55.5	55.6	53.7
–Nonmetropolitan Areas	0.6	0.6	0.2	0.5	8.7	9.6	9.5	10.1

[a]See Appendix A for definitions of regions and metropolitan statistical areas (MSAs).

[b]Includes New York City, Albany, Broome, Erie, Monroe, and Onondaga counties.

Source: New York State Data Center, unpublished population data, and *Official Population Projections for New York State Counties: 1980–2010*, April 1985.

TABLE B-2

Racial Composition of Migration—1980 to 1985: Comparison of New York, Northeast, and Other Regions[a]
(Net In-Migration in Thousands and Percent of 1980 Population)

	Total	*White*	*Black*	*Other Races*	*Hispanic*[b]
New York State	−183	−328	49	96	82
	−1.0%	−2.2%	1.9%	25.0%	4.9%
Other Northeast:	−144	−276	24	108	67
	−0.5%	−1.0%	1.0%	33.6%	7.5%
Connecticut	−6	−19	4	9	3
	−0.2%	−0.7%	1.7%	34.9%	2.6%
Massachusetts	−28	−52	6	18	11
	−0.5%	−1.0%	2.5%	28.9%	8.5%
New Jersey	39	−28	18	50	43
	0.5%	−0.4%	1.9%	40.6%	8.8%
Pennsylvania	−211	−231	−5	25	5
	−1.8%	−2.2%	−0.5%	30.5%	3.9%
Midwest:	−1771	−1798	−92	119	66
	−3.0%	−3.4%	−1.7%	16.5%	5.6%
Ohio	−401	−471	−14	84	−1
	−3.7%	−5.1%	−1.3%	18.1%	−1.0%
Michigan	−496	−484	−23	11	−2
	−5.4%	−6.1%	−1.9%	10.0%	−1.5%
South:	3436	2939	235	262	591
	4.6%	4.9%	1.7%	27.8%	13.8%
Florida	1437	1315	86	36	216
	14.7%	15.8%	6.3%	39.8%	25.3%
Texas	1202	1062	71	70	315
	8.4%	8.6%	4.1%	37.0%	10.5%
West:	2193	1385	105	703	884
	5.1%	3.7%	4.6%	23.5%	14.2%
California	1429	800	79	550	773
	6.0%	3.9%	4.3%	35.0%	17.0%

[a]Net in-migration by region includes intraregional migration between states within a region.

[b]Includes residents classified as white, black, or other races.

Source: U.S. Department of Commerce, Bureau of the Census, *Current Population Reports*, Nos. 998 and 1040-RD-1.

TABLE B-3

Immigration to New York State[a]
and the United States, 1970 to 1988

Year[b]	New York	Annual Percent Change	United States	Annual Percent Change	New York as a Percent of United States
1970	97,821		373,326		26.2
1971	92,478	−5.5	370,478	−0.8	25.0
1972	93,833	1.5	384,685	3.8	24.4
1973	93,626	−0.2	400,063	4.0	23.4
1974	88,068	−5.9	394,861	−1.3	22.3
1975	86,492	−1.8	386,194	−2.2	22.4
1976	85,928	−0.7	398,613	3.2	21.6
1977	88,811	3.4	462,315	16.0	19.2
1978	100,542	13.2	601,442	30.1	16.7
1979	94,401	−6.1	460,348	−23.5	20.5
1982	85,048	−9.9	594,131	29.1	14.3
1983	93,159	9.5	559,763	−5.8	16.6
1984	107,056	14.9	543,903	−2.8	19.7
1985	104,734	−2.2	570,009	4.8	18.4
1986	110,216	5.2	601,009	5.4	18.3
1987	114,194	3.6	601,516	0.1	19.0
1988	109,259	−4.3	643,025	6.9	17.0

[a]Immigration to New York State is defined as those immigrants who name New York as their intended state of residence.

[b]Data for 1980 and 1981 are missing as a result of data processing problems in the Immigration and Naturalization Service.

Source: U.S. Department of Justice, Immigration and Naturalization Service, *Statistical Yearbook of the Immigration and Naturalization Service*, 1978 and 1988 editions.

APPENDIX C

Employment Data

TABLE C-1

New York State Employment Growth Gap[a]
Compared to United States Employment Growth
(Total Nonagricultural Employment, in Thousands)

	New York City	New York City Suburbs	Rest of New York State	Total New York State
1960–70	882.3	−158.9	206.3	929.6
1970–73	517.2	5.1	98.6	620.9
1973–75	261.4	10.8	44.5	316.7
1975–77	334.4	33.2	95.2	462.8
1977–80	192.9	−12.6	130.0	310.3
1970–80	1306.0	36.4	368.3	1710.7
1980–83	−61.9	−83.7	23.0	−122.6
1983–89	434.3	61.1	43.2	538.6
1980–89	372.4	−22.6	66.2	416.0

[a]The growth gap is the difference between actual employment and potential employment if it had grown at the national rate over this time period. The growth gap for 1970 to 1980 and 1980 to 1989 is found by adding up the gap for each on the subblocks of years. For example, the gap for 1980 to 1989 is found by adding the gap for 1980 to 1983 and 1983 to 1989.

Source: U.S. Department of Labor, Bureau of Labor Statistics, *Employment, Hours and Earnings, States and Areas, and Employment and Earnings*, March 1990.

TABLE C-2

Employment Trends and Projections by MSA and Region in
New York (Annual Percent Change)

Region/ Metropolitan Area (MSA)[a]	1970– 75	1975– 80	1970– 80	1980– 83	1983– 89	1980– 89	1990– 2000[b]
Buffalo MSA	–0.5	0.7	0.1	–2.5	2.7	0.9	0.7
Rochester Region	1.0	1.5	1.2	0.3	2.6	1.8	
–Rochester MSA	1.0	1.5	1.2	0.4	2.6	1.9	1.0
Syracuse/Utica Region	0.4	1.5	1.0	0.1	2.7	1.8	
–Syracuse MSA	0.8	2.0	1.4	0.7	2.7	2.0	1.0
–Utica/Rome MSA	–0.7	0.7	0.0	–0.9	2.2	1.2	0.5
Southern Tier Region	0.2	1.7	0.9	–1.1	2.7	1.4	
–Binghamton MSA	–0.9	1.8	0.5	0.1	1.6	1.1	0.9
–Elmira MSA	–0.6	–0.3	–0.4	–3.1	3.6	1.3	0.6
North Country Region[c]	0.5	2.1	1.3	–0.1	4.3	2.4	
–Glen Falls MSA[c]	0.1	2.4	1.3	0.4	4.6	2.8	1.1
Upper Hudson Region	1.4	1.8	1.6	0.4	3.1	2.2	
–Albany MSA	1.4	1.9	1.6	0.3	3.2	2.2	0.8
Mid-Hudson Region[d]	1.9	2.4	2.2	2.1	3.1	2.8	
–Poughkeepsie MSA[d]	2.7	2.3	2.4	2.8	2.2	2.4	1.3
–Orange MSA[d]	1.5	2.6	2.1	0.8	4.5	3.2	1.1
New York City	–2.6	0.1	–1.3	0.5	1.2	1.0	0.6
North NYC Suburbs	0.8	2.7	1.7	1.3	2.3	2.0	1.2
Long Island	1.7	3.0	2.4	2.3	2.6	2.5	1.3
Total New York State	–0.9	1.1	0.1	0.5	2.1	1.5	0.9
–Metropolitan Areas[e]	–0.7	1.0	0.2	0.6	2.4	1.6	
–Nonmetropolitan Areas[e]	0.4	1.6	1.1	–0.7	3.1	1.5	

[a]See Appendix A for definitions of regions and metropolitan statistical areas (MSAs).

[b]Based on projected growth rates for nonfarm employment for metropolitan areas by the U.S. Bureau of Economic Analysis.

[c]Data only available up to 1987. Percent changes end with 1987.

[d]Data for 1970 are not available. Percent changes begin with 1971.

[e]Data only available from 1971 to 1987.

Source: New York State, Department of Labor, "Current Employment Statistics" (Establishment Survey); and U.S. Department of Commerce, Bureau of Economic Analysis, *1985 OBERS BEA Regional Projections.*

TABLE C-3

Unemployment Rate by Sex, Race, and Occupation
for New York State, New York City, and the Nation

	1980			1986		
	United States	New York State	New York City	United States	New York State	New York City
Percent of Labor Force:						
White	87.7	85.6	70.9	89.3	87.3	74.9
Nonwhite	12.3	14.4	29.1	10.7	12.7	25.1
Unemployment Rate by Sex/Race (Percent):						
Men:						
White	6.1	6.6	7.5	6.0	5.5	5.9
Nonwhite	13.3	13.1	12.6	14.8	15.5	15.8
Women:						
White	6.5	7.3	7.9	6.1	5.3	5.3
Nonwhite	13.1	9.8	8.9	14.2	8.9	9.0
Unemployment Rate by Occupation (Percent):						
Professional/ Manager	2.4	3.2	4.1	2.5	2.4	2.8
Clerical/Sales	5.0	5.8	7.0	4.9	4.5	5.4
Blue Collar:	10.0	10.2	11.5	10.4	9.1	10.7
Precision/Craft	6.6	6.6	7.1	7.2	6.9	8.7
Other	12.2	12.5	13.8	13.3	10.7	12.1
Service Workers	7.9	7.6	8.3	8.6	7.4	7.8

Source: U.S. Department of Labor, Bureau of Labor Statistics, *Geographic Profile of Employment and Unemployment*, 1980 and 1986.

TABLE C-4

Employment Growth by Industrial Sector: By Region and Metropolitan Areas in New York State
(Annual Percent Change, Nonagricultural Employees)

Region/Metropolitan Area (MSA)[a]	Total		Manufacturing		Services		Trade		FIRE	
	1975–80	1980–89	1975–80	1980–89	1975–80	1980–89	1975–80	1980–89	1975–80	1980–89
Buffalo MSA	0.7	0.9	–0.9	–3.0	3.0	3.8	1.2	2.2	2.1	3.5
Rochester Region	1.5	1.8	1.5	–1.4	3.2	4.8	1.0	3.6	1.1	4.1
–Rochester MSA	1.5	1.9	1.7	–1.4	3.1	4.9	0.9	3.6	1.2	4.2
Syracuse/Utica Region	1.5	1.8	1.0	–1.6	3.4	3.9	1.7	3.1	2.4	2.8
–Syracuse MSA	2.0	2.0	2.0	–1.2	3.6	4.1	1.6	3.1	2.7	2.4
–Utica/Rome MSA	0.7	1.2	–0.4	–2.4	3.2	3.4	1.8	2.7	1.9	3.2
Southern Tier Region	1.7	1.4	1.4	–1.3	3.6	4.6	2.4	3.0	2.2	2.0
–Binghamton MSA	1.8	1.1	1.9	–1.0	4.9	4.3	2.2	2.7	2.9	1.1
–Elmira MSA	–0.3	1.3	–1.8	–2.5	1.8	4.5	1.5	2.7	0.0	3.8
North Country Region	2.1	2.4	1.8	–1.3	NA	NA	2.2	4.6	2.0	1.8
–Glen Falls MSA	2.4	2.8	1.2	0.0	NA	NA	2.4	4.6	3.5	0.7
Upper Hudson Region	1.8	2.2	–0.4	–2.6	4.1	4.8	3.0	3.1	3.2	4.9
–Albany MSA	1.9	2.2	–0.6	–2.8	4.2	4.9	3.2	3.0	3.3	5.0

Mid-Hudson Region	2.4	2.8	1.9	–0.5	4.0	5.0	2.5	4.4	0.8	5.4
–Poughkeepsie MSA	2.3	2.4	2.0	–0.5	4.0	5.3	1.9	3.6	2.4	6.8
–Orange MSA	2.6	3.2	1.4	–1.5	4.1	5.3	3.0	5.6	–0.6	4.7
New York City	0.1	1.0	–1.6	–3.5	3.0	2.8	–0.7	0.4	1.3	1.9
North NYC Suburbs	2.7	2.0	3.3	–1.9	4.0	4.2	2.8	1.9	2.8	6.0
Long Island	3.0	2.5	3.3	–0.3	4.8	4.5	2.8	2.7	4.0	5.4
Total New York State	1.1	1.5	0.3	–2.1	3.4	3.6	0.9	1.9	1.6	2.7
–Metropolitan Areas[b]	1.0	1.6	0.2	–2.4	NA	NA	0.9	2.0	1.7	3.5
–Nonmetropolitan Areas[b]	1.6	1.5	1.3	–2.1	NA	NA	1.2	3.5	–0.2	3.0

[a]See Appendix A for definitions of regions and metropolitan statistical areas (MSAs).

[b]Data only available up to 1987. Percent changes calculated using 1987 instead of 1989.

Source: U.S. Bureau of Labor Statistics and New York State Department of Labor, "Current Employment Statistics" (Establishment Survey).

TABLE C-5

Distribution of Employment by Industrial Sector: By Region and Metropolitan Areas in New York State (Percent of Total, Nonagricultural Employees)

Region/ Metropolitan Area (MSA)[a]	Manu- facturing		Services		Trade		FIRE	
	1975	1989	1975	1989	1975	1989	1975	1989
Buffalo MSA	28.8	18.6	17.9	25.8	21.9	25.2	4.1	5.6
Rochester Region	37.3	28.0	17.2	24.3	19.0	21.6	3.8	4.6
–Rochester MSA	37.4	28.3	17.6	24.9	19.1	21.5	3.9	4.7
Syracuse/Utica Region	25.0	18.1	17.9	23.7	20.6	23.3	5.1	5.8
–Syracuse MSA	22.8	17.1	18.7	24.3	22.4	24.2	6.0	6.4
–Utica/Rome MSA	28.2	19.2	15.9	21.8	18.3	22.1	4.5	5.7
Southern Tier Region	31.5	24.2	17.7	25.7	17.6	20.8	3.0	3.3
–Binghamton MSA	35.8	29.7	13.1	20.3	17.9	21.0	3.3	3.5
–Elmira MSA	33.2	21.7	17.1	25.1	20.9	25.8	2.7	3.4
North Country Region[b]	21.8	16.6	NA	22.4	19.6	22.9	3.4	3.3
–Glen Falls MSA[b]	28.6	22.2	NA	22.6	21.0	23.7	4.7	4.3
Upper Hudson Region	20.3	11.8	18.5	26.0	18.9	21.7	4.1	5.6
–Albany MSA	19.6	11.0	18.7	26.4	18.9	21.6	4.3	5.8
Mid-Hudson Region	27.7	20.2	17.3	22.8	19.5	22.7	3.8	4.4
–Poughkeepsie MSA	32.8	25.0	17.1	23.7	17.0	18.5	2.7	4.1
–Orange MSA	21.8	13.5	17.0	21.8	22.2	27.7	4.5	4.4
New York City	16.3	10.0	23.4	31.9	19.3	17.5	12.8	14.7

272

TABLE C-5 (continued)

Distribution of Employment by Industrial Sector:
By Region and Metropolitan Areas in New York State
(Percent of Total, Nonagricultural Employees)

Region/ Metropolitan Area (MSA)[a]	Manu- facturing		Services		Trade		FIRE	
	1975	1989	1975	1989	1975	1989	1975	1989
North NYC Suburbs	19.8	14.4	23.0	29.6	23.0	23.0	4.8	6.9
Long Island	18.0	14.2	20.5	26.6	26.3	26.5	5.4	7.3
Total New York State	20.8	14.4	21.2	28.4	20.5	21.0	8.5	9.6
–Metropolitan Areas[b]	20.4	14.7	NA	27.7	20.7	21.0	8.9	10.4
–Nonmetro- politan Areas[b]	26.6	20.3	NA	24.0	19.0	21.3	3.3	3.4

[a]See Appendix A for definitions of regions and metropolitan statistical areas (MSAs).

[b]Data only available up to 1987. Percent of total calculated for 1987 instead of 1989.

Source: U.S. Bureau of Labor Statistics and New York State Department of Labor, "Current Employment Statistics" (Establishment Survey).

APPENDIX D

Personal Income Data

TABLE D-1

Real Personal Income Trends and Projections: For New York, the Northeast Region, and the United States (Constant 1982 Dollars in Millions)[a]

Year	New York State			Other Northeast Region[b]			United States	
	Personal Income	Annual Percent Change	Share of United States (Percent)	Personal Income	Annual Percent Change	Share of United States (Percent)	Personal Income	Annual Percent Change
1970	211,209		10.7	321,628		16.4	1,965,557	
1975	210,136	−0.1	9.5	339,131	1.1	15.4	2,206,546	2.3
1980	219,744	0.9	8.4	388,766	2.8	14.8	2,630,194	3.6
1983	230,971	1.7	8.5	407,929	1.6	15.0	2,727,993	1.2
1987	272,584	4.2	8.5	490,945	4.7	15.3	3,207,900	4.1
1988	285,030	4.6	8.5	516,381	5.2	15.5	3,341,296	4.2
1989	291,924	2.4	8.5	533,805	3.4	15.5	3,452,826	3.3
Business Cycles[c]:								
Expansion 1971–73		1.3			3.4			5.2
Contraction 1973–75		−2.0			−1.0			−0.1
Expansion 1975–79		0.7			2.9			4.0
1980–81		0.8			1.3			1.7

Contraction 1981–82	0.8	0.5	-0.4
Expansion 1982–89	3.9	4.4	3.8
Long-term Trends:			
1970–80	0.4	1.9	3.0
1980–89	3.2	3.6	3.1
BEA Projections:			
1988–2000	1.5	1.7	2.0

[a]Personal income is deflated using the implicit GNP deflator.

[b]Includes Connecticut, Maine, Massachusetts, New Hampshire, New Jersey, Pennsylvania, Rhode Island, and Vermont.

[c]These are only rough approximations of the business cycles because they are based on annual averages.

Source: U.S. Department of Commerce, Bureau of Economic Analysis, unpublished personal income data, and *Survey of Current Business*, May 1990, for projections.

TABLE D-2

Personal Income Trends and Projections: In New York City,
New York City Suburbs, and the Rest of the State
(Constant 1982 Dollars in Millions)[a]

Year	New York City			New York City Suburbs[b]			Rest of New York State		
	Personal Income	Annual Percent Change	Share of New York State (Percent)	Personal Income	Annual Percent Change	Share of New York State (Percent)	Personal Income	Annual Percent Change	Share of New York State (Percent)
1970	98,901		46.8	49,099		23.2	63,209		29.9
1975	93,179	−1.2	44.3	50,646	0.6	24.1	66,311	1.0	31.6
1980	89,943	−0.7	40.9	58,061	2.8	26.4	71,740	1.6	32.6
1983	95,624	2.1	41.4	61,725	2.1	26.7	73,622	0.9	31.9
1987	111,885	4.0	41.0	75,853	5.3	27.8	84,845	3.6	31.1
1988	116,557	4.2	40.9	79,561	4.9	27.9	88,912	4.8	31.2
Business Cycles[c]:									
Expansion 1971–73		0.0			2.2				
Contraction 1973–75		−2.8			−1.3				

Expansion 1975–79	–0.9	2.4	1.5
1980–81	1.3	0.5	0.3
Contraction 1981–82	0.6	1.6	0.4
Expansion 1982–88	4.1	5.0	3.5
Long-term Trends:			
1970–80	–0.9	1.7	1.3
1980–88	3.3	4.0	2.7
BEA Projections[d]:			
1983–90	1.7	2.8	3.0
1990–2000	1.3	1.8	1.7

[a]Personal income is deflated using the implicit GNP deflator.

[b]Includes Nassau, Putnam, Rockland, Suffolk, and Westchester counties.

[c]These are only rough approximations of the business cycles because they are based on annual averages.

[d]Projections for New York State and New York City area are based on projected growth rates for real personal income for 1983 to 1990 and 1990 to 2000 by the U.S. Bureau of Economic Analysis. Distributed between substate areas based on past shares.

Source: U.S. Department of Commerce, Bureau of Economic Analysis, unpublished personal income data, *Survey of Current Business*, April 1990, and *1985 OBERS BEA Regional Projections*.

TABLE D-3

Comparison of Personal Income and Employment Trends and Projections By Region and Metropolitan Areas in New York State
(Annual Percent Change)

Region/Metropolitan Area (MSA)[a]	Total Real Personal Income[b]					Total Nonagricultural Employment				
	1970–80	1980–83	1983–88	1980–88	1990–2000[c]	1970–80	1980–83	1983–88	1980–88	1990–2000[c]
Buffalo MSA	0.6	-1.1	2.6	1.2	1.5	0.1	-2.5	2.6	0.7	0.7
Rochester Region	1.3	1.0	3.5	2.6		1.2	0.3	2.7	1.8	
–Rochester MSA	1.3	1.1	3.5	2.6	1.8	1.2	0.4	2.7	1.8	1.0
Syracuse/Utica Region	1.1	1.2	3.3	2.5		1.0	0.1	2.7	1.7	
–Syracuse MSA	1.4	1.6	3.4	2.7	1.8	1.4	0.7	2.8	2.0	1.0
–Utica/Rome MSA	0.4	1.0	2.8	2.1	1.3	0.0	-0.9	2.2	1.0	0.5
Southern Tier Region	1.2	0.6	3.1	2.2		0.9	-1.1	2.9	1.4	
–Binghamton MSA	0.9	1.8	3.0	2.5	1.7	0.5	0.1	2.2	1.4	0.9
–Elmira MSA	0.6	-0.6	2.6	1.4	1.4	-0.4	-3.1	3.7	1.1	0.6
North Country Region	1.3	0.9	4.8	3.3		1.3	-0.1	NA	NA	
–Glen Falls MSA	1.3	1.1	5.3	3.7	1.9	1.3	0.4	NA	NA	1.1

Upper Hudson Region	1.4	1.4	4.3	3.2		1.6	0.4	3.3	2.2	
–Albany MSA	1.3	1.5	4.4	3.3	0.9	1.6	0.3	3.3	2.2	0.8
Mid-Hudson Region	2.7	3.2	5.4	4.6		2.2	2.1	3.5	2.9	
–Poughkeepsie MSA	2.7	3.5	4.6	4.2	2.0	2.4	2.8	2.6	2.6	1.3
–Orange MSA	3.2	2.9	6.6	5.2	1.2	2.1	0.8	4.8	3.3	1.1
New York City	-0.9	2.1	4.0	3.3	1.3	-1.3	0.5	1.4	1.1	0.6
North NYC Suburbs	1.5	2.1	5.2	4.0	1.4	1.7	1.3	2.7	2.2	1.2
Long Island	1.8	2.0	5.2	4.0	2.0	2.4	2.3	3.1	2.8	1.3
Total New York State	0.4	1.7	4.3	3.3	1.6	0.1	0.5	2.3	1.6	0.9
–Metropolitan Areas	0.3	1.7	4.3	3.3		0.2	0.6	2.4	1.6	
–Nonmetropolitan Areas	1.5	0.8	4.6	3.2		1.1	-0.7	3.1	1.5	

[a]See Appendix A for definitions of regions and metropolitan statistical ares (MSAs).

[b]Personal income is deflated using the implicit GNP deflator.

[c]Based on projected growth rates for personal income and nonfarm employment for metropolitan areas by the U.S. Bureau of Economic Analysis.

Source: U.S. Department of Commerce, Bureau of Economic Analysis, unpublished personal income data, *Survey of Current Business*, April 1990, *1985 OBERS BEA Regional Projections*; and U.S. Bureau of Labor Statistics, unpublished employment data.

TABLE D-4

Annual Percent Change in Real Earnings by Industry[a]:
New York, Northeast Region, and the United States
(Constant 1982 Dollars)[b]

	United States		Other Northeast Region		New York State		New York City		New York City Suburbs[c]		Rest of New York State	
	1975–80	1980–87	1975–80	1980–87	1975–80	1980–87	1975–80	1980–87	1975–80	1980–87	1975–80	1980–87
Total Nonagricultural Earnings	3.4	2.6	2.4	2.3	0.7	3.4	-0.2	3.8	2.3	4.7	1.1	2.0
Goods-Producing Sectors:	3.9	0.1	2.4	0.0	1.2	0.6	-1.3	0.0	3.9	3.4	1.9	-0.6
Mining	7.8	-8.1	4.0	-3.5	8.0	-2.3	7.0	-4.7	14.5	-2.7	5.3	-12.3
Construction	4.4	2.1	4.4	1.6	-0.2	7.8	-0.7	9.1	1.0	8.9	-0.6	6.0
Total Manufacturing	3.5	-0.1	3.5	-0.2	1.3	-0.9	-1.6	-2.4	4.5	2.0	2.2	-1.5
Durable	4.1	-0.4	4.1	-0.5	1.9	-1.0	-2.8	-4.2	4.6	2.0	2.3	-1.8
Nondurable	2.5	0.6	2.5	0.3	0.5	-0.9	-1.2	-1.8	4.2	2.0	2.1	-0.5
Service-Producing Sectors:	3.1	3.7	3.1	3.4	0.5	4.3	0.1	4.5	1.6	5.2	0.5	3.6
Distributive Services:	3.8	1.4	3.8	1.0	1.0	0.3	0.1	-0.9	3.9	4.0	1.6	0.4
Transportation and Public Utilities	3.7	1.2	3.7	0.8	0.8	-0.6	0.3	-1.7	2.3	2.9	1.3	0.8
Wholesale Trade	3.8	1.7	3.8	1.3	1.2	1.2	-0.1	0.0	5.1	4.7	1.9	2.2
Retail Trade	1.7	2.1	1.7	2.2	-1.4	2.9	-2.3	2.3	-0.7	4.3	-0.7	2.5

Consumer Services:	3.8	4.0	3.8	3.4	1.4	3.7	1.3	3.8	1.4	4.4	1.5	3.4
Lodging/Amusement	4.4	4.7	4.4	4.4	1.4	4.5	2.8	5.5	NA	NA	NA	NA
Other	3.6	3.7	3.6	3.6	1.4	3.6	0.6	3.4	NA	NA	NA	NA
Producer Services:	5.8	7.0	5.8	5.8	3.0	7.8	2.8	7.9	4.0	8.8	3.1	5.5
FIRE	4.4	5.9	4.4	4.4	2.2	8.6	2.4	9.2	2.4	7.9	1.0	8.1
Business Services	9.7	9.8	9.7	9.7	5.5	7.8	5.1	6.7	6.5	9.9	6.5	8.8
Other	5.2	6.1	5.2	5.2	2.6	6.3	2.1	6.1	3.6	8.8	3.5	0.4
Nonprofit Services:	4.1	5.7	4.1	4.1	0.0	4.7	-1.2	4.7	1.2	5.0	1.0	5.7
Health Services	5.1	5.8	5.1	5.1	0.9	4.7	-0.7	4.6	2.1	5.3	2.6	5.7
Educational Services	-1.2	4.6	-1.2	-1.2	-3.3	4.7	-2.9	5.2	-3.6	3.3	-3.8	5.6
Government	0.9	2.6	0.9	0.9	-2.3	3.2	-3.9	3.7	-0.4	2.9	-1.1	3.3

[a]For comparison with employment data, only nonagricultural earnings were used (minus farm and agricultural services). See authors for classification methodology.

[b]Personal income is deflated using the implicit GNP deflator.

[c]Includes Nassau, Putnam, Rockland, Suffolk, and Westchester counties.

Source: U.S. Department of Commerce, Bureau of Economic Analysis, unpublished personal income data.

APPENDIX E

Fiscal Data

TABLE E-1

Annual Percent Change in Revenues[a]:
New York's Neighboring States

	Real Per Capita Amounts				Amounts Per $1,000 of Personal Income			
	1970– 1980–	1980–	1983–	1980–	1970–	1980–	1983–	
	80	83	88	88	80	83	88	88
Connecticut:								
General Revenue	1.4	1.6	5.1	3.7	0.7	0.0	1.3	0.8
Own-source Revenue	0.6	3.1	5.4	4.6	–0.1	1.5	1.6	1.6
Total Taxes	0.1	2.3	5.3	4.2	–0.5	0.7	1.5	1.2
Property Taxes	–0.9	1.4	3.8	2.9	–1.6	–0.2	0.0	–0.1
Income Taxes	NA	6.9	7.1	7.0	NA	5.3	3.2	4.0
General Sales Taxes	NA	2.9	7.3	5.6	NA	1.3	3.4	2.6
Federal Aid	5.5	–5.6	3.0	–0.3	4.8	–7.1	–0.7	–3.2
Massachusetts:								
General Revenue	2.9	–2.1	3.5	1.4	2.3	–3.9	–0.6	–1.8
Own-source Revenue	1.8	–1.0	4.7	2.5	1.2	–2.9	0.6	–0.7
Total Taxes	1.4	–2.8	4.3	1.6	0.8	–4.6	0.2	–1.6
Property Taxes	0.2	–8.9	1.4	–2.6	–0.4	–10.6	–2.6	–5.7
Income Taxes	NA	1.5	5.1	3.7	NA	–0.4	1.0	0.5
General Sales Taxes	NA	4.0	8.9	7.0	NA	2.1	4.6	3.6
Federal Aid	7.4	–5.4	–1.4	–2.9	6.8	–7.2	–5.3	–6.0
New Jersey:								
General Revenue	2.7	1.3	4.5	3.3	1.9	–0.7	1.0	0.4
Own-source Revenue	2.1	2.5	4.7	3.9	1.3	0.4	1.2	0.9
Total Taxes	1.5	0.9	4.3	3.1	0.7	–1.1	0.9	0.1
Property Taxes	–0.6	0.7	3.6	2.5	–1.3	–1.3	0.2	–0.4
Income Taxes	NA	3.5	6.9	5.6	NA	1.4	3.4	2.6
General Sales Taxes	NA	3.7	8.2	6.5	NA	1.6	4.7	3.5
Federal Aid	6.6	–4.4	3.3	0.3	5.8	–6.3	–0.1	–2.5

TABLE E-1 (continued)
Annual Percent Change in Revenues[a]:
New York's Neighboring States

	Real Per Capita Amounts				Amounts Per $1,000 of Personal Income			
	1970– 1980–	1980– 83	1983– 88	1980– 88	1970– 80	1980– 83	1983– 88	88
Pennsylvania:								
General Revenue	2.4	0.0	2.3	1.5	1.3	0.3	0.6	0.5
Own-source								
Revenue	1.7	–0.2	3.3	2.0	0.7	0.0	1.5	1.0
Total Taxes	1.1	–1.4	2.5	1.0	0.1	–1.1	0.7	0.0
Property Taxes	–0.4	0.4	2.6	1.8	–1.4	0.6	0.8	0.8
Income Taxes	NA	–2.3	1.8	0.2	NA	–2.1	0.0	–0.8
General Sales								
Taxes	NA	–1.8	5.6	2.8	NA	–1.5	3.7	1.7
Federal Aid	5.3	0.9	–1.7	–0.7	4.2	1.2	–3.4	–1.7

[a]Per capita amounts deflated using the implicit GNP deflator for state and local government purchases.

Source: U.S. Department of Commerce, Bureau of the Census, *Governmental Finances*, various years.

TABLE E-2

State and Local Revenues As a Percent of United States Total[a]: New York's Neighboring States

	Real Per Capita Amounts				Amounts Per $1,000 of Personal Income			
	1970	1975	1980	1988	1970	1975	1980	1988
Connecticut:								
General Revenue	101.2	95.5	95.9	112.8	80.8	80.9	79.7	81.3
Own-source Revenue	105.7	97.7	98.8	115.6	84.3	82.8	82.1	83.4
Total Taxes	113.8	106.2	108.2	128.5	90.8	90.0	89.9	92.7
Property Taxes	142.6	147.2	156.1	169.1	113.9	124.7	129.6	121.9
Income Taxes	NA	38.1	45.6	64.6	NA	32.3	37.8	46.6
General Sales Taxes	NA	101.9	113.8	143.2	NA	86.4	94.5	103.3
Federal Aid	78.9	87.2	85.5	98.2	62.9	73.9	71.0	70.8
Massachusetts:								
General Revenue	105.0	111.2	115.2	112.6	94.1	104.2	108.9	90.1
Own-source Revenue	106.1	113.5	111.4	111.2	95.2	106.3	105.3	89.0
Total Taxes	116.5	124.6	125.5	121.6	104.4	116.7	118.7	97.3
Property Taxes	149.3	181.2	182.7	128.1	133.9	169.7	172.7	102.5
Income Taxes	NA	166.0	169.8	187.8	NA	155.4	160.5	150.2
General Sales Taxes	NA	32.3	57.1	80.0	NA	30.3	54.0	64.0
Federal Aid	99.3	102.5	128.8	119.6	89.1	96.0	121.8	95.7
New Jersey:								
General Revenue	93.9	101.4	101.6	115.4	79.2	87.8	88.2	87.3
Own-source Revenue	98.8	105.1	106.5	118.0	83.3	91.1	92.4	89.2
Total Taxes	104.9	109.7	114.8	124.8	88.5	95.0	99.6	94.4
Property Taxes	144.6	171.4	164.2	173.1	122.0	148.5	142.5	130.9
Income Taxes	NA	25.9	83.0	106.0	NA	22.4	72.1	80.2
General Sales Taxes	NA	77.4	70.4	94.8	NA	67.0	61.1	71.7
Federal Aid	69.7	86.9	84.1	101.7	58.8	75.3	73.0	76.9

TABLE E-2 (continued)

State and Local Revenues As a Percent of United States Total[a]:
New York's Neighboring States

	Real Per Capita Amounts				Amounts Per $1,000 of Personal Income			
	1970	*1975*	*1980*	*1988*	*1970*	*1975*	*1980*	*1988*
Pennsylvania:								
General Revenue	87.1	91.1	90.9	89.5	87.4	91.0	91.4	91.0
Own-source Revenue	88.7	91.1	92.7	88.7	89.0	91.0	93.3	90.2
Total Taxes	93.9	96.0	98.6	91.6	94.2	95.9	99.2	93.2
Property Taxes	70.7	67.6	82.0	81.5	71.0	67.6	82.5	82.8
Income Taxes	NA	130.2	120.6	101.0	NA	130.1	121.3	102.7
General Sales Taxes	NA	78.8	73.9	74.7	NA	78.7	74.3	76.0
Federal Aid	79.2	91.1	84.2	93.6	79.4	91.0	84.7	95.2

[a]Deflated with the implicit GNP deflator for state and local government purchases.

Source: U.S. Department of Commerce, Bureau of the Census, *Governmental Finances*, various years.

TABLE E-3

Federal Aid to State Governments by Program Areas[a]:
Comparison of New York State and All States

Year	Public Welfare	High-ways	Educa-tion	Health and Hospitals	Employ-ment Security	Other	Total
Annual Percent							
Change:							
New York							
1970–75	5.6	−10.1	7.0	8.2	5.3	42.2	6.3
1975–80	1.0	11.3	5.4	8.8	−4.6	2.3	2.4
1980–88	3.6	−2.7	−6.0	−1.1	−1.6	−1.1	1.1
All States							
1970–75	4.4	−4.2	3.3	8.1	6.1	28.9	5.0
1975–80	3.2	2.6	1.9	7.2	−1.8	4.4	3.0
1980–88	3.0	−0.1	−1.1	2.0	−1.2	−2.5	0.7
Percent of							
Total Federal Aid:							
New York							
1975	61.7	5.3	15.0	2.1	4.8	11.1	100.0
1980	57.4	8.0	17.3	2.8	3.3	11.0	100.0
1988	70.0	5.9	9.7	2.4	2.7	9.3	100.0
All States							
1975	39.4	14.6	21.8	3.0	4.2	17.0	100.0
1980	39.9	14.3	20.6	3.7	3.3	18.1	100.0
1988	47.7	13.4	17.9	4.1	2.9	14.0	100.0
New York As							
Percent of Federal							
Aid To All States:							
1970	16.1	5.4	6.3	7.5	12.9	4.4	10.3
1975	17.1	4.0	7.5	7.6	12.4	7.1	10.9
1980	15.3	5.9	8.9	8.1	10.7	6.5	10.6
1984	16.9	4.2	6.5	8.4	10.1	7.6	11.4
1988	16.1	4.8	5.9	6.3	10.4	7.3	11.0

Note: Numbers may not add to 100% due to rounding.

[a]Federal aid deflated using the implicit GNP deflator for state and local government purchases.

Source: U.S. Department of Commerce, Bureau of the Census, *State Government Finances*, various years.

TABLE E-4

Analysis of Changes in ACIR Tax Capacity and Effort Measures
Real Per Capita Values[a]

| Tax Type | New York State | | | | | | | | Total United States | | | |
| | Tax Capacity | | | | Tax Revenue | | | | Tax Revenue/Capacity | | | |
	1979	1988	Percent Change	Annual Percent Change	1979	1988	Percent Change	Annual Percent Change	1979	1988	Percent Change	Annual Percent Change
General Sales	235.9	349.0	47.9	4.4	330.4	442.5	33.9	3.3	271.5	341.1	25.6	2.6
Selective Sales	134.8	129.1	-4.2	-0.5	145.4	128.5	-11.6	-1.4	150.0	142.9	-4.7	-0.5
Total License Taxes	34.5	27.6	-20.1	-2.5	30.2	27.3	-9.6	-1.1	43.1	38.2	-11.3	-1.3
Personal Income	221.9	385.2	73.6	6.3	430.1	680.3	58.2	5.2	212.3	279.1	31.5	3.1
Corporate Income	66.2	89.4	35.0	3.4	130.5	176.7	35.5	3.4	73.3	81.9	11.7	1.2
Total Property	280.2	440.9	57.4	5.2	619.6	667.5	7.7	0.8	357.5	417.4	16.8	1.7
Estates and Gifts	15.1	19.4	27.9	2.8	11.3	19.9	76.4	6.5	11.6	10.3	-10.8	-1.3
Severance	0.4	0.3	-8.5	-1.0	0.0	0.0	NA	NA	18.8	14.2	-24.4	-3.1
Total Taxes	989.1	1500.6	51.7	4.7	1697.4	2278.0	34.2	3.3	1138.1	1376.2	20.9	2.1

[a]Deflated using the implicit GNP deflator for state and local government purchases. The capacity is calculated by using representative (national average) tax rates and standard tax bases in each state.

Source: Advisory Commission on Intergovernmental Relations, *Tax Capacity of the Fifty States: Methodology and Estimates,* Report M-134, March 1982, and unpublished estimates for 1988 provided by the ACIR.

TABLE E-5

Annual Percent Change for Selected Objects of Expenditure[a]:
New York's Neighboring States

	Real Per Capita Amounts				Amounts Per $1,000 of Personal Income			
	1970–80	1980–83	1983–88	1980–88	1970–80	1980–83	1983–88	1980–88
Connecticut:								
Total Expenditures	0.7	0.2	6.0	3.8	0.0	–1.4	2.1	0.8
Operating Expenditures	2.1	1.3	5.1	3.7	1.4	–0.3	1.3	0.7
Capital Expenditures	–6.1	–9.8	13.9	4.3	–6.7	–11.2	9.8	1.4
Total Payroll	0.2	–0.5	3.7	2.1	–0.9	–1.5	1.1	0.1
Employment[b]	0.3	0.1	1.3	0.8	NA	NA	NA	NA
Payroll per Employee	–1.7	–0.5	2.7	1.5	NA	NA	NA	NA
Long-term Debt Outstanding	–0.9	0.7	4.3	3.0	–1.5	–0.8	0.6	0.0
Massachusetts:								
Total Expenditures	1.8	–2.0	4.9	2.2	1.3	–3.8	0.7	–1.0
Operating Expenditures	2.9	–1.9	4.4	2.0	2.3	–3.8	0.3	–1.2
Capital Expenditures	–5.1	–2.5	9.3	4.7	–5.6	–4.3	5.0	1.4
Total Payroll	1.8	–3.6	2.4	0.1	0.8	–4.9	–0.6	–2.2
Employment[b]	0.5	0.3	1.4	1.0	NA	NA	NA	NA
Payroll per Employee	–0.8	0.1	0.9	0.6	NA	NA	NA	NA
Long-term Debt Outstanding	1.3	1.5	5.6	4.0	0.7	–0.4	1.4	0.7
New Jersey:								
Total Expenditures	2.5	–0.2	5.1	3.1	1.7	–2.3	1.7	0.2
Operating Expenditures	3.7	0.3	4.6	3.0	2.9	–1.7	1.1	0.1
Capital Expenditures	–3.8	–5.3	9.8	3.9	–4.5	–7.2	6.2	1.0
Total Payroll	2.5	–0.9	1.6	0.6	1.2	–2.3	–0.7	–1.3
Employment[b]	0.3	0.0	1.2	0.7	NA	NA	NA	NA
Payroll per Employee	–0.8	0.0	1.2	0.7	NA	NA	NA	NA
Long-term Debt Outstanding	1.7	2.9	7.5	5.7	0.9	0.8	3.9	2.7

TABLE E-5 (continued)

Annual Percent Change for Selected Objects of Expenditure[a]: New York's Neighboring States

	Real Per Capita Amounts				Amounts Per $1,000 of Personal Income			
	1970– 80	*1980– 83*	*1983– 88*	*1980– 88*	*1970– 80*	*1980– 83*	*1983– 88*	*1980– 88*
Pennsylvania:								
Total Expenditures	1.2	–1.3	3.1	1.4	0.2	–1.0	1.3	0.4
Operating								
Expenditures	2.7	–0.7	3.3	1.7	1.6	–0.5	1.5	0.7
Capital Expenditures	–5.4	–5.8	1.5	–1.3	–6.4	–5.6	–0.3	–2.3
Total Payroll	0.9	–1.8	–0.5	–1.0	–0.6	–0.9	–1.1	–1.0
Employment[b]	0.5	0.4	1.7	1.2	NA	NA	NA	NA
Payroll per								
Employee	–0.5	–0.9	–0.3	–0.5	NA	NA	NA	NA
Long-term Debt								
Outstanding	0.4	–5.6	8.6	3.0	–0.6	–5.4	6.7	2.0

[a]Expenditures are direct general expenditures. Per capita amounts deflated using the implicit GNP deflator for state and local government purchases except payroll, which is deflated by the implicit GNP deflator for state and local government compensation.

[b]Full-time equivalent employment.

Source: U.S. Department of Commerce, Bureau of the Census, *Governmental Finances and Public Employment*, various years.

TABLE E-6

State and Local Expenditures by Selected Objects of Expenditures
As a Percent of United States Total[a]:
New York's Neighboring States

	Real Per Capita Amounts				Amounts Per $1,000 of Personal Income			
	1970	1975	1980	1988	1970	1975	1980	1988
Connecticut:								
Total Expenditures	105.2	99.5	97.4	114.1	84.0	84.3	80.9	82.3
Operating Expenditures	102.7	99.7	100.9	115.3	82.0	84.5	83.8	83.1
Capital Expenditures	114.8	98.3	76.4	105.9	91.7	83.3	63.4	76.4
Total Payroll	98.7	96.3	91.6	106.2	78.8	81.6	76.0	76.6
Employment[b]	90.3	89.8	90.8	96.1	NA	NA	NA	NA
Payroll per Employee	109.3	107.0	100.9	110.5	NA	NA	NA	NA
Long-term Debt Outstanding	133.9	141.3	120.8	111.1	106.9	119.7	100.3	80.1
Massachusetts:								
Total Expenditures	106.5	111.7	110.2	114.8	95.5	104.6	104.2	91.8
Operating Expenditures	111.1	117.4	117.8	117.9	99.6	109.9	111.4	94.3
Capital Expenditures	88.9	84.7	65.5	93.4	79.8	79.3	61.9	74.8
Total Payroll	96.8	103.2	105.3	103.9	86.8	96.6	99.6	83.1
Employment[b]	96.2	99.5	103.2	99.9	NA	NA	NA	NA
Payroll per Employee	100.6	103.8	102.2	104.0	NA	NA	NA	NA
Long-term Debt Outstanding	99.6	114.2	111.2	110.7	89.4	106.9	105.1	88.6
New Jersey:								
Total Expenditures	93.6	103.1	103.6	115.2	79.0	89.4	89.9	87.1
Operating Expenditures	93.6	108.2	107.7	116.5	79.0	93.7	93.5	88.1
Capital Expenditures	93.9	79.2	79.2	106.1	79.2	68.6	68.7	80.2
Total Payroll	92.8	107.5	107.8	111.3	78.3	93.1	93.6	84.2
Employment[b]	88.2	97.1	102.0	102.1	NA	NA	NA	NA
Payroll per Employee	104.8	110.5	105.7	109.1	NA	NA	NA	NA
Long-term Debt Outstanding	94.0	114.5	109.1	123.8	79.3	99.2	94.7	93.6

TABLE E-6 (continued)

State and Local Expenditures by Selected Objects of Expenditures As a Percent of United States Total[a]: New York's Neighboring States

	Real Per Capita Amounts				Amounts Per $1,000 of Personal Income			
	1970	1975	1980	1988	1970	1975	1980	1988
Pennsylvania:								
Total Expenditures	92.3	93.7	90.1	87.9	92.6	93.6	90.6	89.4
Operating								
Expenditures	88.7	95.0	92.6	91.0	89.0	94.9	93.1	92.5
Capital								
Expenditures	106.3	87.6	75.4	66.8	106.6	87.5	75.8	68.0
Total Payroll	84.6	85.2	84.4	76.6	84.9	85.1	84.8	77.9
Employment[b]	85.2	85.1	82.0	79.6	NA	NA	NA	NA
Payroll per								
Employee	99.4	100.1	103.1	96.3	NA	NA	NA	NA
Long-term Debt								
Outstanding	112.8	124.5	115.7	106.8	113.2	124.3	116.3	108.6

[a]Expenditures are direct general expenditures. Per capita amounts deflated using the implicit GNP deflator for state and local government purchases except payroll, which is deflated by the implicit GNP deflator for state and local government compensation.

[b]Full-time equivalent employment.

Source: U.S. Department of Commerce, Bureau of the Census, *Governmental Finances and Public Employment*, various years.

TABLE E-7

Percent Distribution of Expenditures[a]
for New York State and the United States

	New York State			Total United States		
	1975	1980	1988	1975	1980	1988
Expenditure by Object:						
Current Expenditures	84.4	90.5	90.2	82.6	85.6	87.3
Salaries and Wages	NA	41.0	42.7	NA	42.7	42.1
Capital Outlay	15.6	9.5	9.8	17.4	14.4	12.7
Expenditure by Function:						
Education	30.7	30.4	28.9	38.3	36.3	34.6
Environment and Housing	NA	8.7	7.9	NA	8.5	8.4
Government Administration	NA	5.3	4.9	NA	5.0	5.3
Health	11.9	8.9	10.3	8.2	8.8	8.8
Highways	5.3	5.6	5.3	9.8	9.1	7.9
Public Safety	NA	8.0	9.5	NA	7.6	8.8
Public Welfare	14.4	16.2	16.8	11.8	12.4	12.3
Other	NA	16.8	16.4	NA	12.4	13.8
Total	100.0	100.0	100.0	100.0	100.0	100.0

[a]Direct general expenditures. Percentages may not add to 100 due to rounding. Breakdowns of expenditures into some catgories were not available in Census publications for 1975.

Source: U.S. Department of Commerce, Bureau of the Census, *Governmental Finances*, various years.

TABLE E-8

Annual Percent Change for Selected Expenditure Functions[a]:
New York's Neighboring States

	Real Per Capita Amounts				Amounts Per $1,000 of Personal Income			
	1970– 80	1980– 83	1983– 88	1980– 88	1970– 80	1980– 83	1983– 88	1980– 88
Connecticut:								
Total Expenditures	0.7	0.2	6.0	3.8	0.0	–1.4	2.1	0.8
Education	–0.2	–1.0	4.3	2.3	–0.8	–2.5	0.5	–0.6
Health	0.5	4.1	7.9	6.4	0.3	1.5	3.9	3.0
Highways	–3.9	–2.0	13.4	7.4	–4.8	–3.5	9.1	4.2
Public Safety	NA	2.2	6.1	4.6	NA	0.6	2.0	1.5
Public Welfare	3.6	2.1	3.2	2.8	2.9	0.5	–0.6	–0.2
Massachusetts:								
Total Expenditures	1.8	–2.0	4.9	2.2	1.3	–3.8	0.7	–1.0
Education	1.9	–4.7	4.3	0.8	1.3	–6.5	0.2	–2.4
Health	2.1	3.3	5.3	4.5	2.1	0.4	1.1	0.9
Highways	–3.8	–3.8	4.8	1.5	–4.5	–5.9	0.6	–1.9
Public Safety	NA	–1.9	5.5	2.6	NA	–4.1	1.3	–0.8
Public Welfare	0.8	–2.0	4.3	1.9	0.3	–3.8	0.2	–1.3
New Jersey:								
Total Expenditures	2.5	–0.2	5.1	3.1	1.7	–2.3	1.7	0.2
Education	1.6	–1.7	4.2	1.9	0.8	–3.7	0.8	–0.9
Health	2.1	–1.7	4.9	2.4	1.8	–4.5	1.5	–0.8
Highways	–5.1	2.1	10.7	7.4	–6.0	0.2	6.7	4.2
Public Safety	NA	3.2	4.2	3.8	NA	1.3	0.4	0.8
Public Welfare	6.1	–0.6	4.0	2.2	5.2	–2.6	0.6	–0.6
Pennsylvania:								
Total Expenditures	1.2	–1.3	3.1	1.4	0.2	–1.0	1.3	0.9
Education	–0.2	–2.8	4.5	1.7	–1.2	–2.5	2.6	0.7
Health	1.8	3.9	–2.7	–0.3	1.3	3.2	–4.4	–1.6
Highways	–6.7	7.6	4.2	5.5	–7.7	7.8	2.2	4.2
Public Safety	NA	1.2	1.5	1.4	NA	1.5	–0.5	0.2
Public Welfare	4.6	–0.2	1.2	0.7	3.5	0.1	–0.6	–0.3

[a]Expenditures are direct general expenditures. Per capita amounts deflated using the implicit GNP deflator for state and local government purchases.

Source: U.S. Department of Commerce, Bureau of the Census, *Governmental Finances*, various years.

TABLE E-9

State and Local Expenditures by Selected Functional Areas
As a Percent of United States Total[a]:
New York's Neighboring States

	Real Per Capita Amounts				Amounts Per $1,000 of Personal Income			
	1970	1975	1980	1988	1970	1975	1980	1988
Connecticut:								
Total Expenditures	105.2	99.5	97.4	114.1	84.0	84.3	80.9	82.3
Education	99.4	94.1	93.6	102.7	79.3	79.7	77.8	74.1
Health	86.2	74.3	69.2	95.9	68.8	63.0	57.5	69.1
Highways	96.5	95.4	78.1	134.0	77.6	81.2	64.0	95.8
Public Safety	NA	NA	103.9	109.5	NA	NA	85.2	78.3
Public Welfare	94.5	92.0	105.2	114.8	75.4	78.0	87.3	82.8
Massachusetts:								
Total Expenditures	106.5	111.7	110.2	114.8	95.5	104.6	104.2	91.8
Education	82.7	100.0	95.3	93.2	74.2	93.6	90.1	74.6
Health	110.0	101.3	103.6	124.3	98.7	94.9	98.0	99.5
Highways	89.5	75.0	73.1	79.9	80.3	70.4	68.5	63.3
Public Safety	NA	NA	126.3	114.4	NA	NA	118.3	90.6
Public Welfare	184.0	170.1	155.4	158.7	165.0	159.3	146.9	126.9
New Jersey:								
Total Expenditures	93.6	103.1	103.6	115.2	79.0	89.4	89.9	87.1
Education	91.5	105.2	102.3	109.3	77.2	91.2	88.8	82.6
Health	80.9	68.8	75.8	77.1	68.2	59.6	65.8	58.3
Highways	100.7	83.0	72.1	123.4	84.8	72.0	61.9	92.5
Public Safety	NA	NA	117.0	116.1	NA	NA	100.5	87.1
Public Welfare	73.5	109.1	103.0	108.0	62.0	94.5	89.4	81.7
Pennsylvania:								
Total Expenditures	92.3	93.7	90.1	87.9	92.6	93.6	90.6	89.4
Education	93.1	92.1	87.3	91.4	93.5	92.1	87.8	92.9
Health	71.8	75.8	65.7	54.0	72.1	75.7	66.0	54.9
Highways	107.1	102.9	64.7	96.2	107.5	102.5	65.0	97.7
Public Safety	NA	NA	78.2	64.1	NA	NA	78.6	65.1
Public Welfare	95.9	113.2	116.9	108.3	96.3	113.1	117.5	110.1

[a]Expenditures are direct general expenditures. Per capita amounts deflated using the implicit GNP deflator for state and local government purchases.

Source: U.S. Department of Commerce, Bureau of the Census, *Governmental Finances*, various years.

TABLE E-10

Expenditure Effort Index for New York and Its Neighboring States[a]

	Total	Public Education	Health	Highways	Public Safety	Public Welfare
New York	147.5	142.6	156.4	152.9	141.4	182.4
Connecticut	114.9	117.2	93.4	114.0	107.6	174.9
Massachusetts	114.8	109.5	119.3	86.6	114.2	182.6
New Jersey	117.8	130.5	79.1	101.6	134.8	131.9
Pennsylvania	94.4	107.6	68.3	106.5	93.3	131.3

[a]Average for the United States equals 100. Calculated by dividing direct general expenditures by function by the estimate of representative expenditures.

Source: Robert Rafuse, "A Representative-Expenditure Approach to Measurement of the Cost of the Service Responsibilities of the States," in *Federal-State-Local Fiscal Relations, Technical Papers*, Vol. 1 (Washington, D.C.: Department of the Treasury, 1986), Table 3, p. 164.

TABLE E-11

Major Discretionary State Tax Actions During the 1980s
in New York and Its Neighboring States

PERSONAL INCOME TAX

1982   Pennsylvania: Reduced tax rate from 2.2 to 2.0 percent, to be phased in by
        fiscal year 1984.

1983   Connecticut: Instituted interest income tax for income more than $50,000
        and raised tax rate on dividend income.

        Massachusetts: Carried out minor base broadening for capital income part of
        tax.

        Pennsylvania: Raised tax rate temporarily from 2.2 to 2.45 percent. Will
        drop to 2.35 percent by July 1984.

1984   Pennsylvania: Allowed temporary increase to drop to 2.35 percent as
        planned.

1985   New York: Reduced personal income tax rates: (1) unearned income: 14 to
        13 percent and (2) earned income: 10 to 9 percent, phased in over three
        years.

        Pennsylvania: Reduced tax rate from 2.35 to 2.2 percent.

1986   Pennsylvania: Reduced tax rate from 2.2 to 2.1 percent.

1987   New York: Major tax reform that included: (1) base broadening to conform
        to federal reform and (2) reduced tax rates that will drop to 7 percent by
        1991.

        Pennsylvania: Increased income tax relief for the poor.

1988   Massachusetts: Allowed base to conform to federal tax reform.

1989   Connecticut: Allowed capital gains tax to conform to federal tax reform.

        Massachusetts: Increased tax rate on earned income from 5.0 to 5.75
        percent.

TABLE E-11 (continued)

Major Discretionary State Tax Actions During the 1980s
in New York and Its Neighboring States

CORPORATE INCOME TAX

1982   The major issue was whether states were going to conform to the accelerated depreciation (ACRS) passed by the federal government.

All northeastern states decoupled except Vermont, Rhode Island, Massachusetts, and New Hampshire.

Pennsylvania: Reduced tax rate from 10.5 to 9.5 percent, to be phased in by fiscal year 1984.

1983   Connecticut: Increased corporate profit tax rate from 10.0 to 11.5 percent.

1984   Pennsylvania: Delayed scheduled rate reduction to fiscal year 1985.

1985   No major tax action.

1986   Pennsylvania: Reduced tax rate from 9.5 to 8.5 percent.

1987   New York: Passed "The Business Tax Reform and Rate Reduction Act of 1987," which reduced the tax rate from 10 to 9 percent (8 percent for small businesses) and broadened the tax base.

1988   No major tax action.

1989   Connecticut: Imposed 20 percent surcharge on corporate income tax.

GENERAL SALES TAX

1982   New Jersey: Raised tax rate from 5 to 6 percent.

1983   Connecticut: Extended sales tax to food less than $1 and other items.

Pennsylvania: Eliminated sales tax exemption on cigarettes.

1984   No major tax action.

1985   Connecticut: Exempted clothing with price less than $75 and certain nonprescription drugs.

1986   Connecticut: Exempted meals less than $2 from sales tax.

TABLE E-11 **(continued)**

Major Discretionary State Tax Actions During the 1980s
in New York and Its Neighboring States

1987	No major tax action.
1988	Massachusetts: Brought cigarettes into general sales tax base.
1989	Connecticut: Increased sales tax rate from 7.5 to 8.0 percent and extended base to numerous services, out-of-state mail-order sales, meals less than $2, and other items.
	New York: Extended sales tax to out-of-state mail-order sales and floor coverings.

SELECTIVE SALES TAXES

1982	New Jersey: Raised cigarette tax.
1983	Connecticut: Raised cigarette, alcohol, and gasoline taxes.
	Massachusetts: Raised cigarette and gasoline taxes.
	New York: Raised cigarette and alcohol taxes.
	Pennsylvania: Raised cigarette and gasoline taxes.
1984	Connecticut: Passed legislation authorizing raising gasoline taxes 1 cent per year until 1993.
1985	Connecticut: Raised cigarette tax and allowed 1 cent increase in gas tax.
	New Jersey: Raised diesel tax.
	New York: Made permanent the increases in cigarette and alcohol taxes passed in 1983.
1986	No major tax action.
1987	Connecticut: Allowed 1 cent increase in gas tax.
1988	Connecticut: Allowed 1 cent increase in gas tax.
	New Jersey: Raised gasoline and diesel taxes.

TABLE E-11   (continued)

Major Discretionary State Tax Actions During the 1980s
in New York and Its Neighboring States

1989   Connecticut: Allowed 1 cent increase in gas tax and raised cigarette and
            alcohol taxes.

            New York: Passed major increases in cigarette and alcohol taxes.

Source: National Conference of State Legislatures, *State Budget Actions*,
various years.

Bibliography

Adams, Terry K., Gregg J. Duncan, and Willard R. Rodgers. "Persistent Urban Poverty: Prevalence, Correlates and Trends." Paper presented at "The Kerner Report: 20 Years Later," a conference held in Racine, Wisconsin, on February 22 to 29, 1988.

Advisory Commission on Intergovernmental Relations. "Preliminary Estimates of the Effect of the 1986 Federal Tax Reform Act on State Personal Income Tax Liabilities," Staff Information Report (Washington, D.C.: ACIR, December 8, 1986).

_____. *Significant Features of Fiscal Federalism, 1990*, Vol. 1 (Washington, D.C.: ACIR, 1990).

_____. *1986 State Fiscal Capacity and Effort* (Washington, D.C.: ACIR, March 1989).

Alba, Richard, and Michael Batutis. *The Impact of Migration on New York State* (Albany: Business Council of New York State and New York State Job Training Partnership Council, September 1984).

Alba, Richard, and Katherine Trent. *The People of New York: Population Dynamics of a Changing State; New York State Project 2000, Report on Population* (Albany: Rockefeller Institute of Government, 1986).

_____. "Population Loss and Change in the North: An Examination of New York's Migration to the Sunbelt," *Social Science Quarterly* 67 (December 1986): 690–706.

Allen, Steven. "Productivity Levels and Productivity Change Under Unionism," NBER Working Paper No. 2304 (Cambridge: National Bureau of Economic Research, July 1987).

Armstrong, Regina. "Immigration," *Citizens Budget Commission Quarterly* 9 (Winter 1989): 5.

Associated General Contractors of America. *America's Infrastructure: A Plan to Rebuild* (Washington, D.C.: Associated General Contractors, 1983).

Aten, Robert. "Gross State Product: A Measure of Fiscal Capacity," in *Measuring Fiscal Capacity*, ed. H. Clyde Reeves (Boston: Oelgeschlager, Gunn & Hain, 1986).

Bahl, Roy. *Financing State and Local Government in the 1980s* (New York: Oxford University Press, 1984), p. 37.

———. "Industrial Policy and the States: How Will They Pay?" *Journal of the American Planning Association* 52 (Summer 1986): 310–318.

———. "Measuring the Creditworthiness of State and Local Governments: Municipal Bond Ratings," in *1971 Proceedings of the Sixty-Fourth Annual Conference on Taxation of the National Tax Association* (Columbus: National Tax Association, 1971).

———. "The New York Economy: 1960–1978 and the Outlook," Metropolitan Studies Program Occasional Paper, No. 37 (Syracuse: Maxwell School, Syracuse University, 1979).

Bahl, Roy, and William Duncombe. "State and Local Government Finances: Was There a Structural Break in the Reagan Years?" *Growth and Change* 19 (Fall 1988): 30–48.

Bahl, Roy, and David Greytak. "The Response of City Government Revenues to Changes in Employment Structures," *Land Economics* 52 (November 1976): 415–434.

Bailey, Thomas, and Roger Waldinger. "A Skills Mismatch in New York's Labor Market?" *New York Affairs* 8 (1984): 3–29.

Barro, Stephen. "Improved Measures of State Fiscal Capacity: Short-Term Changes in the PCI and RTS Indexes," in *Federal-State-Local Fiscal Relations: Technical Papers*, Vol. 1 (Washington, D.C.: U.S. Department of the Treasury, 1986).

Bartel, Ann P. *Location Decisions of the New Immigrants to the United States*, NBER Working Paper No. 2049 (Cambridge: National Bureau of Economic Research, October 1986).

Battelle-Columbus Division. *Development of High Technology Industries in New York State* (Albany: New York State Science and Technology Foundation, 1982).

Baumol, William. "Macroeconomics of Unbalanced Growth: The Anatomy of Urban Crisis," *American Economic Review* 57 (June 1967): 415–426.

Bawden, D. Lee, and John Palmer. "Social Policy: Challenging the Welfare State," in *The Reagan Record*, eds. John Palmer and Isabel Sawhill (Cambridge: Ballinger Publishing Co., 1984).

Berne, Robert, and Richard Schramm. *The Financial Analysis of Governments* (Englewood Cliffs, NJ: Prentice Hall, 1986).

Berry, William, and David Lowery. *Understanding United States Government Growth: An Empirical Analysis of the Post-War Era* (New York: Praeger, 1987).

"Big Drop in Jobs in New York City Is Predicted by Its Budget Director," *New York Times* (January 22, 1988).

Birch, David. "Who Creates Jobs?" *The Public Interest* 65 (Fall 1981): 3–14.

Bluestone, Barry, and Bennett Harrison. *The Deindustrialization of America* (New York: Basic Books, 1982).

"Bond Market Woe for New York City," *New York Times* (October 9, 1990), p. A16.

Bradbury, Katherine. "Urban Decline and Distress: An Update," *New England Economic Review* (July/August 1984): 39–55.

Bradford, David, Robert Malt, and Wallace Oates. "The Rising Cost of Local Public Services: Some Evidence and Reflections," *National Tax Journal* 22 (June 1969): 185–202.

Brecher, Charles, and Raymond Horton. "Retrenchment and Recovery: American Cities and the New York Experience," *Public Administration Review* 45 (March/April 1985): 267–274.

Britto, Karen. "The Family Support Act of 1988: Welfare Reform," *State Federal Issue Brief*, National Conference of State Legislatures, Vol. 2 (February 1989).

Browne, Lynn. "High Technology and Business Services," *New England Economic Review* (July/August 1983): 5–17.

———. "Shifting Regional Fortunes: The Wheel Turns," *New England Economic Review* (May/June 1989): 29–40.

Bush, Winston, and Arthur Denzau. "The Voting Behavior of Bureaucrats and Public Sector Growth," in *Budgets and Bureaucrats: The Sources of Government Growth*, ed. Thomas Borcherding (Durham, N.C.: Duke University Press, 1977).

Cameron, David. "The Expansion of the Public Economy: A Comparative Analysis," *American Political Science Review* 72 (December 1978): 1243–1261.

Carroll, Robert. "An Analysis of Corporate Income Taxation in

Nebraska and Comparison with the 50 States," Metropolitan Studies Program, Occasional Paper No. 123 (Syracuse: Maxwell School, Syracuse University, 1988).

Cebula, Richard J. *The Determinants of Human Migration* (New York: D.C. Heath and Co., 1979).

Chall, Daniel. "New York City's 'Skills Mismatch,'" *Federal Reserve Bank of New York Quarterly Review* 10 (Spring 1985): 20–27.

Choate, Pat. "House Wednesday Group Special Report on U.S. Economic Infrastructure," unpublished manuscript.

Choate, Pat, and Susan Walter. *America in Ruins: Beyond the Public Works Pork Barrel* (Washington, D.C.: Council of State Planning Agencies, 1981).

Citizens Budget Commission. *New York State's Road to Fiscal Soundness: The Detours and Guidelines for a Return* (New York: Citizens Budget Commission, January 1989).

————. "Review of New York's 1990 Preliminary Budget" (New York: Citizens Budget Commission, 1989).

————. "Review of the City of New York's 1990 Preliminary Budget" (New York: Citizens Budget Commission, March 1989).

————. "The State of Municipal Services: Hospital and Social Services between 1983 and 1988" (New York: Citizens Budget Commission, February 1989).

City of New York. *Comprehensive Annual Financial Report of the Comptroller for the Fiscal Year Ended June 30, 1985* (New York: City of New York, 1985).

Cluff, George, and Paul Farnham. "A Problem of Discrete Choice: Moody's Municipal Bond Ratings," *Journal of Economics and Business* 37 (December 1985): 277–302.

————. "Standard & Poor's versus Moody's: Which City Characteristics Influence Municipal Bond Ratings?" *Quarterly Review of Economics and Business* 24 (Autumn 1984): 72–94.

Coleman, James, Ernest Campbell, and Carol Hobson. *Equality of Educational Opportunity* (Washington, D.C.: U.S. Government Printing Office, 1966).

Congressional Budget Office. *Reducing Poverty Among Children* (Washington, D.C.: U.S. Government Printing Office, May 1985).

Cornell Institute for Social and Economic Research and Public Policy Institute of New York State. *Patterns of Migration in New York*

State, 1980 to 1985 (Albany: Public Policy Institute, July 1987).

Coughlin, Cletus, and Phillip Cartwright. "An Examination of State Foreign Export Promotion and Manufacturing Exports," *Journal of Regional Science* 27 (August 1987): 439–449.

Courant, Paul N., and Daniel Rubinfeld. "Tax Reform: Implications for the State-Local Public Sector," *Journal of Economic Perspectives* 1 (Summer 1987): 87–100.

Courant, Paul, Edward Gramlich, and Daniel Rubinfeld. "Public Employee Market Power and the Level of Government Spending," *American Economic Review* 69 (December 1979): 806–817.

"Cuomo to Urge Shifting Burden of Budget Gap," *New York Times* (December 28, 1989), p. 1.

Cuomo, Governor Mario M. "Message to the Legislature" (Albany: State of New York, January 4, 1989).

Danziger, Sheldon. "Fighting Poverty and Reducing Welfare Dependency," in *Welfare Policy for the 1990s*, eds. Phoebe Cottingham and David Ellwood (Cambridge: Harvard University Press, 1989).

Danziger, Sheldon, and Peter Gottschalk. "A Framework for Evaluating the Effects of Economic Growth and Transfers on Poverty," *American Economic Review* 75 (March 1985): 153–161.

———. "Work, Poverty, and the Working Poor: A Multifaceted Problem," *Monthly Labor Review* 109 (September 1986): 17–21.

DaVanzo, Julie. "Repeat Migration in the United States: Who Moves Back and Who Moves On?" *Review of Economics and Statistics* 65 (November 1983): 552–559.

Dearborn, Philip. "Fiscal Conditions in Large American Cities, 1971–1984," in *Urban Change and Poverty*, eds. Michael McGeary and Laurence Lynn (Washington, D.C.: National Academy Press, 1988).

Diesel, R. Wayne. "Federal Tax Reform: The Impact on New York State," *Citizens Budget Commission Quarterly* 5 (Summer-Fall 1985): 2.

Doolittle, Fred. "Adjustments in Buffalo's Labor Market," *Federal Reserve Bank of New York Quarterly Review* 10 (Winter 1985–86): 28–37.

Drennan, Matthew. "Local Economy and Local Revenues," in *Setting Municipal Priorities, 1988*, eds. Charles Brecher and Raymond Horton (New York: New York University Press, 1988).

Duncombe, William. *Evaluation of Factors Affecting the Cost of Public Services with an Application for Fire Protection*, doctoral dissertation (Syracuse: Syracuse University, 1989).

Eckstein, Albert, and Dale Heien. "Causes and Consequences of Service Sector Growth," *Growth and Change* 16 (April 1985): 12–17.

Ehrenhalt, Samuel. "Looking to the 1990s: Continuity and Change." Paper presented at the 20th Annual Institute of Challenges of the Changing Economy of New York City, sponsored by the New York City Council of Economic Education, July 1987, pp. 5, 12–14, 19.

Federal Emergency Management Agency. *Fire in the United States, 1984* (Washington, D.C.: U.S. Government Printing Office, 1987).

Feldstein, Martin, and Gilbert Metcalf. "The Effect of Federal Tax Deductibility on State and Local Taxes and Spending," *Journal of Political Economy* 95 (August 1987): 710–736.

Ferejohn, John. *Pork Barrel Politics* (Stanford: Stanford University Press, 1974).

Follain, James R., and Patric H. Hendershott. *Tax Reform and Real Estate: The Impact of the Senate Finance Committee Plan* (Washington, D.C.: Urban Institute, 1986).

Fox, William F., and Matthew Murray. "Economic Aspects of Taxing Services," *National Tax Journal* 41 (March 1988): 19–36.

Freeman, R. L., and J. L. Medoff. *What Do Unions Do?* (New York: Basic Books, 1984).

Garnick, Daniel. "Accounting for Regional Differences in Per Capita Personal Income Growth: An Update and Extension," *Survey of Current Business* 70 (January 1990): 29–40.

Gold, Steven. "Developments in State Finances, 1983 to 1986," *Public Budgeting & Finance* 7 (Spring 1987): 5–23.

_____. "State Government Fund Balances, Financial Assets, and Measures of Budget Surplus," in *Federal-State-Local Fiscal Relations, Technical Papers*, Vol. 2 (Washington, D.C.: U.S. Department of the Treasury, 1986).

Goldman, Mark. *High Hopes: The Rise and Decline of Buffalo, New York* (Albany: State University of New York Press, 1983).

Gould, Frank. "The Growth of Public Expenditures: Theory and Evidence from Six Advanced Democracies," in *Why Governments Grow: Measuring Public Sector Size*, ed. Charles Taylor (Beverly Hills: Sage Publications, 1983).

Governor's Project on Trade and Competitiveness. *The Impact of the National Trade Deficit on New York State Employment* (Albany: New

York State Industrial Cooperation Council, June 1987).

Governor's Task Force on Poverty and Welfare. *A New Social Contract: Rethinking the Nature and Purposes of Public Assistance* (Albany: Governor's Task Force on Poverty and Welfare, December 1986).

Gramlich, Edward. "The Deductibility of State and Local Taxes," *National Tax Journal* 38 (December 1985): 447–464.

_____. "The New York City Fiscal Crisis: What Happened and What Is to Be Done?" *American Economic Review* 2 (May 1976): 415–429.

Green, Cynthia. "State Aid," in *Setting Municipal Priorities, 1986*, eds. Charles Brecher and Raymond Horton (New York: New York University Press, 1985).

Greenwood, Michael J. "Human Migration: Theory, Models, and Empirical Studies," *Journal of Regional Science* 25 (November 1985): 521–544.

Gurwitz, Aaron, and Julie Rappaport. "Structural Change and Slower Employment Growth in the Financial Services Sector," *Federal Reserve Bank of New York Quarterly Review* 9 (Winter 1984–85): 39–45.

Hanushek, Eric. "The Economics of Schooling: Production and Efficiency in Public Schools," *Journal of Economic Literature* 3 (September 1986): 1141–1177.

Harriman, Linda, and Jeffrey Straussman. "Do Judges Determine Budget Decisions? Federal Court Decisions in Prison Reform and State Spending for Corrections," *Public Administration Review* 43 (July/August 1983): 343–351.

Harrison, Bennett, Chris Tilly, and Barry Bluestone. "Wage Inequality Takes a Great U-Turn," *Challenge* 29 (March/April 1986): 26–32.

Henderson, Vernon, Peter Mieszkowski, and Yvon Sauvageau. "Peer Group Effects and Education Production Functions," *Journal of Public Economics* 10 (1978): 97–106.

Hilke, John. "The Impact of Volunteer Firefighters on Local Government Spending and Taxation," *Municipal Finance Journal* 7 (Winter 1986): 33–44.

Holahan, John, and Joel Cohen. *Medicaid: The Trade-Off Between Cost Containment and Access to Care* (Washington, D.C.: Urban Institute Press, 1986).

Holcombe, Randall G., and Asghar Zardkoohi. "The Determinants of Federal Grants," *Southern Economic Journal* 48 (October 1981): 393–399.

Holloway, Thomas, and Jane Reed. "Sources of Changes in Federal Transfer Payments to Persons: An Update," *Survey of Current Business* 66 (June 1986): 21–25.

Horvath, Francis. "The Pulse of Economic Change: Displaced Workers of 1981–85," *Monthly Labor Review* 110 (June 1987): 3–12.

Howe, Wayne. "The Business Services Industry Sets Pace in Employment Growth," *Monthly Labor Review* 109 (April 1986): 29–36.

Howell, Embry, David Baugh, and Penelope Pine. "Patterns of Medicaid Utilization and Expenditures in Selected States: 1980–84," *Health Care Financing Review* 10 (Winter 1988): 1–15.

Hulten, Charles, and George Peterson. "The Public Capital Stock: Needs, Trends and Performance," *American Economic Review* 74 (May 1984): 166–173.

Ihlanfeldt, Keith, and David Sjoquist. "The Impact of Job Decentralization on the Economic Welfare of Central City Blacks," *Journal of Urban Economics* 26 (July 1989) 110–130.

Inman, Robert. "Does Deductibility Influence Local Taxation?" NBER Working Paper, No. 1714 (Cambridge: National Bureau of Economic Research, October 1985).

International Monetary Fund. *International Finance Statistics, 1989 Yearbook* (Washington, D.C.: International Monetary Fund, 1989).

"Job Outlook After Stock Collapse Rated Cloudy in New York," *New York Times* (December 12, 1987).

Kamensky, John. "Budgeting for State and Local Infrastructure: Developing a Strategy," *Public Budgeting & Finance* 4 (Autumn 1984): 3–17.

Kasarda, John D. "The Implications of Contemporary Redistribution Trends for National Urban Policy," *Social Science Quarterly* 61 (December 1980): 373–400.

_____. "Jobs, Migration, and Emerging Urban Mismatches," in *Urban Change and Poverty*, eds. Michael McGeary and Laurence Lynn (Washington, D.C.: National Academy Press, 1988), pp. 148–188.

Kasarda, John D., Michael Irwin, and Holly Hughes. "Demographic and Economic Shifts in the Sunbelt." Paper presented at the Sunbelt Research Conference, Miami, Florida, November 3 to 6, 1985.

Kenyon, Daphne. "Direct Estimates of the Effects of Tax Deductibility on State Tax Mix and the Level of State Taxing and Spending," unpublished paper, 1985.

Kirk, Robert. "Are Business Services Immune to the Business Cycle?" *Growth and Change* 18 (Spring 1987): 15–23.

Klein, Bruce, and Philip Rones. "A Profile of the Working Poor," *Monthly Labor Review* 112 (October 1989): 3–13.

Krugman, Paul, and George Hatsopoulos. "The Problem of U.S. Competitiveness in Manufacturing," *New England Economic Review* (January/February 1987): 18–29.

Kutscher, Ronald, and Valerie Personick. "Deindustrialization and the Shift to Services," *Monthly Labor Review* 109 (June 1986): 3–13.

Ladd, Helen, and John Yinger. *America's Ailing Cities: Fiscal Health and the Design of Urban Policy* (Baltimore: Johns Hopkins University Press, 1989).

Larkey, Patrick, Chandler Stolp, and Mark Winer. "Theorizing About Government Growth: A Research Assessment," *Journal of Public Policy* 1 (May 1981): 157–220.

Lawrence, Robert. *Can America Compete?* (Washington, D.C.: Brookings Institution, 1984).

Lewis, Gregg. *Unionism and Relative Wages in the United States: An Empirical Inquiry* (Chicago: University of Chicago Press, 1963).

Lichter, Daniel, and Glenn V. Fuguitt. "The Transition to Nonmetropolitan Population Deconcentration," *Demography* 19 (May 1982): 211–221.

Liebschutz, Sarah F. "The City and the State in Washington," in *The Two New Yorks: State-City Relations in the Changing Federal System*, eds. Gerald Benjamin and Charles Brecher (New York: Russell Sage Foundation, 1988).

Littman, Mark. "Poverty in the 1980s: Are the Poor Getting Poorer?" *Monthly Labor Review* 112 (June 1989): 13–18.

―――. "Reasons for Not Working: Poor and Nonpoor Householders," *Monthly Labor Review* 112 (August 1989): 16–21.

Long, Larry. *Migration and Residential Mobility in the United States* (New York: Russell Sage Foundation, 1988).

Loveman, Gary W., and Chris Tilly. "Good Jobs or Bad Jobs: What Does the Evidence Say?" *New England Economic Review* (January/February 1988): 46–65.

Lowery, David, and William Berry. "The Growth of Government in the United States: An Empirical Assessment of Competing Explanations," *American Journal of Political Science* 27 (November 1983): 665–691.

Lynch, Gerald, and Thomas Hyclak. "Cyclical and Noncyclical Unemployment Differences among Demographic Groups," *Growth and Change* 15 (January 1984): 9–17.

Lynch, James. "Changes in Police Organization and Their Effects on the Divergence of the UCR and NCS Trends." Unpublished paper presented at the 35th Annual Meeting of the American Society of Criminology, Denver, Colorado, November 9–13, 1983.

Macsherry, Cathy Daicoff. "Assessing Revenue-Raising Ability: A Private-Sector View of Changes," in *Measuring Fiscal Capacity*, ed. H. Clyde Reeves (Boston: Oelgeschlager, Gunn & Hain, 1986).

Malecki, Edward. "Research and Development and the Geography of High-Technology Complexes," in *Technology, Regions and Policy*, ed. J. Rees (Totowa, N.J.: Rowman & Littlefield, 1986), pp. 51–74.

Manrique, Gabriel. "Foreign Export Orientation and Regional Growth in the U.S.," *Growth and Change* 18 (Winter 1987): 1–12.

Markusen, Ann, Peter Hall, and Amy Glasmeier. *High Tech America* (Boston: Allen & Unwin, 1986).

McClelland, Peter. *Crisis in the Making: The Political Economy of New York State Since 1945* (Cambridge: Cambridge University Press, 1981).

McLure, Charles, Jr. *Economic Perspectives on State Taxation of Multijurisdictional Corporations* (Arlington: Tax Analysts, 1986).

————. "The Elusive Incidence of the Corporate Income Tax: The State Case," *Public Finance Quarterly* 9 (October 1981): 395–413.

McUsic, Molly. "U.S. Manufacturing: Any Cause for Alarm?" *New England Economic Review* (January/February 1987): 3–17.

Meltzer, Alan, and Scott Richard. "A Rational Theory of the Size of Government," *Journal of Political Economy* 89 (October 1981): 914–927.

Mieszkowski, Peter, and George Zodrow. "The Incidence of a Partial State Corporate Income Tax," *National Tax Journal* 38 (December 1985): 489–496.

Migue, Jean-Luc, and Gerald Belanger. "Toward a General Theory of Managerial Discretion," *Public Choice* 17 (1974): 27–47.

Moffitt, Robert. *Has State Redistribution Policy Grown More Conservative? AFDC, Food Stamps and Medicaid, 1960-84,* Institute for Research on Poverty Discussion Paper, DP No. 851–88 (Madison: University of Wisconsin, January 1988).

Moody's Investors Service. *Moody's on Municipals* (New York: Moody's Investors Service, 1989).

Morrison, Peter A., and Julie DaVanzo. "The Prism of Migration: Dissimilarities Between Return and Onward Movers," *Social Science Quarterly* 67 (September 1986): 504–516.

Musgrave, Richard. "Leviathan Cometh—Or Does He?" in *Tax and Expenditure Limitations,* eds. Helen F. Ladd and T. Nicholaus Tideman (Washington, D.C.: Urban Institute Press, 1981), pp. 77–120.

Musgrave, Richard, and Peggy Musgrave. *Public Finance in Theory and Practice,* 5th ed. (New York: McGraw-Hill Book Co., 1989).

Nathan, Richard, and Charles Adams. "Understanding Central City Hardship," *Political Science Quarterly* 91 (Spring 1976): 47–62.

National Commission on Excellence in Education. *A Nation at Risk: The Imperative for Educational Reform* (Washington, D.C.: U.S. Government Printing Office, April 1983).

National Conference of State Legislatures. *State Budget Actions* (Denver: NCSL, various years).

National League of Cities. *City Fiscal Conditions* (Washington, D.C.: National League of Cities, 1986 and 1987).

Nelson A. Rockefeller Institute of Government. *1985-86 New York State Statistical Yearbook* (Albany: Nelson A. Rockefeller Institute of Government, 1986).

———. *1986-87 New York State Statistical Yearbook* (Albany: Nelson A. Rockefeller Institute of Government, 1987).

Netzer, Dick. "What Should Governors Do When Economists Tell Them That Nothing Works?" *New York Affairs* 9 (1986): 19–36.

New York City. *Small Retail Business Study Commission: Final Report* (New York: Small Retail Business Study Commission, June 1986).

New York Council on Children and Families. "Household Projections: New York State," unpublished manuscript, 1984.

New York Department of Social Services. *Statistical Supplement to the Annual Report* (Albany: New York State Department of Social Services, various years).

New York Department of State, Office of Fire Prevention and Control. *Fire in New York 1986* (Albany: New York Department of State, 1987).

New York Department of Transportation. *Pavement Condition of New York's Highways* (Albany: New York Department of Transportation, various years).

New York State, Division of the Budget. "Five-Year Projections, Fiscal Years 1986–87 through 1990–91" (Albany: New York State Division of the Budget, 1986), pp. 20–24.

New York State. "Offering Statement: 1989–1990 Tax and Revenue Anticipation Notes" (Albany: New York State, March 27, 1990), pp. 26–27.

New York State. "Official Statement: 1990 Tax and Revenue Anticipation Notes" (Albany: New York State, June 8, 1990).

New York State Assembly Ways and Means Committee. "Fiscal Change and Financial Sense: Budgetary and Financial Reform in New York State" (Albany: New York State Legislature, February 1989).

New York State Data Center. *Official Population Projections for New York State Counties: 1980–2010* (Albany: New York State Department of Commerce, 1985).

New York State Department of Commerce. *Financial Services Industries in New York State: A Statistical Profile* (Albany: New York State Department of Commerce, May 1986).

New York State Department of Economic Development. "New York State: Opportunities for Business" (Albany: New York State Department of Economic Development, 1989).

New York State Department of Labor. *High-Technology Industries in New York State* (Albany: New York State Department of Labor, 1988).

New York State Department of Taxation and Finance. "New York State's Tax Reform and Reduction Act of 1987," No. 900 (Albany: New York State Department of Taxation and Finance, May 1987).

New York State Department of Taxation and Finance, Office of Tax Policy Analysis. *Statistical Report* (Albany: New York State Department of Taxation and Finance, various years).

_____. "Sales and Use Tax Information for Consumers," No. 760 (Albany: New York State Department of Taxation and Finance, 1986).

_____. "Sales Tax Information on Selected Services in New York City," No. 846 (Albany: New York State Department of Taxation and Finance, 1989).

New York State Financial Control Board. *New York City Financial Plan, Fiscal Years 1988–91* (New York: New York State Financial Control Board, July 14, 1987).

New York State Industrial Cooperation Council. "New York Is Working This Labor Day: New Data on Business and Labor Growth in NY" (Albany: New York State Industrial Cooperation Council, August 1987).

New York State Legislative Commission on State-Local Relations. *New York's Fire Protection System, Services in Transition* (Albany: New York State Legislative Commission on State-Local Relations, February 1988).

_____. *New York's Highway System, a Vital Economic Asset* (Albany: New York State Legislative Commission on State-Local Relations, 1986).

_____. *New York's Police Service, Perspectives on the Issues* (Albany: New York State Legislative Commission on State-Local Relations, November 1985).

Niskanen, William. *Bureaucracy and Representative Government* (New York: Aldine, Atherton, 1971).

Office of the State Comptroller. "The Potential Impact of Federal Tax Law Changes on New York City and New York State" (Albany: New York State Comptroller, 1987).

_____. *Special Report on Municipal Affairs* (Albany: New York State Comptroller, 1988).

Orzechowski, William. "Economic Models of Bureaucracy: Survey, Extensions, and Evidence," in *Budgets and Bureaucrats: The Sources of Government Growth*, ed. Thomas Borcherding (Durham, N.C.: Duke University Press, 1977).

Pascal, Anthony, Marilyn Cuitanic, and Charles Bennett, et al."State Policies and the Financing of Acquired Immunodeficiency Syndrome Care," *Health Care Financing Review* 11 (Fall 1989): 91–104.

Passel, Jeffrey S., and David L. Word. "Problems in Analyzing Race and Hispanic Origin Data for the 1980 Census: Solutions Based on Constructing Consistent Populations from Micro-Level Data." Paper presented at the 1987 Annual Meeting of the Population Association of America, Chicago, April-May 1987.

Pencavel, John, and Catherine Hartsog. "A Reconsideration of the Effects of Unionism on Relative Wages and Employment in the United States, 1920–80," NBER Working Paper No. 1316 (Cambridge: National Bureau of Economic Research, March 1984).

Perna, Norman. "The Shift from Manufacturing to Services: A Concerned View," *New England Economic Review* (January/February 1987): 30–38.

Personick, Valerie. "Industry Output and Employment: A Slower Trend for the Nineties," *Monthly Labor Review* 112 (November 1989): 25–41.

Peters, Donald. "Receipts and Expenditures of State Governments and of Local Governments: Revised and Updated Estimates, 1985–88," *Survey of Current Business* 69 (October 1989): 24–25.

Plotnick, Robert. "How Much Poverty Is Reduced by State Income Transfers?" *Monthly Labor Review* 112 (July 1989): 21–26.

"Population's Rise in the Northeast Reverses a Trend," *New York Times* (April 7, 1985), p. 1.

Port Authority of New York and New Jersey. "The Regional Economy: Review 1988, Outlook 1989 for the New York–New Jersey Metropolitan Region" (New York: Port Authority of New York and New Jersey, March 1989).

———. *Regional Perspectives: The Regional Economy* (New York: Port Authority of New York and New Jersey, September 1987).

Public Citizen Health Research Group. *Poor Health Care for Poor Americans: A Ranking of State Medicaid Programs* (Washington, D.C.: Public Citizen Health Research Group, 1987).

Rafuse, Robert. "A Representative-Expenditure Approach to the Measurement of the Cost of the Service Responsibilities of the States," in *Federal-State-Local Fiscal Relations: Technical Papers*, Vol. 1 (Washington, D.C.: U.S. Department of the Treasury, 1986).

———. *A Representative Expenditure Index for State and Local Governments* (Washington, D.C.: Advisory Commission on Intergovernmental Relations, unpublished, 1989).

Ram, Rati. "Government Size and Economic Growth: A New Framework and Some Evidence from Cross-Section and Time-Series Data," *American Economic Review* 76 (May 1986): 191–203.

Rappaport, Peter. "Inflation in the Service Sector," *Federal Reserve Bank of New York Quarterly Review* 12 (Winter 1987): 35–45.

Ratcliffe, Kerri, Bruce Riddle, and John Yinger. "The Fiscal Condition of School Districts in Nebraska: Is Small Beautiful?" *Economics of Education Review* 9 (January 1990): 81–99.

Rees, John, and Howard Stafford. "Theories of Regional Growth and Industrial Location: Their Relevance for Understanding High-Technology Complexes," in *Technology, Regions and Policy*, ed. John Rees (Totowa: Rowman & Littlefield, 1986).

Regional Plan Association. *The Region in the Global Economy* (New York: Regional Plan Association, May 1988).

Reischauer, Robert. "The Welfare Reform Legislation: Directions for the Future," in *Welfare Policy for the 1990s*, eds. Phoebe Cottingham and David Ellwood (Cambridge: Harvard University Press, 1989).

Renshaw, Vernon, Edward Trott, Jr., and Howard Freidenberg. "Gross State Product by Industry, 1963–86," *Survey of Current Business* 68 (May 1988): 30–46.

Riche, Richard, Daniel Hecker, and John Burgan. "High Technology Today and Tomorrow: A Small Slice of the Employment Pie," *Monthly Labor Review* 106 (November 1983): 50–58.

Rubinfeld, Daniel. "Credit Ratings and the Market for General Obligation Municipal Bonds," *National Tax Journal* 26 (March 1973): 17–27.

Rymer, Marilyn, and Gerald Adler. "Children and Medicaid: The Experience in Four States," *Health Care Financing Review* 9 (Fall 1987): 1–20.

Sawhill, Isabel V. "Poverty in the U.S.: Why Is It So Persistent?" *Journal of Economic Literature* 26 (September 1988): 1073–1119.

Schachter, Joseph, and Paul G. Althaus. "An Equilibrium Model of Gross Migration," *Journal of Regional Science* 29 (May 1989): 143–160.

Schwartz, Joe, and Thomas Exter. "All Our Children," *American Demographics* 11 (May 1989): 34–37.

Shaw, R. Paul. *Migration Theory and Fact* (Philadelphia: Regional Science Research Institute, 1975).

Shepsle, Kenneth. "Institutional Arrangements and Equilibrium in

Multidimensional Voting Models," *American Journal of Political Science* 23 (February 1979): 23–57.

Silvestri, George, and John Lukasiewicz. "Projections of Occupational Employment, 1988–2000," *Monthly Labor Review* 112 (November 1989): 42–65.

Smith, Brian. "An Investigation of the High Technology Section: Prospects for New York State and Syracuse," Master's thesis (Syracuse: Syracuse University, December 1983).

Social Security Administration. *Social Security Bulletin, Annual Statistical Supplement, 1987* (Washington, D.C.: U.S. Department of Health and Human Services, 1987).

Stanback, Thomas. *Services: The New Economy* (Totowa, N.J.: Allenheld, Osmun & Co., 1981).

———. *Understanding the Service Economy* (Baltimore: Johns Hopkins University Press, 1979).

Standard & Poor's Corporation. *Credit Overview* (New York: Standard & Poor's Corp., 1983).

———. "New Jersey on CreditWatch," *Creditweek* (March 19, 1990), p. 10.

———. "New York State Lowered to 'A'," *Creditweek* (April 2, 1990), p. 15.

Straussman, Jeffrey, and Kurt Thurmaier. "Budgeting Rights: The Case of Jail Litigation," *Public Budgeting & Finance* 9 (Summer 1989): 30–42.

Sullivan, David. "State and Local Fiscal Position in 1989," *Survey of Current Business* 70 (February 1990): 26–28.

Summers, Anita, and Barbara Wolfe. "Do Schools Make a Difference?" *American Economic Review* 67 (September 1977): 639–652.

Survey Research Center. *User Guide to the Panel Study of Income Dynamics* (Ann Arbor: University of Michigan, 1984).

Swan, James, Charlene Harrington, and Leslie Grant. "State Medicaid Reimbursement for Nursing Homes, 1978–86," *Health Care Financing Review* 9 (Spring 1988): 33–50.

Tobier, Emanuel, with Walter Stafford. "People and Incomes," in *Setting Municipal Priorities 1986*, eds. Charles Brecher and Raymond Horton (New York: New York University Press, 1985).

Troy, Leo, and Neil Sheflin. *Union Sourcebook: Membership, Structure, Finance, Directory* (West Orange, N.J.: Industrial Relations Data and Information Service, 1985).

Twentieth Century Fund. *The Rating Game* (New York: Twentieth Century Fund, 1974).

U.S. Bureau of Economic Analysis. *Local Area Personal Income: 1978–83, Methodology* (Washington, D.C.: U.S. Government Printing Office, 1985).

————. "State Personal Income, 1969–85: Revised Estimates," *Survey of Current Business* 66 (August 1986): 21–23.

————. *1985 OBERS BEA Regional Projections* (Washington, D.C.: U.S. Government Printing Office, 1985).

U.S. Bureau of Labor Statistics. *CPI Detailed Report* (Washington, D.C.: U.S. Department of Labor, October 1986).

————. *Geographic Profiles of Employment and Unemployment* (Washington, D.C.: U.S. Department of Labor, 1986).

U.S. Bureau of the Census. *Annual Housing Survey: 1983, New York, NY* (Washington, D.C.: Government Printing Office, May 1985).

————. "Estimates of the Population of the United States, by Age, Sex and Race: 1980 to 1986," *Current Population Reports*, Series P-25, No. 1000 (Washington, D.C.: U.S. Government Printing Office, February 1987).

————. "Experimental County Estimates by Age, Sex, Race and Year" (Washington, D.C.: National Cancer Institute, 1980 and 1984).

————. "Fertility of American Women: June 1988," *Current Population Reports*, Series P-20, No. 436 (Washington, D.C.: U.S. Government Printing Office, May 1989).

————. "General Population Characteristics: New York," *1970 Census of Population*, Report PC(1)-B34 (Washington, D.C.: U.S. Government Printing Office, 1971).

————. "Geographic Mobility for States and the Nation," *1980 Census of Population*, Report PC80-2-2A (Washington, D.C.: U.S. Department of Commerce, September 1985).

————. "Geographic Mobility: 1987," *Current Population Reports*, Series P-20, No. 430 (Washington, D.C.: U.S. Government Printing Office, April 1989).

————. *Governmental Finances* (Washington, D.C.: U.S. Government Printing Office, various years).

————. "Household and Family Characteristics," *Current Population Reports*, Series P-20, Nos. 366 and 437 (Washington, D.C.: U.S. Government Printing Office, March 1980 and May 1989).

————. "Households, Families, Marital Status, and Living Arrangements: March 1989 (Advanced Report)," *Current Population Reports,* Series P-20, No. 441 (Washington, D.C.: U.S. Government Printing Office, November 1989).

_____. *Local Government Finances in Major County Areas* (Washington, D.C.: U.S. Government Printing Office, various years).

_____. *Local Government Finances in Selected Metropolitan Areas and Large Counties* (Washington, D.C.: U.S. Government Printing Office, various years).

_____. "Methodology for Experimental Estimates of the Population of Counties, by Age and Sex: July 1, 1975," *Special Studies,* Series P-23, No. 103 (Washington, D.C.: U.S. Government Printing Office, May 1980).

_____. "Money Income and Poverty Status in the United States 1988," *Current Population Reports,* Series P-60, No. 166 (Washington, D.C.: U.S. Government Printing Office, October 1989).

_____. "Patterns of Metropolitan Area and County Population Growth: 1980 to 1987," *Current Population Reports,* Series P-25, No. 1039 (Washington, D.C.: U.S. Government Printing Office, June 1989).

_____. "Population Estimates by Race and Hispanic Origin for States, Metropolitan Areas, and Selected Counties: 1980 to 1985," *Current Population Reports,* Series P-25, No. 1040-RD-1 (Washington, D.C.: U.S. Government Printing Office, May 1989).

_____. "Poverty in the United States, 1987," *Current Population Reports,* Series P-60, No. 163 (Washington, D.C.: U.S. Government Printing Office, February 1989).

_____. "Projections of the Population of States, by Age, Sex and Race: 1988 to 2010," *Current Population Reports,* Series P-25, No. 1017 (Washington, D.C.: U.S. Government Printing Office, October 1988).

_____. *State Government Finances* (Washington, D.C.: U.S. Government Printing Office, various years).

_____. "State Population and Household Estimates: July 1, 1989," *Current Population Reports,* Series P-25, No. 1058 (Washington, D.C.: U.S. Government Printing Office, March 1990).

_____. "State Population and Household Estimates, with Age, Sex, and Components of Change: 1981–88," *Current Population Reports*, Series P-25, No. 1044 (Washington, D.C.: U.S. Government Printing Office, August 1989).

————. *Statistical Abstract of the United States, 1990* (Washington, D.C.: U.S. Government Printing Office, 1989).

————. *1980 Census of Population* (Washington, D.C.: U.S. Government Printing Office, 1983 and 1984).

————. *1986 Survey of Manufactures* (Washington, D.C.: U.S. Government Printing Office, 1988).

————. *1982 Census of Manufactures* (Washington, D.C.: U.S. Government Printing Office, 1984).

U.S. Congress, Joint Economic Committee. *Poverty, Income Distribution, the Family and Public Policy* (Washington, D.C.: U.S. Government Printing Office, December 1986).

U.S. Department of Education, National Center for Education Statistics. *Digest of Education Statistics, 1989* (Washington, D.C.: U.S. Government Printing Office, 1989).

————. *Digest of Education Statistics, 1983–84,* (Washington, D.C.: U.S. Government Printing Office, 1985).

U.S. Department of Health and Human Services, Health Care Financing Administration. *Medicare and Medicaid Data Book* (Washington, D.C.: U.S. Government Printing Office, 1983 and 1988).

U.S. Department of Justice, Bureau of Justice Statistics. *Census of Local Jails, 1983* (Washington, D.C.: U.S. Government Printing Office, 1988).

————. *Criminal Victimization in the United States, 1985* (Washington, D.C.: U.S. Government Printing Office, May 1987).

————. Office of Justice Programs, *1988 Drug Use Forecasting Annual Report* (Washington, D.C.: U.S. Department of Justice, March 1990).

————. *1984 Census of State Adult Correctional Facilities* (Washington, D.C.: U.S. Government Printing Office, 1987).

U.S. Department of Justice, Immigration, and Naturalization Service. *1988 Statistical Yearbook of the Immigration and Naturalization Service* (Washington, D.C.: U.S. Department of Commerce, August 1989).

U.S. Department of Transportation, Federal Highway Administration.

Highway Bridge Replacement and Rehabilitation Program (Washington, D.C.: U.S. Government Printing Office, various years).

_____. *Highway Statistics* (Washington, D.C.: U.S. Government Printing Office, various years).

U.S. Office of Management and Budget. *Budget of the United States Government*, Fiscal Year 1991 (Washington, D.C.: U.S. Government Printing Office, 1990).

Wagner, Adolph. *Finanzwissenschaft* (Leipzig: C. F. Winter, 1977).

Wallace-Moore, Sally. "The Effects of Interstate Tax Differentials on Wages with an Application to Interstate Migration," doctoral dissertation (Syracuse: Syracuse University, 1988).

Wasylenko, Michael. "Business Climate, Industry and Employment Growth: A Review of the Evidence," Metropolitan Studies Program Occasional Paper, No. 98 (Syracuse: Maxwell School, Syracuse University, 1985).

_____. "The Effect of Business Climate on Employment Growth," Report to the Minnesota Tax Study Commission (St. Paul: Butterworths, June 28, 1984).

_____. "Employment Growth and the Business Climate in New York and Neighboring States," Metropolitan Studies Program Occasional Paper, No. 140 (Syracuse: Maxwell School, Syracuse University, 1990).

Wetzel, James. "American Families: 75 Years of Change," *Monthly Labor Review* 113 (March 1990): 4–13.

Wilson, William Julius. "The Urban Underclass in Advanced Industrial Society," in *The New Urban Reality*, ed. Paul E. Peterson (Washington, D.C.: Brookings Institution, 1985), pp. 129–160.

Wojtkiewicz, Roger, Sara McLanahan, and Irwin Garfinkel. "The Growth of Families Headed by Women: 1950–80," *Demography* 27 (February 1990): 19–30.

World Bank. *World Development Report 1988* (New York: Oxford University Press, 1988).

Yago, Glenn, and Richard McGahey. "Can the Empire State Strike Back? The Limits of Cyclical Recovery in New York," *New York Affairs* 8 (1984): 23–25.

Young, Ruth. "Industrial Location and Regional Change: The United States and New York State," *Regional Studies* 20 (August 1986): 341–369.

Zimmerman, Dennis. "Federal Tax Reform and State Use of the Sales Tax," in *Proceedings of the 79th Annual Meeting of the National Tax Association–Tax Institute of America* (Columbus: National Tax Association, November 1986), pp. 325–331.

Index

WIDENER UNIVERSITY
WOLFGRAM
LIBRARY
CHESTER, PA.